Global Financial Markets series

Global Financial Markets is a series of practical guides to the latest financial market tools, techniques and strategies. Written for practitioners across a range of disciplines it provides comprehensive but practical coverage of key topics in finance covering strategy, markets, financial products, tools and techniques and their implementation. This series will appeal to a broad readership, from new entrants to experienced practitioners across the financial services industry, including areas such as institutional investment; financial derivatives; investment strategy; private banking; risk management; corporate finance and M&A, financial accounting and governance, and many more.

Titles include:

Cyril Demaria
PRIVATE EQUITY FUND INVESTMENTS
New Insights on Alignment of Interests, Governance, Returns and Forecasting

Erik Banks
DARK POOLS, 2nd Edition
Off-Exchange Liquidity in an Era of High Frequency, Program, and Algorithmic Trading

Erik Banks
LIQUIDITY RISK, 2nd Edition
Managing Funding and Asset Risk

Felix Lessambo
THE INTERNATIONAL CORPORATE GOVERNANCE SYSTEM
Audit Roles and Board Oversight

Sandy Chen
INTEGRATED BANK ANALYSIS AND VALUATION
A Practical Guide to the ROIC Methodology

Jawwad Farid
MODELS AT WORK
A Practitioner's Guide to Risk Management

Frances Cowell
RISK-BASED INVESTMENT MANAGEMENT IN PRACTICE, 2nd Edition

Daniel Capocci
THE COMPLETE GUIDE TO HEDGE FUNDS AND HEDGE FUND STRATEGIES

Guy Fraser-Sampson
INTELLIGENT INVESTING
A Guide to the Practical and Behavioural Aspects of Investment Strategy

Michael Hünseler
CREDIT PORTFOLIO MANAGEMENT
A Practitioner's Guide to the Active Management of Credit Risks

Ross K. McGill
US WITHHOLDING TAX
Practical Implications of QI and FATCA

David Murphy
OTC DERIVATIVES, BILATERAL TRADING AND CENTRAL CLEARING
An Introduction to Regulatory Policy, Trading Impact and Systemic Risk

Gianluca Oricchio
PRIVATE COMPANY VALUATION
How Credit Risk Reshaped Equity Markets and Corporate Finance Valuation Tools

---

Global Financial Markets series
Series Standing Order ISBN: 978–1–137–32734–5
(outside North America only)

You can receive future titles in this series as they are published by placing a standing order. Please contact your bookseller or, in case of difficulty, write to us at the address below with your name and address, the title of the series and the ISBN quoted above.

Customer Services Department, Macmillan Distribution Ltd, Houndmills, Basingstoke, Hampshire RG21 6XS, England

---

An Option Greeks Primer

Building Intuition Using Delta Hedging and Monte Carlo Simulation in Excel

Jawwad Farid
Fellow Society of Actuaries

palgrave
macmillan

Softcover reprint of the hardcover 1st edition 2015 978-1-137-37166-9

First published 2015 by
PALGRAVE MACMILLAN

Palgrave Macmillan in the UK is an imprint of Macmillan Publishers Limited, registered in England, company number 785998, of Houndmills, Basingstoke, Hampshire RG21 6XS.

Palgrave Macmillan in the US is a division of St Martin's Press LLC, 175 Fifth Avenue, New York, NY 10010.

Palgrave Macmillan is the global academic imprint of the above companies and has companies and representatives throughout the world.

Palgrave® and Macmillan® are registered trademarks in the United States, the United Kingdom, Europe and other countries

This book is printed on paper suitable for recycling and made from fully managed and sustained forest sources. Logging, pulping and manufacturing processes are expected to conform to the environmental regulations of the country of origin.

A catalogue record for this book is available from the British Library.

A catalogue record for this book is available from the Library of Congress.

ISBN 978-1-349-47572-8 ISBN 978-1-137-37167-6 (eBook)
DOI 10.1057/9781137371676

For Amin, Salwa and Taha.
As promised.
May you be blessed with teachers
who broaden your minds and
change your lives.

Contents

Part IV Hedging Higher-Order Greeks

Part V Applications

List of Figures

Preface

A word of fair warning. This is a trivial book by quantitative standards.

It is trivial because as a handbook it doesn't present proof, pose revolutionary solutions or spend time deriving interesting partial differential equations. If you were looking for any of these three items, please feel free to put the book down now. We won't hold it against you.

We however do assume that you have some familiarity with options, derivative pricing, the Black–Scholes–Merton model and Monte Carlo simulations in Excel.

This is a book about teaching intuition – intuition for a topic that despite its importance to trading desks doesn't get fair coverage in business school textbooks or on the student side of the academic world. This morning when I asked a colleague about the coverage of Vega, Vanna and Volga in his examination materials for a well-respected risk management exam, I was informed that the materials added up to just under three paragraphs, only one of which was relevant; the other two were for background. Only Vega was mentioned; Vanna and Volga were not covered.

It's just as bad as it used to be for convexity in the 1990s.

The interesting part is that there is really no shortage of material on the subject. When it comes to option Greeks, the topic catches the fancy of PhD students all over the world. We have an abundance of high-quality research papers, practitioner handbooks and publications – but not enough class time for entry-level students or professionals. The challenge is compounded further by the terminology chasm; God forbid if you are a fresh arrival in the field, a recent hire at a trading desk, or even worse, at the internal risk management group – learning and getting comfortable with the language is a real task. To survive you must scale the wall of notation and context before you can decipher the literature available in the field.

On building intuition

Trading requires a combination of discipline, process and intuition. Of the three, intuition is the most difficult to teach, since discipline and process are an incentives and control game. While individual intuition can be built over years of experience, there are tools that make it easier to pick and transfer intuition faster.

Institutional intuition gets passed on between generations of traders through shadowing, standards, trader's lore and floor legends. This passage becomes easier if you have a knack for the subject, if you already know some of the rules or if you are familiar with the trading language.

The sales and trading language has many dimensions dealing with execution, trading strategy, customer behaviour and product variations. This book focuses on just one very limited aspect of that language – the aspect dealing with option Greeks and hedging.

The issue with this part of the language lies partly with terminology (a range of Greek symbols), partly with presentation (partial differential equations), with calculations (a combination of Greek symbols and partial differential equations) and with interpretation (please say that again in a language that we can all understand).

Most business school derivative courses run out of time and patience before the derivative product universe has been covered, let alone spending time on how to read, predict or forecast the behaviour of exotic Greek symbols. We certainly manage to touch them (briefly) and talk about them superficially, but we have never had time to do justice to the topic.

Advanced derivative courses only cover pricing (and if you are lucky spend a little time on sensitivities and Greeks) because of conflicts with other topics in the outline. Sometimes as a business school student, all you will get are case notes and text references that are long on definitions and calculations but short on guidance and practical applications.

This is unfortunate, because the option price sensitivity topic, given its non-linear nature, is difficult to grasp for any audience. It takes time to think comfortably in the non-linear world. We understand simple, straightforward, single-dimensional relationships very well. But when asked to envision a new dimension or even worse to collate reactions from multiple dimensions into a single trading decision, our mental framework tends to break down. And frankly speaking, the partial differential equations don't help at all. Just over a decade ago, it was an interview question on the behaviour of the third moment of a derivative security that stumped me on Fleet Street. Not much has changed since then.

To develop an appreciation for this topic you need at least a few weeks of hands-on modelling experience followed by a few months of active application of the same concepts on a trading desk in shadow mode. The reason you are reading this book is that you don't have a few weeks or a few months – you possibly have just a few hours or a night before that interview or risk presentation is due.

We can't teach intuition or a new language in a few hours. But we can certainly get you started. The book uses a tutorial template. Primary lessons are compressed into short, bite-sized pieces. There are some equations, but we limit ourselves to brief references; we don't spend time on them or their derivations. We do spend time on ground rules and behaviour.

As an interviewer, I am more likely to ask you about how Gamma is going to behave under a given scenario and the relevant trade when that scenario occurs. I may ask you how that is different from Vega's reaction rather than ask for its partial differential equation (though I may ask for the latter too, depending on my mood and how much I dislike you). If you really push me, I may also ask that third moment question. I am more interested in how you think, in your ability to grasp a concept, in your awareness of the context and your capacity to appreciate how positions may flip directions; in your intuition, rather than your memory.

The only way to do this is to make you walk through thought experiments dressed as Excel spreadsheets. Read the chapter, dissect the model, build it in your own time, follow up with exercises and the "what is next?" questions. Repeat. Numbers, models and graphs that we have tweaked ourselves have a higher chance of being retained by us than those on printed papers or electronic screens.

What do we cover?

The book is organized into five parts.

Part I – The refresher

The first part consists of two chapters (Introduction and Chapter 1) as background and refresher on basic materials that can easily be skipped by more experienced readers. They cover basic themes, a few relationships and numerical examples to reinforce the calculation and usage conventions of Greeks.

Part II – Delta hedging simulations

The second part begins with a simple Delta hedging simulation for a vanilla call option. The simulation is used to examine the components of hedging P&L. We extend the model to vanilla put options. We use the P&L model to build a better understanding of the behaviour of Delta and two minor Greeks.

Part III – Volatility surfaces

The third part is dedicated to volatility. My personal demons as a student in the field were volatility surfaces and hedging higher-order Greeks. Volatility, Vega and Gamma surfaces, therefore, make an extended appearance.

Part IV – Hedging higher-order Greeks

We begin with hedging a single position with deep out of money options, and then graduate to a portfolio of short positions and more sophisticated Solver models. Solver is used to illustrate multiple scenarios, objective functions and hedging perspectives for Gamma and Vega neutral hedging models.

Part V – Applications

The fifth part ties up a few loose ends by reviewing two application questions, spending some additional time on Theta and Rho, and closing up with appendices.

And now let's go waltz with our Greek friends.

Jawwad Farid
June 2014
Karachi, Pakistan
FinanceTrainingCourse.com

Acknowledgements

This book is partly based on a four-part MBA course on derivative pricing and risk management that I taught for seven years in Dubai and Singapore at the SP Jain School of Management.

There is no substitute for feedback from smart students on my teaching material and lecture notes. Without the students and their questions at SP Jain, spread across multiple batches in both campuses (you know who you are), these pages would have never evolved beyond the original PowerPoint slides.

The practitioner's touch came from the risk and treasury consulting practice I have run since 2003, working with banking and investment management professionals in the region. Our clients made it possible for us to work across markets, with interesting transactions and incomplete data. Many of the Excel-based training tools used here were first developed to teach advanced treasury concepts to treasury sales and corporate banking teams using our signature hands-on, equations-off mode.

Whatever intuition I have picked up over the years I owe to the course-work done with Mark Broadie, Maria Vassalou and Harvey Corb at Columbia Business School in 1999 and the time spent on the Prime Brokerage desk in Goldman's Fleet Street office in 1998. These four influences acted as connecting bridges that made it possible for me to build risk and valuation systems that ultimately led to these pages. That journey was helped along the way by many readings of John C. Hull, Nassim Nicholas Taleb and Paul Wilmott.

I would say the original inspiration for this book was my first reading of Taleb's *Dynamic Hedging*, three years after the book came out. Taleb took the first step in demystifying the practice of dynamic hedging and the behaviour of Greeks as viewed by a practitioner. If you were an outsider, recently hired by the risk function (as I was), the maps that Taleb drew guided many a lost soul; I owe a personal debt of gratitude to my tattered copy.

A number of examples shared in this book were originally presented and discussed on the FinanceTrainingCourse.com blog. I am grateful for their permission to reuse the material.

Option pricing and implied volatility data was provided by ivolatility.com. It is a fantastic and convenient source of volatility data when you no longer have access to your Bloomberg terminal.

Agnes and Uzma made it possible to write, test, tweak and publish much of the analysis presented in this book. Without Agnes' support as a sounding board and a peer reviewer, we would never have had the confidence to share our work with the world. Sohail A. Shaikh at Heriot Watt University was kind enough to review the entire manuscript and suggest a number of changes that helped improve readability and flow. Some of the Greek modelling work you will see in this book was actually used to scare away interns and prospective employees in their first few months at our firm. A number of thought experiments posed in hedging chapters originally debuted as interview questions. Farhan Anwaar survived many of our torturous rituals, and the edition you hold in your hands is significantly better because of his patience, suggestions and contribution.

Finally, Fawzia, collaborator, partner in crime and life, and a lifelong sufferer of my odd writing habits and timings – without you there wouldn't be a beginning.

The mistakes, as always, remain mine.

About the Author

Photo credit – Sana Saleem

Jawwad Farid has been building and implementing risk models and back office systems since August 1998. Working with clients on four continents, he helps bankers, board members and regulators take a market relevant approach to risk management.

Jawwad's expertise includes investment management, product development and risk models. His specialty is customizing risk and valuation models for effective use in emerging and illiquid markets.

He has advised multiple due diligence teams on risk assessment and valuation in banking and insurance sectors, has set up FX and commodity hedging desks, has built fair value models for illiquid securities for FAS 157 disclosures, and has helped a US$3 billion life insurance fund on allocation and bid patterns for 10-, 20- and 30-year bonds, ALM mismatch and fixed income portfolio strategy. He has worked with securities and banking regulators as well as with the Asian Development Bank on assessing the state of the corporate bond market, and has issued valuation opinions on cross currency swaps, interest rate swaps, caps, floors, participating forwards and contingent liabilities for Exchange Guarantee Funds in the region.

Jawwad is a Fellow of the Society of Actuaries (FSA, Schaumburg, IL); he holds an MBA from Columbia Business School, and is a computer science graduate from NUCES FAST. He is also an adjunct faculty member at the SP Jain Global School of Management in Dubai and Singapore, where he teaches Risk Management, Derivative Pricing and Entrepreneurship.

He is the founder and consulting actuary at Alchemy Technologies, a risk consulting practice that works with clients in the MENA region, and he writes regularly on the FinanceTrainingCourse.com blog.

Glossary

Alpha: Gamma rent or Theta per Gamma ratio.

Arbitrage: The practice of making risk-free profits at zero cost due to the inefficiencies present between two or more markets by entering into simultaneous instantaneous deals designed to take advantage of these imbalances.

Call at the money option: The point at which the strike price of the call option equals the current spot price.

Call in the money option: The point at which the strike price of the call option is lower than the current spot price (the opposite is true for put options).

Call obligation for writers: The writer of the call option is the seller of the call option. When the underlying price rises the buyer of the option exercises their right to buy the underlying and the writer of the option is obligated to sell the underlying at the strike price.

Call option: Call option for buyers: the right (but not the obligation) to buy an underlying security on a future date at a price agreed today.

Call out of money option: The strike price of the call option is higher than the current spot price (the opposite is true for put options).

Convenience yield: The benefit or return from holding the underlying instrument or physical asset rather than the derivative product. The benefits include having easy access to the asset to keep a production process running during or to profit from temporary shortages of that product in the market. In simple terms *Convenience yield = Final price* (P_t) *– Purchase price* (P_0)

Convexity: A second-order (non-linear) derivative that adjusts the linear sensitivity measure to account for the curvature in the price yield relationship.

Cost of short position: In the context of this text, the total cost from prior periods less the short sale cost from positions that are closed in the prior period, plus the cost of any incremental short sales for the current period.

Delivery price: Price at which the forward contract will be settled for, at some future date.

Delta: Measures the change in the value of the option due to a change in price of the underlying. It is also defined as the *conditional* probability of the terminal value of S (denoted by S_t) being greater than the Strike (X) given that $S_t > X$ for a call option.

Delta Normal method: In the context of this text, this refers to an approach that uses approximations; for each Greek we shock the variable in question and calculate the impact on the price of the option predicted by the Greek.

Duration: A first-order (linear) rate of change in the price of an interest-rate-sensitive instrument (a bond) because of a change in the yield to maturity or reference rate of the instrument.

Empirical or historical volatility: Volatility measured using actual historical price data.

Forward implied volatility or forward-forward volatility for the period $[t_1, t_2]$: Given the spot implied volatilities for the period t_0 to t_1 ($\sigma_{t0,\, t1}$) and t_0 to t_2 ($\sigma_{t0,\, t2}$), respectively, it is possible to infer the expected volatility between t_1 and t_2 ($\sigma_{t1,\, t2}$). The forward implied volatility between two points is the 'local volatility' between two points. The generalization of this formula gives Dupire–Derman–Kani's local volatility, which is a function of time to expiry and option moneyness.

Forward rate: The forward rate is the rate of interest that would be applicable from one point in time in the future to another point in time in the future. These rates are implicit in the current quoted spot rates. Typically, forward interest rates are expressed as single-period rates, but they could also be applied to several time periods. The rates are inferred from available data.

Full Valuation approach: In the context of this text, this refers to the approach which values the option using the Black–Scholes formula and the revised parameter input. The difference between this value and the original value will be the impact on option price.

Gamma: Measures a change in the value of Delta based on a change in the price of the underlying.

Gamma correction: Rather than using the Black–Scholes formal definition of Gamma, numerically estimate Gamma using the modified Gamma methodology by observing the actual change in Delta and using that as an input to Gamma approximation.

Greeks/option price sensitivities (OPS): Approximations used to determine the change in price of the option due to a unit change in the value of one of the drivers.

Gross P&L: A P&L calculation that excludes trading losses.

Hedge: An investment position created to offset the potential losses/gains from another investment position so as to ensure a more stable income stream or reduce the risk of losses/volatility.

Hedging for Gamma and Vega exposures: Hedging of Gamma and Vega is carried by buying other options with similar maturities. The rebalancing frequency is less than in Delta hedging. The final hedge is a mix of exposure to the underlying (partial Delta hedge) and cheaper options with similar maturities.

Holding period: The number of trading days that an investor holds a given investment.

Implied volatility: A mixture of future expectations of realized volatility and the level of volatility at which a trader is comfortable taking a position. In simple terms, pick an option, use its currently quoted price, plug in the Black–Scholes equation and solve for the value of volatility that would lead to that price.

Incremental amount borrowed: In the context of this text, this refers to the difference between the two Deltas for the two time periods multiplied by the new price of the underlying stock.

Incremental short position: In the context of this text, this refers to the units short sold multiplied by the price.

Interest paid per period: In the context of this text, this refers to the interest accrued on the balance of the previous period. The interest accrual factor is: $\text{EXP}(\textit{Risk-free rate} \times \textit{Delta}_t) - 1$

Local volatility: Calculates volatilities for different combination of strike prices (K) and expiries (T). Done in a market-consistent no-arbitrage manner. This means that for a given date, time and underlying spot price combination, local volatilities are calculated in such a fashion that the resultant option prices match market prices.

Local volatility surface: A surface that makes it possible to generalize a "local" volatility value for all combinations of strike prices and expiries.

Log normal distribution: A probability distribution in which the logarithm of a variable has a normal distribution. It is an asymmetric distribution, and is always positive with a single peak.

Long position: The buy side of a transaction or a contract.

Modified Theta: Price of an option at current volatility less the price of the same option a day later at the day-later maturity.

Modified Vega: Weighted average Vega (by maturity buckets) taking into consideration the maturity bucket volatility.

Monte Carlo simulation (MC simulation): A random series of prices that are used to test the effectiveness of a hedge, the profitability of a position and the distribution of profits and losses.

$N(d_1)$: A Black–Scholes–Merton model probability. $N(d_1)$ accounts for the probability of exercise as given by $N(d_2)$ and the fact that exercise or rather receipt of stock on exercise is dependent on the *conditional* future values that the stock price takes on the expiry date.

$N(d_2)$: The probability that the terminal price will exceed the strike.

Naked option (open position): An unhedged option position.

Net P&L: P&L calculation that includes trading losses.

Normal distribution: A probability distribution that is centred on mean. It is a symmetric distribution and has a bell-shaped density distribution with a single peak on mean.

Omega: Option duration or expected life for vanilla American options or expected exit for binaries and knockouts.

Path-dependent: In relation to options and their payoffs, path dependency refers to the way payoffs are tied to how the prices of the underlying have moved over the tenure of the derivative contract, and not simply on the price at maturity.

Put: Put options for buyers: the right to sell an underlying security on a future date at a price agreed upon today. It gives the buyer the right to walk away if the market price is greater than the strike price.

Replication: Creating a hedge for short option position that follows changes in option values.

Rho: Measures the change in the value of the option due to a change in interest rates.

Shadow Gamma: A calculation that takes into account changes in volatility in addition to changes in the price of the underlying.

Shadow down-Gamma: In the context of this text, this refers to

$$\frac{Delta\,(revised\ vol) - Delta\,(original\ vol)}{revised\ vol - original\ vol}$$

where the underlying asset price is assumed to go down.

Shadow up-Gamma: In the context of this text, this refers to

$$\frac{Delta\,(original\ vol) - Delta\,(revised\ vol)}{original\ vol - revised\ vol}$$

where the underlying asset price is assumed to go up.

Short position: The counterparty on the sell side of a transaction, who has agreed to sell the contract.

Squaring: In order for trading desks to buy and sell at a spread, they need to offset (hedge) their client positions. This process of matching or offsetting positions is called squaring.

Standard deviation: This is a measure of the deviation of observed values from the mean or expected value.

Standard normal distribution: A probability distribution that is centred on zero and has a standard deviation of 1. It is a symmetric distribution, and has a bell-shaped density distribution with a single peak on zero.

Stock: Equity ownership where the claims are subordinate to those of bondholders, creditors and preferred shareholders. There may be different classes of common stock that have different voting rights and profit-sharing percentages. Dividends on common stocks will only be paid after all preferred stock dividends are paid.

Strike price: The predetermined price at which the derivative contract will settle for at some predetermined future date.

Term structure of volatility: A curve that shows the movement of implied volatilities against changing time to maturity.

Terminal price: Price of the underlying security on the maturity of the option.

Theta: Measures the change in the value of the option due to a change in the time to expiry or maturity.

Time premium: Represents the change in the value of the option as the option approaches expiration. It is calculated as the difference between the value of the option at inception and its value at expiry.

Vanilla option: A derivative instrument that gives us the right to buy or sell an underlying security on a future date at a price agreed upon today. It gives us the right to walk away if the market price is not in our favour.

Vanna: A second-order cross-Greek; measures the change in Vega because of a change in underlying price, the change in Delta because of a change in volatility and the second derivative of option value with respect to a joint move in volatility and underlying asset price.

Vega: Measures the change in the value of the option due to a change in volatility of the underlying.

Volatility smile: A term structure of volatility in which the volatility for out of money and in the money options changes slower than the volatility for at the money options.

Volatility surface: A volatility surface plots market-consistent volatilities across moneyness (strike prices) and maturity (time to expiry).

Volatility: Within the options world, volatility is a measure of relative price changes.

Volga: A second-order Greek; measures the change in Vega because of a change in volatility and the second derivative of option value with respect to volatility.

Part I
Refresher

Introduction: Context

1 Options

A vanilla option is a derivative instrument that gives us the right to buy or sell an underlying security on a future date at a price agreed upon today. Unlike a forward or future contract, an option gives us the right to walk away if the market price is not in our favour. If we do decide to walk away, our loss is limited to the upfront premium we paid when we purchased the option.

The right to buy an underlying security is known as a call. The right to sell an underlying security is known as a put. When we sell an option we write it, and our obligation is very different from that of the buyer; while the buyer has the right to walk away, the writer is obligated to perform.

For a more detailed treatment of the Options and derivatives world, see John C. Hull, Paul Wilmott and Jawwad Farid.[1]

2 Option price drivers

Option prices are determined by a range of methods. Three of the methods that we will refer to in this book are the Black–Scholes equation (also known as the Black–Scholes–Merton Model or BSM for short) for European options; Binomial Trees for American options; and the Monte Carlo simulation.

Irrespective of the method used, the price of an option is determined by the following factors:[2]

- Spot price of the underlying security
- Strike or Exercise Price of the option
- Time to Maturity or Expiry of the option
- Price volatility of the underlying security
- Price volatility of the underlying security
- Reference risk free interest rate
- Dividend or earnings yield on the underlying security

A natural follow-up question is: How does the price of an option change when any of the above variables changes? And then: Which of these variables has the biggest price impact, and which the least?

3 Greeks

Greeks are approximations used to determine the change in price of the option due to a unit change in the value of one of the above drivers. They are also known as option price sensitivities (OPS) or option factor sensitivities. They are called Greeks because their names reference the Greek alphabet: Delta, Gamma, Vega, Theta and Rho.

If you are familiar with the world of fixed income investment you will have heard of the terms 'duration' and 'convexity', which measure the change in the value of a treasury bond for a change in the underlying interest rates. Duration is a first-order (linear) rate of change in the price of an interest-rate-sensitive instrument (a bond) because of a change in the yield to maturity or reference rate of the instrument. Convexity is a second-order (non-linear) derivative that adjusts the linear sensitivity measure to account for the curvature in the price–yield relationship. In like manner, there are multiple option price sensitivities because of multiple option price drivers. Some, like duration for fixed income securities, are linear (e.g. Delta). Others, like convexity for fixed income securities, are non-linear (e.g. Gamma).

4 Hedging and squaring

Trading desks make money by taking (running) positions for their account, buying and selling at a spread (buying low, selling high) or market making (providing liquidity by holding an instrument on their balance sheet temporarily). In order for them to buy and sell at a spread they need to offset (hedge) their client positions. This process of matching or offsetting positions is called squaring. The spread is booked and realized when they buy (**long**) from the client at a slightly lower price and then sell (**short**) in the market at a slightly higher price, and vice versa.

If no appropriate counterparty or security is available to hedge a position, a trader needs to hedge their exposure by using basic principles. An unhedged position is known as an open (or naked) position.

5 Empirical and implied volatility

Within the options world, volatility is a measure of relative price changes. These changes can be measured on a daily, weekly, monthly or annualized basis. When volatility is measured using actual historical price data, we call it empirical or historical volatility. Figure 1 illustrates the behaviour of historical volatility for Gold, Silver, WTI and the EUR-USD exchange rate.

The volatility used as an input to determine option prices is not historical or empirical volatility, but implied volatility. While historical volatility is the historical average, implied volatility represents a mixture of future expectations of realized volatility and the level of volatility at which a trader is comfortable taking a position.

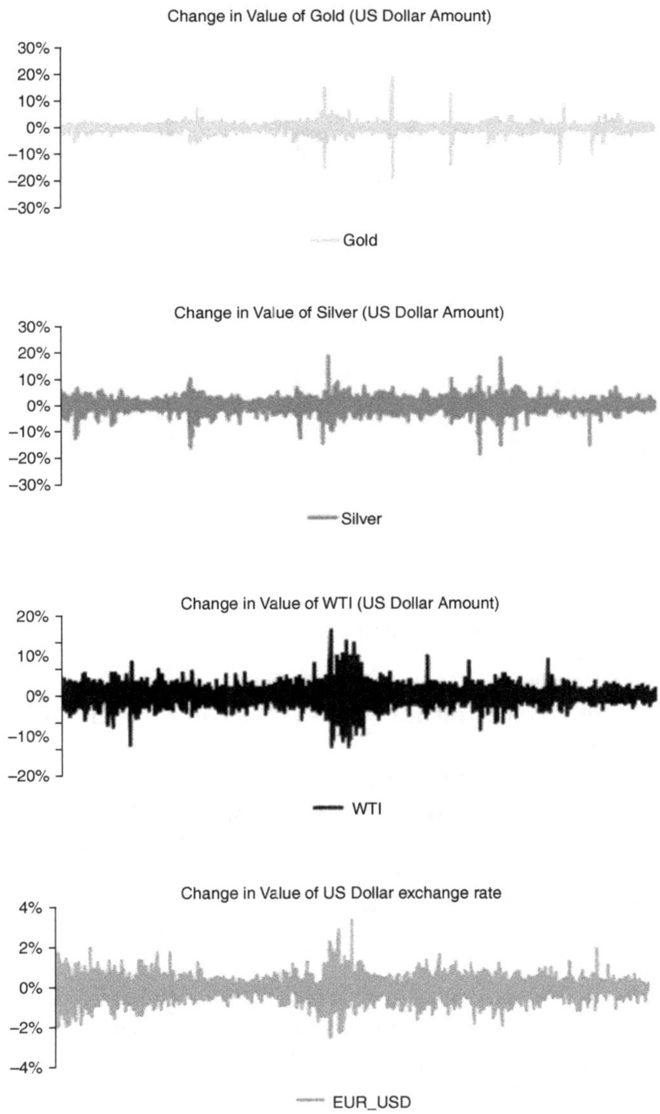

Figure 1 Changes in gold, silver, WTI and US dollar prices
Source: The Greeks against Spot. FinanceTrainingCourse.com

One of the reasons why implied volatility differs and varies from historical volatility is that, just like prices, it is not constant. It moves, it goes up and down. For a trader to improve the odds of making money on an option position it is important that the volatility at which they sell an option position to a client is higher than the volatility at which they square it in the market. If the trader runs a book of exposure and does not square it, it is important that the actual realized level of volatility in the underlying security is lower than the volatility they charge their clients.

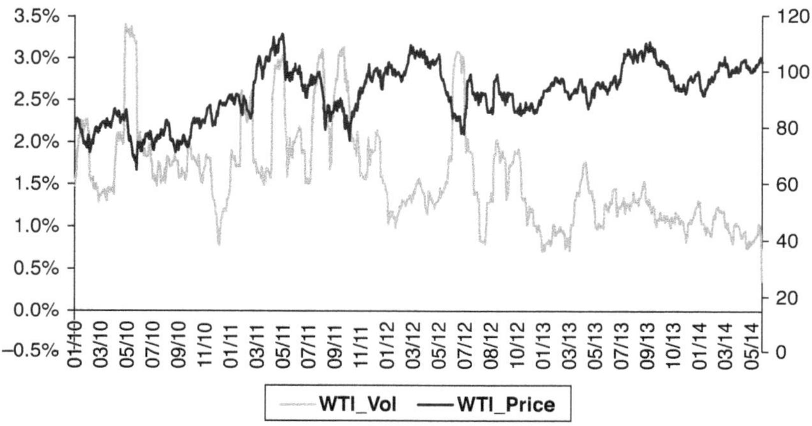

Figure 2 WTI prices and trading volatility
Source: FinanceTrainingCourse.com

6 In and out of money options

Let's consider a simple call option that gives us the right to buy one barrel of the WTI blend of crude oil at US$100 a barrel, one month down the road. Let's also assume that the spot price of the underlying security (crude oil) for immediate delivery is US$90 per barrel. The price at which we can buy crude oil using our option is the strike price. In this specific case the strike price of the call option is significantly higher than the current spot price, hence the option is trading out of money. As a buyer to the option, you would not exercise the option, as it would not make economic sense to do so. If the spot price fell further – to US$80 per barrel for example – the option would be trading deep out of money.

Conversely, if the spot price rose from US$90 per barrel to US$108 per barrel, the option would now be in the money. If it moved higher, to US$120 per barrel, it would be deep in the money. As the spot price moves closer to the strike price, the option moves closer to being at or near money.

While the empirical volatility for an underlying security is the same for, and not impacted by, the option being in or out of money, the implied volatilities for deep out of money options are different from the implied volatilities for at or near money options.

Compared to the values of at or near money options, the value of deep out of money options also react very differently to changes in volatility.

7 Deep out of money options and lottery tickets

A deep out of money option is like a lottery ticket. If you used the at money estimate of implied volatility to hedge it, you would be in for a rude shock when volatility moved against you, but if your timing was right and you had bought the option before market volatility moved in your favour, you would really strike it rich.

Here is a simplified and contrived example that illustrates the point.

Let's assume that we are interested in buying call and put options on the OIL ETF. Oil has not recently been particularly volatile, and we believe that there is going to be a significant jump in volatility given the cyclicality of this market. Current implied volatility is at a historical low of 6.75%. To keep our model simple, we assume that the convenience yield is zero.

Out of Money Call and Put Prices

Spot	100	100	100	100	100	100	100	100
Strike	**120**	**110**	**105**	**101**	**100**	**95**	**85**	**70**
Vol	6.75%	6.75%	6.75%	6.75%	6.75%	6.75%	6.75%	6.75%
Riskfree	1%	1%	1%	1%	1%	1%	1%	1%
Maturity	**1.00**	**1.00**	**1.00**	**1.00**	**1.00**	**1.00**	**1.00**	**1.00**
PVF	0.990	0.990	0.990	0.990	0.990	0.990	0.990	0.990
Calls – Price	**0.012**	**0.342**	**1.202**	**2.686**	**3.196**	**6.585**	**15.852**	**30.693**
Puts – Price	**18.824**	**9.253**	**5.162**	**2.686**	**2.206**	**0.644**	**0.010**	**0.000**

Figure 3 Example OIL ETF – call and put prices at a historically low implied volatility
Source: FinanceTrainingCourse.com

The above grid presents the option price drivers, and calculates the options prices for eight at, out, and in the money call and put options. Focus on the five areas circled below. When we play the scenario we have in mind, the values in these cells will change. Right now, you can buy a call on your ETF for 1.2 cents at a strike price of 120 with an implied volatility of 6.75%. A deep out of money put struck at US$70 is currently worth zero.

Let's assume that Libya implodes again, driving Brent prices through the roof. There is a change of heart in Saudi Arabia against pumping 11 million barrels a day, and so they decide to cut production by a few million barrels – and then Russia, peeved by the burden of Western sanctions, decides to impose a unilateral oil and gas embargo on Western Europe after finding a new market for petrochemical products in China.

Out of Money Call and Put Prices								
Spot	100	100	100	100	100	100	100	100
Strike	120	110	105	101	100	95	85	70
Vol	6.75%	6.75%	6.75%	6.75%	6.75%	6.75%	6.75%	6.75%
Riskfree	1%	1%	1%	1%	1%	1%	1%	1%
Maturity	1.00	1.00	1.00	1.00	1.00	1.00	1.00	1.00
PVF	0.990	0.990	0.990	0.990	0.990	0.990	0.990	0.990
				FinanceTrainingCourse.com				
Calls – Price	0.012	0.342	1.202	2.686	3.196	6.585	15.852	30.693
Puts – Price	18.824	9.253	5.162	2.686	2.206	0.644	0.010	0.000
Legend	Deep Out of Money							At or Near Money

Figure 4 Example OIL ETF – areas of focus
Source: FinanceTrainingCourse.com

The implied volatility jumps from 6.75% to 25%. Here is the corresponding change in the value of our options:

Out of Money Call and Put Prices								
Spot	100	100	100	100	100	100	100	100
Strike	120	110	105	101	100	95	85	70
Vol	25.00%	25.00%	25.00%	25.00%	25.00%	25.00%	25.00%	25.00%
Riskfree	1%	1%	1%	1%	1%	1%	1%	1%
Maturity	1.00	1.00	1.00	1.00	1.00	1.00	1.00	1.00
PVF	0.990	0.990	0.990	0.990	0.990	0.990	0.990	0.990
Calls – Price	3.925	6.507	8.261	9.923	10.377	12.886	19.143	31.340
Puts – Price	22.737	15.418	12.221	9.923	9.387	6.945	3.301	0.647
Legend	Deep Out of Money							At or Near Money

Figure 5 Example OIL ETF – impact of higher implied volatility assumption; unchanged spot price
Source: FinanceTrainingCourse.com

Since this is a contrived scenario, you can see that there is no change in the underlying spot price. We will change that in the next panel. When you plug in the impact of changes in spot price on account of the oil volatility scenario playing out, the revised value of your option positions is shown below:

Out of Money Call and Put Prices								
Spot	125	125	125	125	125	125	125	125
Strike	120	110	105	101	100	95	85	70
Vol	25.00%	25.00%	25.00%	25.00%	25.00%	25.00%	25.00%	25.00%
Riskfree	1%	1%	1%	1%	1%	1%	1%	1%
Maturity	1.00	1.00	1.00	1.00	1.00	1.00	1.00	1.00
PVF	0.990	0.990	0.990	0.990	0.990	0.990	0.990	0.990
Calls – Price	15.439	21.365	24.822	27.813	28.591	32.644	41.452	55.763
Puts – Price	9.251	5.276	3.783	2.813	2.601	1.703	0.610	0.070
Legend	Deep Out of Money							At or Near Money

Figure 6 Example OIL ETF – impact of higher implied volatility assumption; change in spot price
Source: FinanceTrainingCourse.com

So our 1.2 cent deep out of money call option is now worth US$15.439. If you had sold this option and had hedged it with the at money implied volatility estimate at time zero, and the change in volatilities caught you by surprise, your original Delta would be out of sync with the new market-based Delta determined using the new volatilities. With volatilities, if prices also moved with the same speed you would not get a chance to purchase the underlying at the price recommended by your model.

From an option investing point of view this also creates an interesting question. If you are allowed to trade premiums, as you are with American options, from a pure risk–return perspective, which option positions are you likely to favour? At or near money options, or deep out of money options? How does that preference change when implied volatility is at historical highs versus historical lows? How do these preferences vary across novices and experienced professionals, and how does it impact the supply and demand for deep out of money options? If these questions interest you see the recent research on informed trading.[3]

8 Monte Carlo simulations in Excel

We assume that our readers have a basic understanding of the topic, but for a more detailed and in-depth treatment of building Monte Carlo simulators in Excel, see *Models at Work*.[4]

We essentially use a series of random numbers to simulate prices. The simulated prices represent a make-believe world where changes in prices follow a normal distribution (symmetric, balanced and positive as well as negative), while prices themselves follow the log normal distribution (asymmetric and always positive).

The Monte Carlo simulation, given its limiting assumptions, is not very good at predicting or forecasting the future. However, it is a great tool for building an understanding of possible future behaviour of positions as well as for testing multi-dimensional relationships that cannot be tested through data tables, which are ordinary tools of sensitivity analysis. The Monte Carlo simulation does this by generating a random series of prices that can then be used to test the effectiveness of a hedge, the profitability of a position and the distribution of profits as well as losses.

9 Model and methodology basics

We use a simple Monte Carlo simulation model to simulate the underlying price and evaluate the effectiveness of our hedges for options we have written. The diagram below shows the simulated changes in our position (the option written) and ability of the hedge to track it:

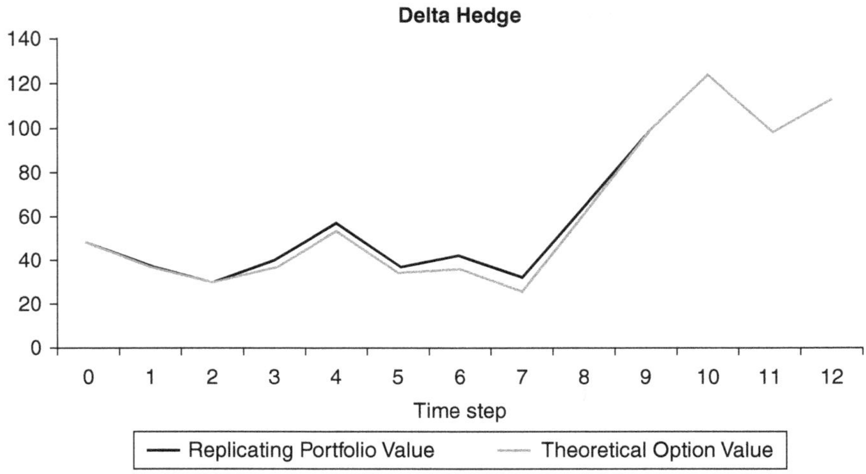

Figure 7 Option value versus value of hedge

Source: Delta Hedging Tracking Error. FinanceTrainingCourse.com

The hedge simulation sheet also calculates a P&L for our position per simulation iteration. The P&L is calculated on a cash basis.

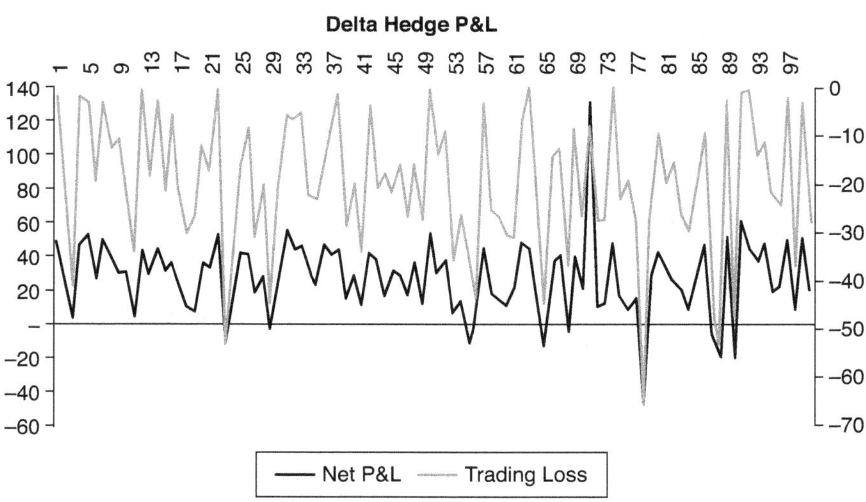

Figure 8 P&L and trading gain (loss) across 100 simulated iterations

Source: Delta Hedging Tracking Error. FinanceTrainingCourse.com

While the above P&L simulation plot is useful as a rough estimate, it is only when we generate a histogram of our P&L simulation results that we will see if our hedge is effective. The histogram will also give us the range for our hedge tracking error.

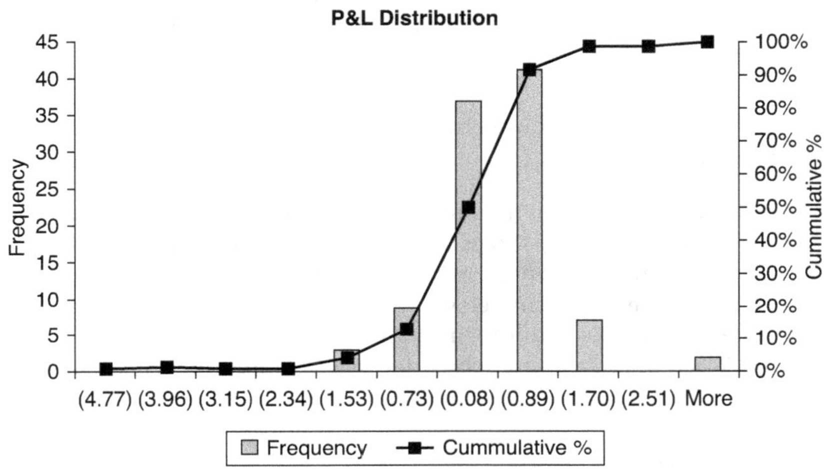

Figure 9 Histogram – distribution of P&L across simulated runs
Source: Delta against Spot price. FinanceTrainingCourse.com

Our P&L histogram is generated using 100 iterations from our simulation engine. The horizontal axis shows the P&L range, while the vertical axis shows the cumulative probability.

In later chapters, we will use this distribution of P&L to build a more intuitive understanding of option pricing drivers, as well as their impact on option Greeks.

10 The Black–Scholes–Merton pricing model

The Black–Scholes–Merton (BSM) pricing model is one of the tools used for pricing options. While the holes in the BSM model are well documented,[5] we rely on the underlying model for building our intuitive understanding. The one big variation where models on the street vary from the original Black–Scholes derivation is the assumption of constant volatility.

Whatever flavour of the model is in season and used by your team or your bank, the framework used in this book can easily be extended to those models. In most instances, the Greeks produced by the original model tend to match those produced by the revised variation.

11 $N'(d_1)$ and $N'(d_2)$

In differential calculus, when you take the rate of change (differential), of a given equation or relationship with respect to a given factor or variable, the resulting equation is denoted with a prime – the symbol ′ . In the material that follows, when we use $N'(d_1)$ or $N'(d_2)$, the N prime denotes the differential (of $N(d_1)$ or $N(d_2)$) with respect to a given variable. You will see N' in the formula for Gamma and Vega.

12 Understanding Black–Scholes: an intuitive derivation of $N(d_1)$ and $N(d_2)$

Of all the intimidating equations and formulas (PDEs and otherwise) out there, the derivation of the Black–Scholes formula for a European option easily takes first prize for the most unapproachable of topics for new arrivals in this field. The objective in the treatment below is not to derive the equation but simply to get more comfortable with the intuition behind it.

The Black–Scholes solution for the value of a call option takes the following form:

$$c = S_0 e^{-qT} N(d_1) - K e^{-rT} N(d_2)$$

where

- c is the value of a European call option
- $N(x)$ is the cumulative probability distribution function (pdf) for a standardized normal distribution
- S_0 is the price of the underlying asset at time zero
- K is the strike or exercise price
- r is the continuously compounded risk-free rate
- σ is the volatility of the asset price
- T is the time to maturity of the option
- q is the yield rate on the underlying asset. (Alternatively, if the asset provides cash income instead of a yield, q will be set to zero in the formula and the present value of the cash income during the life of the option will be subtracted from S_0.)
- e Euler number, the natural exponential e

And,

$$d_1 = \frac{\ln(S_0 / K) + (r - q + \sigma^2 / 2)T}{\sigma \sqrt{T}}$$

$$d_2 = \frac{\ln(S_0 / K) + (r - q + \sigma^2 / 2)T}{\sigma \sqrt{T}} = d_1 - \sigma \sqrt{T}$$

In the material that follows we will spend a fair bit of time with $N(d_1)$ and $N(d_2)$. For that time to be effective, it is important that we are comfortable with the basics behind $N(d_1)$ and $N(d_2)$.

Let's begin with answering some very basic questions:

(a) What is the setting and context for the Black–Scholes formula?
(b) What is the easiest and simplest way for deriving $N(d_2)$ that does not require half a textbook on the mathematics of computational finance?

The following treatment is based on material presented in Lars Nielsen's excellent and highly recommended textbook on the subject.

i Underlying assumptions

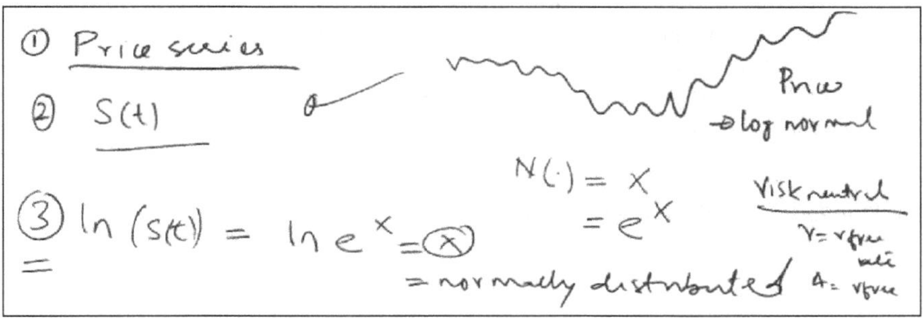

Figure 10 Representation of the underlying assumptions in a Black–Scholes world
Source: Delta against Spot price. FinanceTrainingCourse.com

Within the Black–Scholes world, we will assume that there is an available price series of non-dividend-paying financial security, given by $S(t)$. We assume that $S(t)$ is distributed log normally, which simply means that if Y represents the price series and X represents a normally distributed random variable, then:

$$Y = e^x, \text{ and } \ln(Y) = \ln(e^x) = x$$

The take away from the above equations is that while $S(t)$ is log normally distributed, ln $(S(t))$ is normally distributed. We also assume that the standard deviation and expected return for $\ln(S(t))$ is given by:

$$\textit{Expected Return} = Ln(S_0) + (r - \frac{1}{2}\sigma^2)(T - t)$$

$$\textit{Standard Deviation} = \sigma\sqrt{T - t}$$

And $\mathrm{Ln}(S_t/S_0)$ is normally distributed with:

$$\textit{Expected Return} = (r - \frac{1}{2}\sigma^2)(T - t)$$

$$\textit{Standard Deviation} = \sigma\sqrt{T - t}$$

Why have we used the risk-free rate? Because in the risk-neutral world, investors are content with earning the risk-free rate and all assets earn the risk-free rate; in our illustrations, $(T–t)$ will be simplified to just t.

ii Estimating the price move

For a European call option, we know that the option will only be exercised if the terminal price $S(t)$ is greater than the strike price X. Therefore the first probability that we are interested in is the probability that $S(t) > X$ or $N(d_2)$. But to calculate the probability for our series, (remember we are dealing with $\ln(S(t))$ and not $S(t)$), we first need to convert our series to a standard normal distribution and estimate a Z score.

$$\textit{Standard normal random variable} = \frac{X_i - \overline{X}}{\sigma}$$

Where
X_i is a normally distributed random variable
X_bar is the mean of the random variable
σ is the standard deviation of the random variable

The Z score is basic statistics. As long as we have the values that need to be compared with the mean and standard deviation of the distribution, we can simply plug them into the equation above. We already have the mean and standard deviation (see above discussion). The value that needs to be compared with the mean, X_i, is the price move required for the option to be exercised. How high does $\ln(S(t))$ need to move for the option to be in the money? $\mathrm{Ln}(S(t))$ must be at least as high as the natural log of the strike, $\ln(X)$.

So in the standard normal variable formula,

$$\frac{X_i - \overline{X}}{\sigma}$$

$$\overline{X} = \ln(S_0) + \left(r - \frac{1}{2}\sigma^2\right)t$$

$$\sigma = \sigma\sqrt{t}$$

$$X_i = \ln(X)$$

Once we have the standard normal variable, or z-score, then calculating the probability is a simple call to the normal distribution function in Excel.

iii Plugging in the values

We now take the jump and our estimates of expected return and standard deviation, and plug these into the standard normal variable equation to get the following results:
Standard normal variable or z-score,

$$y = \frac{X_i - \overline{X}}{\sigma} = \frac{\left[\ln(X) - (\ln(S_0)) + (r - \sigma^2/2)t\right]}{\sigma\sqrt{t}} = \frac{\ln(X/S_0) - (r - \sigma^2/2)t}{\sigma\sqrt{t}}$$

But there is a small tweak that needs to be made before our work is complete for determining $N(d_2)$.

$N(y)$, the cumulative probability distribution for a standardized normal distribution, is the probability that the variable will be less than y, that is, $\Pr(Y \leq y) = N(y)$. This is graphically depicted below:

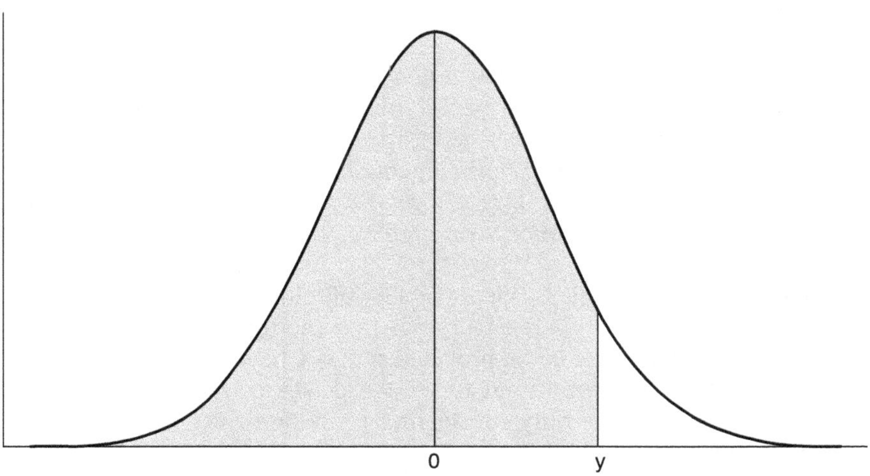

Figure 11 Cumulative probability distribution of a standard normal distribution
Source: The Greeks against Spot. FinanceTrainingCourse.com

However for $N(d_2)$ we are interested in $P(Y>y) = 1-N(y)$, that is, the probability that the terminal price will exceed the strike. It is not a big hurdle to obtain d_2 from our derived value of y above; we use $-y$ (as $1-N(y) = N(-y)$), and our job is done. We multiply our result, y, above with (–1) and simplify the result to the now very familiar Black–Scholes value of d_2.

$$-y = \frac{-1\times\left[\ln(X)-(\ln(S_0)+(r-\sigma^2/2)t)\right]}{\sigma\sqrt{t}} = \frac{\ln(S_0/X)+(r-\sigma^2/2)t}{\sigma\sqrt{t}} = d_2$$

And Probability $(S(t) > X) = N(-y) = N(d_2)$.

iv Receipt of stock and $N(d_1)$

The explanation of $N(d_1)$ is a bit more complex. We begin with the expected value of the contingent receipt of stock.

The expected value of the receipt of stock is contingent on exercise of the option. It is therefore the product of the conditional expected value of the receipt of S_T, given that exercise has occurred, times the probability of exercise:

Statistically this is written as:

$$E(S_T|S_T > X) \times P(S_T > X)$$

This equation can also be written as follows:

$$E(S_T|S_T > X) \times N(d_2)$$

Note that the first term in this equation is a conditional expectation. It is the expected value of S_T, given that we are now only considering those future values of S_T which exceed the exercise price X. If this constraint were not added, we would have $E(S_T) = Se^{rt}$, the unconditional expectation of S_T. Given the conditionality, therefore, $E(S_T|S_T > X)$ will always be greater than $E(S_T)$. We may understand this concept through the following simple probability example.

A six-sided fair die is rolled. The probability of rolling 4 is 1/6. Now suppose we have additional information telling us that the number rolled is greater than 3. In this case, what is the probability of a 4 having being rolled? The conditional probability works out to 1/3 > 1/6. The conditional probability is higher, because we are only considering those outcomes that exceed the number 3 in our calculation.

In a similar fashion, $E(S_T|S_T > X) > E(S_T)$ because the expected value will only consider those stock prices which exceeds the exercise price in the calculation of the expectation. Hence $E(S_T|S_T > X) \times N(d_2) > E(S_T) \times N(d_2) = Se^{rt} \times N(d_2)$.

Let us now consider the present value of this expected value by discounting it with the risk-free rate over the time remaining to option expiry. We have:

$$E(S_T|S_T > X) \times N(d_2) \times e^{-rt} > E(S_T) \times e^{-rt} \times N(d_2) = S \times N(d_2)$$

Comparing the left-hand side of this inequality with first portion of the Black–Scholes equation for the call option, $SN(d_1)$, we have:

$$SN(d_1) = E(S_T|S_T > X) \times N(d_2) \times e^{-rt} > E(S_T) \times e^{-rt} \times N(d_2) = S \times N(d_2).$$

In other words $N(d_1)$ ensures that the discounted expected value of the contingent stock price received on exercise will be greater than this current value of stock.

v **Difference between $N(d_1)$ and $N(d_2)$**

Given $SN(d_1) > SN(d_2)$, we have $N(d_1) > N(d_2)$. As mentioned above, $N(d_2)$ is simply the risk-adjusted probability that the option will be exercised. The linkage to X suggests that this depends solely on when the event $S_T > X$ occurs.

On the other hand, $N(d_1)$ will always be greater than $N(d_2)$. This is because in linking it with the contingent receipt of stock in the Black–Scholes equation, $N(d_1)$ must not only account for the probability of exercise as given by $N(d_2)$ but must also account for the fact that exercise, or rather receipt of stock on exercise, is dependent on the *conditional* future values that the stock price takes on the expiry date. In particular, this means that when calculating the expected future value of stock on the expiry date, the stock prices being greater than the exercise price are taken as a given.

UNDERSTANDING RISK ADJUSTED PROBABILITIES THROUGH THE VALUE OF A CALL OPTION		
	PAYMENT OF EXERCISE PRICE	RECEIPT OF STOCK
Payment /Receipt amount:		
Exercise	–X	S_1
Not exercise	0	0
Payment /Receipt type on exercise	Deterministic – can only take one value	Probabilistic – Must therefore consider expecteed value of S_T. Values of S_T must be >X
Expectation of amount on exercise	–X	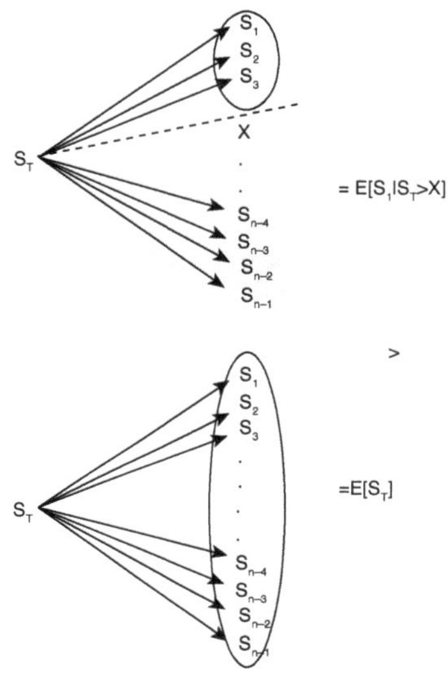
Probability:		
Of exercise	$P(S_T>X)$	$P(S_T>X)$
Of not being exercised	$P(S_T<=X)$	$P(S_T<=X)$
Discount factor	e^{-rt}	e^{-rt}
Present Value=Expection* Discount Factor* Probability	$-xe^{-rt}P(S_T>X)$	$E[S_1 \| S_T>X]e^{-rt}e^{-rt}P(S_T>X) > E[S_T]P(S_T>X) = SP(S_T>X)$
Comparison with Black–Scholes call option calue formula components	$-xe^{-rt}N(d_2)$	$SN(d_1)$
RESULTS	**$P(S_T>x)=N(d_2)$**	**$N(d_1) > N(d_2)$**

Figure 12 $N(d_1)$ and $N(d_2)$ risk-adjusted probabilities explained

Source: The Greeks against Spot. FinanceTrainingCourse.com

1
Delta and Gamma

1 The five Greeks

There are five primary factor sensitivities that we will cover in this book.

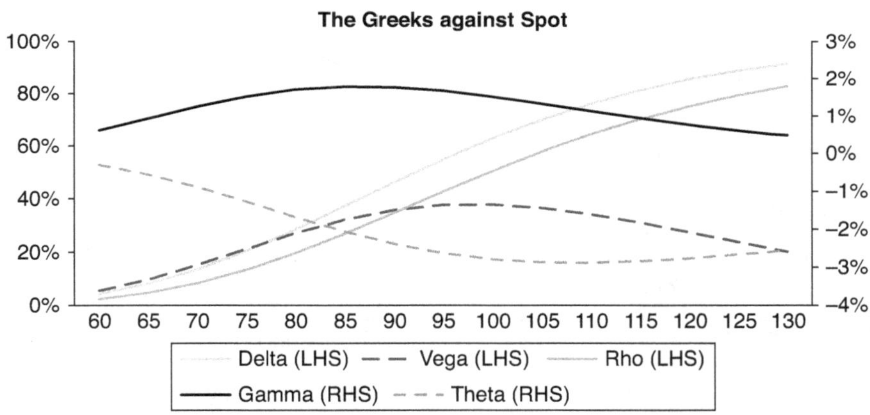

Figure 13 The five Greeks plotted against changing spots
Source: FinanceTrainingCourse.com

The image above presents a plot of the five price-factor sensitivities for a European call option. The first four are linked to four option price determinants – the underlying spot price, volatility, interest rates and time to maturity (shown in brackets with the corresponding Greek below).

Delta (Spot Price) – Measures the change in the value of the option due to a change in price of the underlying.

Vega (Volatility) – Measures the change in the value of the option due to a change in volatility of the underlying.

Rho (Interest Rates) – Measures the change in the value of the option due to a change in interest rates.

Theta (Time to Expiry) – Measures the change in the value of the option due to a change in the time to expiry or maturity.

The fifth and final sensitivity is a little different, as it measures not a change in the option price, but in one of the sensitivities, based on a change in the price of the underlying.

Gamma – Measures a change in the value of **Delta**, based on a change in the price of the underlying. If you are familiar with fixed income analytics, think of Gamma as convexity.

As promised earlier, we won't hit you with any equations. However, a quick notation summary is still required to appreciate the shape of the curves you are about to see. For a review of the notation, see Appendix 2.

Delta, Vega, Theta and Rho are first-order changes, while Gamma is a second-order change. If you take a quick look at the plot of the five factors presented above, you will see that the shape of the curves are similar for Delta and Rho (the slanting S) and similar for Gamma, Vega and Theta (the hill or inverted U). We will revisit the discussion on shapes later in the book.

The other Greeks[1]

Taleb mentions a number of additional Greeks with different utility[2] in his book *Dynamic Hedging*. They include:

- **Shadow Gamma.** A Gamma calculation that takes into account changes in volatility in addition to changes in the price of the underlying.
- **Omega.** Option Duration; the expected life of vanilla American options or expected exit for binaries and knockouts.
- **Alpha.** Gamma Rent; Theta per Gamma ratio.
- **Modified Vega.** Weighted average Vega by maturity buckets, taking into consideration the maturity bucket volatility.
- **Modified Theta.** Price of option at current volatility less the price of the same option a day later at the day-later maturity.
- **Vanna and Volga.** The two cross Greeks increasingly come up w.r.t. to FX options, and are discussed further in the hedging higher-order Greeks section of this book.

Why do we need option price sensitivities?
A vanilla call option has six determinants of value. If we want to guess the impact of a small change in any of these factors on option value, we have two choices. One is to plug in the revised value in the Black–Scholes model (also known as Full Valuation) and get the accurate price; the other is to do a quick and dirty estimate based on how the value of the option will react given the change in this specific factor.

2 Introducing Delta

i Let's talk about Delta

If you sold a call option today, how would you go about hedging your exposure?

As a call option writer, your risk is that option prices will rise and so you will be unable to create an offsetting position in time at the right price; one that would match the price at which you are obligated to deliver.

Imagine a simple world where you have sold 100 call options to a customer. The options give the buyer the right to buy the underlying security – a barrel of crude oil – from you at the price of US$100. The current price of a barrel of oil is US$92. The call option is priced at US$5. How should we hedge this position?

In our simple world, there are no transaction costs, prices do not move suddenly and without notice (jumps), and volatility remains constant throughout the life of the option.

Given these assumptions, our hedging strategy is equally simple. As soon as the underlying security touches US$100, we will purchase the underlying, locking our cost at exactly US$100. If it falls below US$100, we will sell it. We will repeat this process as many times as the security moves across our defined buy–sell threshold.

The core idea behind our hedge is this: as long as the dollar cost average of our purchases is less than the sum of the strike price and premium, we will make money on this trade.

If we remove some of the simpler assumptions behind our model world, we need a better execution strategy; one that can handle price jumps, uncertainty and transaction costs. In this world, prices are not going to wait for us to complete our purchases. They may move well beyond the price threshold of US$100 before our orders are placed and executed.

In our revised and updated hedging strategy, rather than using a single purchase at a single price point, we distribute our purchases around the target price threshold. We start buying when the likelihood of the option being exercised goes up, and we start selling when it goes down. The questions now are:

(1) How much should we buy?
(2) How much should we sell?
(3) What factor or driver should drive these decisions?

One possibility would be to take a look at the change in the value of the option based on the change in the value of the underlying.

If the option increases in value, our hedge should also increase in value. If the change in value in our hedge does not match the change in value of the option, we should buy more units of the underlying until the two changes in values (option and hedge) match. Once again, our primary objective is to keep our dollar cost average less than the sum of the strike price and the premium received.

Creating a hedge for our short option position that follows changes in option values is also known as replication. Our hedge replicates the behaviour of the option we have sold, so that in the case of exercise, as well as expiry without exercise, our replicating hedge is sufficient to pay off our obligation. We use hedge and replicating portfolio interchangeably.

In our original simple world strategy, we bought 100 units of the underlying (because we sold 100 options). In our revised approach, we buy smaller amounts depending on changes in option value based on changes in underlying prices. Our revised strategy is directionally sound. If the underlying price increases, the option value increases, so we buy more; if the underlying price falls, the option value falls, so we reduce the amount of our holdings.

The driver in this model is the change in option value because of a unit change in the underlying price. This change is known as Delta, the hedge ratio that determines how many units of the underlying we need to purchase to create a partial hedge to our options exposure above.

Delta has a handful of interpretations.

The most common interpretation is the one we have just covered above; Delta tracks option price sensitivity to changes in the price of the underlying, which is used to determine the hedge ratio for hedging the exposure of an option position on that security. We use Delta to create our replicating portfolio.

The second interpretation is a conditional probability. The probability of terminal value of S (denoted by S_t) being greater than the Strike (X) given that $S_t > X$ for a call option. In the Black–Scholes world this probability is given by $N(d_1)$. We gave a brief introduction to $N(d_1)$, the conditional probability, in our introductory chapter.

We use $S * N(d_1)$ to represent the conditional expectation (expected present value adjusted for time, probability and interest) of the terminal value of S_t for all those instances where $S_t > X$. In simpler words it is the conditional average of those values of S_t where we know that $S_t > X$.

a $N(d_1)$ revisited; a simple example

For example, for a 1-year European call option, the spot price (S) is US\$30, the strike price (X) is US\$35, the risk-free rate (r) is 10% and the annualized volatility (σ) is 30%. In order to illustrate the concept of $SN(d_1)$ we use a Monte Carlo simulator to generate and then average results over 30 iterations. The results are an approximation to what would be determined using the closed form Black–Scholes formula.

The simulator generates a path of randomly simulated price series using a BSM model.

D26 | fx | =C2*EXP((C6-0.5*C4^2)*C8+C4*SQRT(C8)*C26)

	A	B	C	D	J
24	**Simulator**				
25	**Time Step**	**Random Number**	**Normally scaled Random Number**	**Simulated Stock Price**	
26	1	0.6499	0.38514	**30.5278**	
27	2	0.6812	0.47113	**31.1784**	
28	3	0.0097	−2.33756	**28.2658**	
29	4	0.8126	0.88765	**29.3829**	
30	5	0.8494	1.03396	**30.7343**	
31	6	0.5900	0.22760	**31.0667**	
32	7	0.2938	−0.54240	**30.3933**	
33	8	0.9157	1.37681	**32.2570**	
34	9	0.1745	−0.93635	**31.0348**	
35	10	0.5895	0.22632	**31.3687**	
36	11	0.5784	0.19775	**31.6678**	
37	12	0.5145	0.03635	**31.7516**	
38	13	0.8375	0.98432	**33.1421**	
39	14	0.9114	1.34924	**35.1333**	

Figure 14 Model simulator
Source: FinanceTrainingCourse.com

The price series is calculated using the Black–Scholes terminal price formula:

$$S_t = S_0 e^{\left(r-\frac{1}{2}\sigma^2\right)t+\sigma\sqrt{t}z_t}$$

where
S_0 is the stock price from the previous time step
r is the risk-free rate
σ is the annualized volatility
t is the length of the time step
z_t is the normally scaled random variable.

The terminal price of this series at Time Step 50 is used in the calculation of the Black–Scholes probabilities mentioned below. The next part of the model is a logical test that is applied to the terminal price. The test returns a value of one if the simulated terminal price is greater than the strike price and zero if it is not.

	B	C
1	**Drivers/Inputs**	
2	**Spot**	30
3	**Strike**	35
4	**Volatility**	30%
5	**Time to Maturity**	1
6	**risk free rate**	10%
7	**n**	50
8	**Delta_T**	0.02
9	**PV Factor (PVF)**	0.90483742
10		
11	**Logical Test**	
12	**ST**	30.48
13	**Is ST > X ? (1 if Yes, 0 if No)**	=IF(C12>C3,1,0)

Figure 15 Logical test
Source: FinanceTrainingCourse.com

The average of the results from this test is used to calculate the conditional average terminal price (and probability), given that it exceeds the strike price at expiry.

The final part of the model uses Excel's data table functionality to create a results warehouse. In effect, what the data table does is store the results of each simulation run. In our data table, after each iteration, the results for terminal price (S_T), logical test result and conditional terminal price ($S_T|S_T > X$) are stored. The latter is calculated as the value of S_T if it is greater than zero, otherwise it is given as zero.

	B	C	K	L	M	N
1	**Drivers/Inputs**			**Data Table - Results Warehouse**		
2	**Spot**	30		Total number of iterations		30
3	**Strike**	35		**Unconditional Average Terminal Price**	**Unconditional probability, N(d2)**	**Conditional Average Terminal Price**
4	**Volatility**	30%	**Average across iterations**	-	0.00%	#DIV/0!
5	**Time to Maturity**	1	**Sum across Iterations**	-	0	0
6	**risk free rate**	10%		ST	Logical Test	ST | ST>X
7	n	50	0	24.44	-	0
8	**Delta_T**	0.02	1			
9	**PV Factor (PVF)**	0.904837418	2			
10			3			
11	**Logical Test**		4			
12	**ST**	24.44	5			
13	**Is ST > X ? (1 if Yes, 0 if No)**	–	6			

Figure 16 Building a data table – part 1
Source: FinanceTrainingCourse.com

	K	L	M	N
2		Total number of iterations		30
3		**Unconditional Average Terminal Price**	**Unconditional probability, N(d2)**	**Conditional Average Terminal Price**
4	**Average across iterations**	**35.08**	**53.33%**	**43.03**
5	**Sum across Iterations**	**1,052.5**	**16**	**16**
6		**ST**	**Logical Test**	**ST | ST>X**
7	0	**31.65**	–	**0**
8	1	40.0	1.00	40.00
9	2	25.6	–	–
10	3	33.8	–	–
11	4	39.6	1.00	39.62
12	5	18.8	–	–
13	6	53.9	1.00	53.90
14	7	19.9	–	–
15	8	47.7	1.00	47.74
16	9	31.7	–	–

Figure 17 Building a data table – part 2
Source: FinanceTrainingCourse.com

"Sum Across Iterations" sums the results across all 30 iterations, and "Average Across Iterations" calculates the average result across the iterations. For the conditional average terminal price, it must be noted that the average is only taken across iterations where the value of $S_T|S_T > X$ is greater than zero. Once the table is populated, we present the results from the data table and calculate the values of $N(d_1)$ and $N(d_2)$.

	B	C
15	**Average Results**	
16	**Unconditional Average Terminal Price**	32.55
17	**Conditional Average Terminal Price**	42.54
18	**Unconditional probability, $N(d_2)$**	0.3333
19	**$SN(d_1)$**	12.83
20	**Conditional probability, $N(d_1)$**	0.4277

Figure 18 Model results

We have determined:

- the unconditional probability that the terminal price (ST) will exceed the strike price is 0.3333 (this is the average of the instances when the terminal price exceeded the strike price, and is calculated over the total number of iterations), and
- the average value of terminal price over the strike price, given that the terminal price exceeds the strike price, is US$ 42.54. (In this instance, only 10 out of the total 30 iterations met the condition of terminal price being greater than the strike price, so the average terminal price was calculated across these 10 iterations only, and not over the 30. Because of this, the average is said to be conditional.)

The conditional expectation, $SN(d_1)$ = Unconditional probability × Conditional average of terminal prices × Present value factor = 0.333 × 42.54 × $e^{-1\times 1}$ = 12.83.

Therefore $N(d_1)$, the conditional probability, equals $SN(d_1)/S$ = 12.83/30 = 0.4277.

ii Using Delta: creating the replicating portfolio

If we are to simulate the option replicating and hedging portfolio using Delta, we need two separate components;

a. A long position in S equivalent to $N(d_1)$, and
b. A short position in cash required to fund our position in (a) since the premium by itself is not sufficient to fund the purchase of $S*N(d_1)$.

Together the two pieces (one long, one short) represent our hedge. If we plot the value of the call option that we have just sold and the value of the hedge that we have described, we will see a graph similar to the one below.

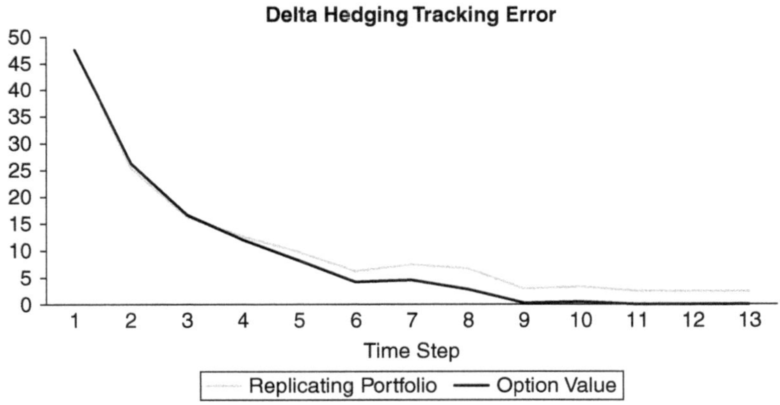

Figure 19 Replicating portfolio for call option using option Delta
Source: FinanceTrainingCourse.com

Given the ability of the hedge to closely track the value of the option, we can now see why we used the term replicating portfolio to describe it earlier.

As a seller of a call option we would like to hedge our exposure (short call option) so that when (or if) the call option is actually exercised, our loss is offset by the value of the hedge. Theoretically speaking, in an ideal world the change in value of our exposure should be completely offset by the change in value of our replicating portfolio.

We formally define the hedge as:

> A long position in the underlying given by Delta x S, less a borrowed amount.
>
> Or more formally,
>
> Call Premium (Spot, Strike, Volatility, Risk-Free Rate, Time to maturity) = $\delta S - B$

where for a European call option

$$\text{Delta}(\delta) = N(d_1)$$

B = Borrowed Amount or Borrowing.

If we adjust Delta, and with it the borrowing, at suitably discrete time intervals, we will find that our replicating portfolio will actually shadow or match the value of the option position. The adjustment and changes are required because of changes in the remaining time to maturity and the price of the underlying. As the option comes closer to maturity and the underlying price rises or falls above the strike price, the value of Delta changes.

At the point when the option is finally exercised (or not) the two positions will offset each other.

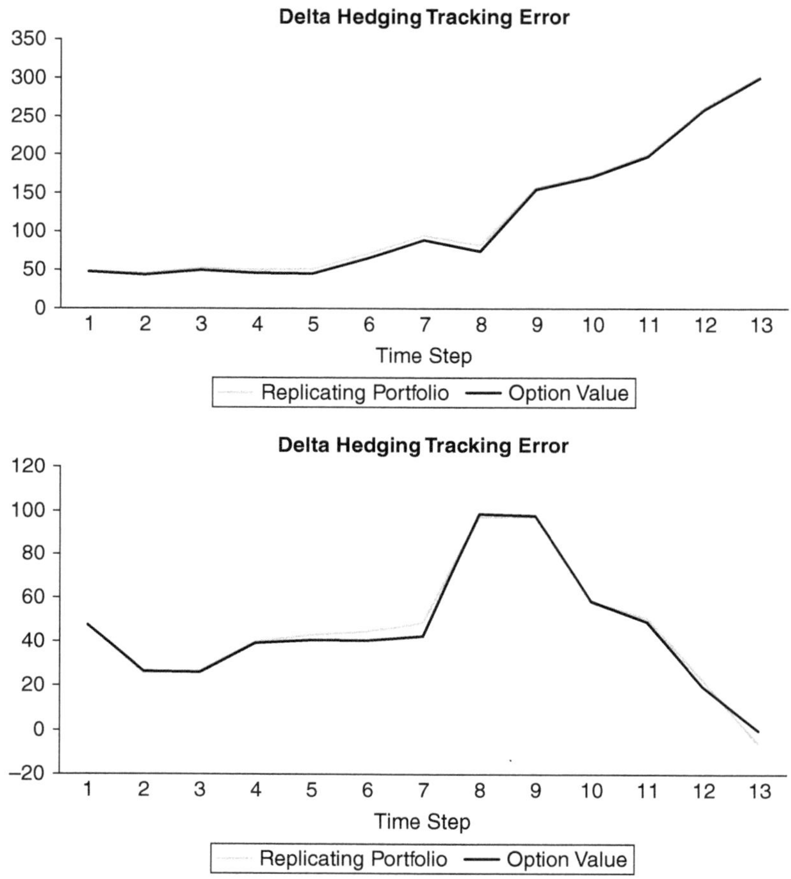

Figure 20 Replicating portfolio performance for hedging a short call option exposure
Source: FinanceTrainingCourse.com

The two replications snapshots above show how closely the two portfolios move with changes in the underlying price over a one-year time interval with monthly rebalancing (12 time steps). The tracking error will reduce if the rebalancing frequency is increased, but it will also increase the cost of maintaining the hedge.

More formally:

$$Delta_{call} = \frac{\partial C}{\partial S} = N(d_1)$$

$$d_1 = \frac{\ln\left(\frac{S}{K}\right) + \left(r + \frac{\sigma^2}{2}\right)(T-t)}{\sigma\sqrt{T-t}}$$

where
S = Stock spot price
σ = Implied volatility
r = Risk-free rate
T = Time to maturity in years
t = Current time

What is the source of the tracking error? Because Delta is a linear estimate and the price function for an option is non-linear, the Delta predicted change in price will either under- or overestimate the actual price change. The bigger the change (jump) in prices, the higher the error.

iii Dissecting Delta

How does this measure of option price sensitivity change as we change the following four key variables:

a. Spot
b. Strike
c. Time to expiry, and
d. Volatility?

Where relevant, we will add more context by also looking at how Delta's behaviour changes if the option is in, at, near or out of money.

a Against spot

How does Delta behave across a range of spot prices?

Assume that we have purchased or sold a call option on a non-dividend paying stock with a strike price of US$100. The underlying is currently trading at a spot price of US$100. The time to expiry or maturity is one year.

The graph above shows the change in the value of Delta as spot prices move higher or lower than the original US$100.

In this specific instance, while we have moved spot prices we have held maturity constant. As a result, while the spot price for the underlying changes from 60 to 130, the option's Delta does not touch zero (0%) or 1 (100%), since

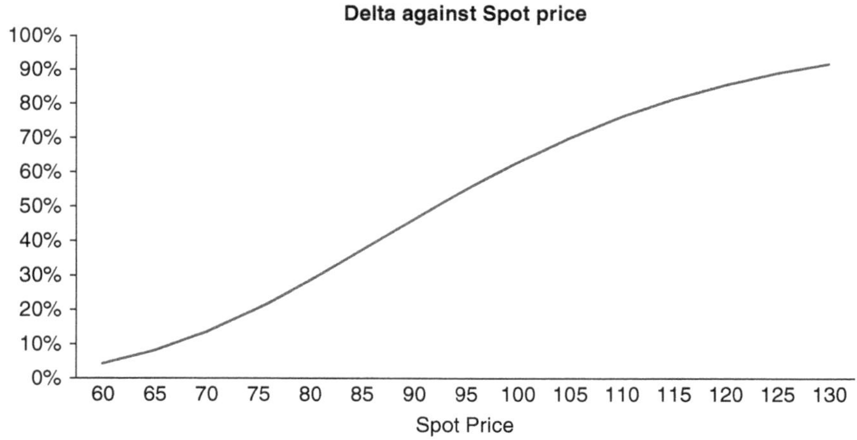

Figure 21 Delta plotted against a range of spot prices
Source: FinanceTrainingCourse.com

there is a chance that in the time remaining the underlying prices may still suddenly go the other way.

How does the behaviour of Delta change if you move across near money options to options that are deep out of money or deep in the money? Think about this for a second before you move forward. Would you expect to see a different curve? Or a different shape? If so, how different?

For at money or near money options, the shape remains the same. For options that are deep in the money, it becomes asymptotic before finally touching 1.

From our hedging definition above, this means that the seller of the option should now own the exact numbers of shares of the underlying committed to the call option (Delta = 1) since the option will most certainly expire in the money. From a probability perspective, for a call option a conditional probability of 1 indicates that the option is very likely to expire in the money, hence the recommendation to fully hedge the position.

How does Delta behave for deep out of money options?

We answer this question by plotting all five Greeks for a European call option written with strike price of US$200 while the current spot price is only at US$100. In a price ranging between US$60 and US$130, the value of Delta touches zero and then slowly rises to about 80% as the underlying spot price reaches US$130.

The overall shape of the curve that plots Delta remains the same. All we are doing for options with different moneyness is looking at a different pane of the option sensitivity window. Slide a little further or put the following two figures side by side, and you should be able to see the complete picture.

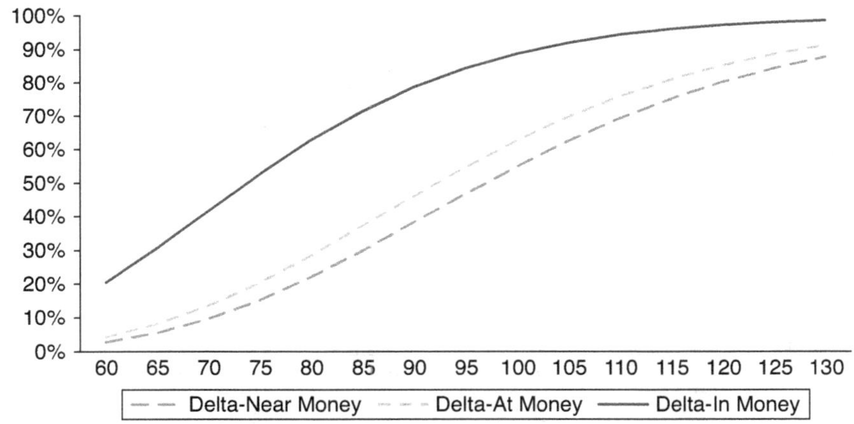

Figure 22 Delta against spot: at, in and near money options
Source: FinanceTrainingCourse.com

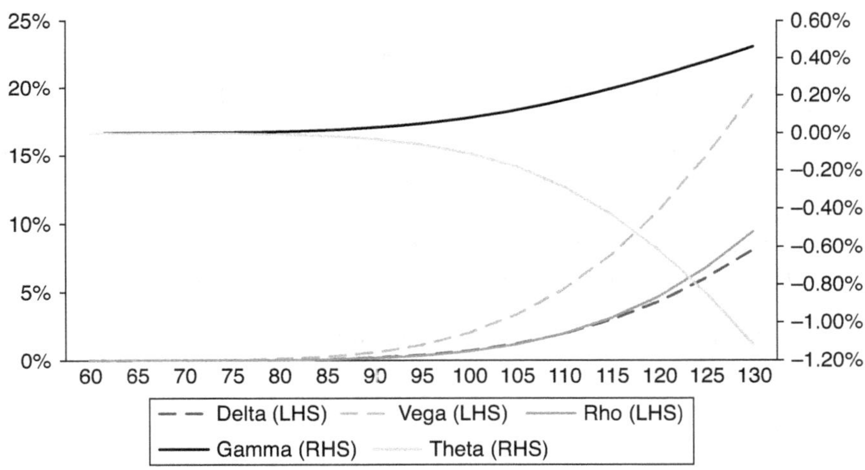

Figure 23 The Greeks against spot – deep out of money call options – strike price US$200
Source: FinanceTrainingCourse.com

What is the valid range of values that Delta is expected to take? For a call option the range is between 0 and 1, as demonstrated above. Zero for deep out of money options, one for deep in money options, and in between for all other shades.

For put options, Delta ranges between 0 and −1. Deep in money put options touch a Delta of −1, and deep out of money put options reach a Delta of

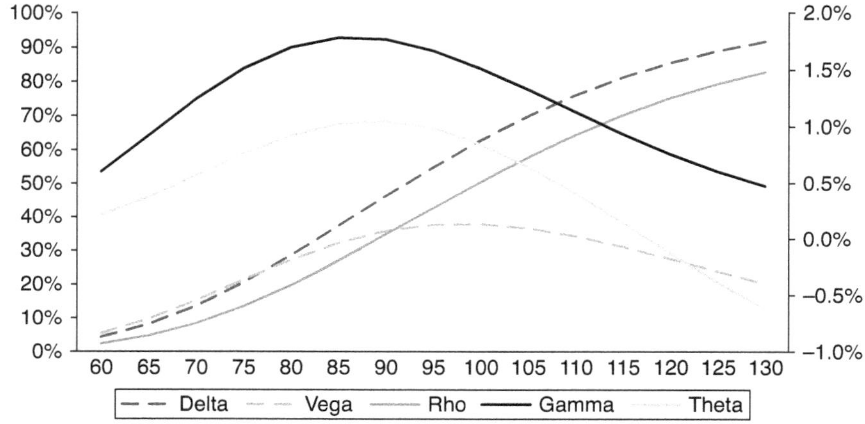

Figure 24 The Greeks against spot – strike price US$100
Source: FinanceTrainingCourse.com

zero. The negative sign corresponds to the negative change in the value of option when underlying increases by a unit price. A negative Delta further corresponds to taking a short position in underlying asset to hedge the short position of put option.

To hedge a put, unlike a call, we short the underlying and invest the proceeds, rather than buying the underlying by borrowing the difference. In the terminology used earlier, this is a long position in a riskless investment security, and a short position in the underlying.

Formally, the hedge for a short position in a European put option is:

$$\text{Put premium (Spot, Strike, Vol, Int Rate, Time)} = I - \delta S$$

where
$\delta = N(d_1) - 1$
S = Spot price
I = Investment portfolio.

3 Introducing Gamma

Gamma is the second derivative of the option price with respect to the price of an underlying asset. Alternatively, it is the rate of change in the option Delta due to a change in the underlying asset price.

What does that mean in simpler language?

In the image above, the Gamma peak corresponds to at money options while the dips at the two ends correspond to deep out and deep in money options.

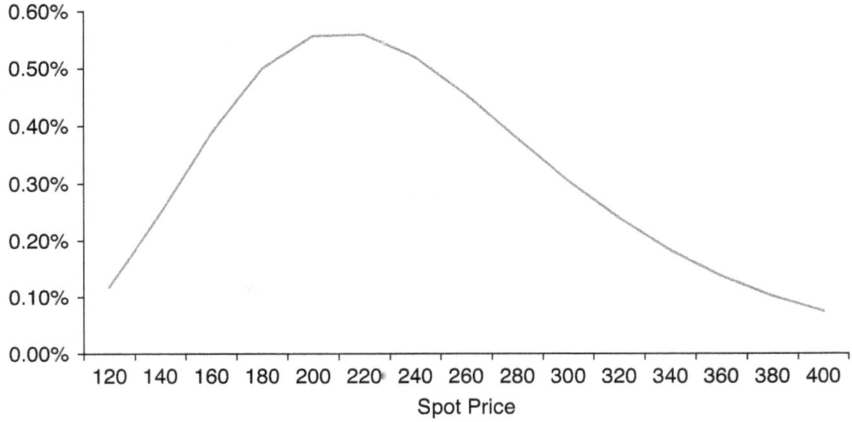

Figure 25 Gamma against spot
Source: FinanceTrainingCourse.com

If you hedge your Delta but ignore your Gamma, your hedge may remain effective as long as prices do not move – but a large movement in the underlying will move Delta as well as your underlying exposure. For at money options the risk of large moves impacting Delta is higher (higher Gamma); for deep in and deep out of money options, the risk of large moves impacting Delta is lower.

i Against strike

We examine the relationship between Delta and Gamma, between Gamma and moneyness, and between Gamma and time to expiry in a series of images below:

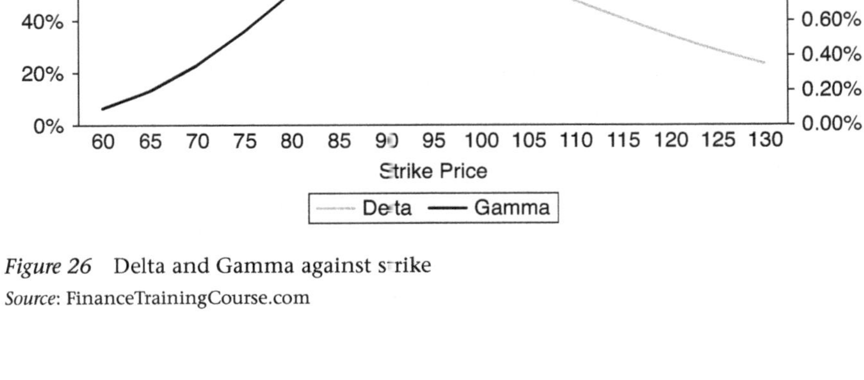

Figure 26 Delta and Gamma against strike
Source: FinanceTrainingCourse.com

The above graph plots Delta and Gamma against changing strike price. We use a plot of both Delta and Gamma to reinforce the relationship between the two variables. Once again, before you proceed further, think about why you see the two curves behaving the way they do.

The answer lies in the relationship between Delta and Gamma. Gamma is the rate of change in Delta with respect to change in the price of the underlying. As the rate of change in Delta rises, Gamma will rise as well; as the rate of change in Delta declines, Gamma will also decline.

In the figure above, as the strike price moves from the left to the right, the option gets deeper and deeper out of money. As it goes further into the deep out territory, the probability of its exercise and the amount required to hedge the exposure fall. Thus the rate of change in Delta also slows down, hence the steady decline in Delta as the strike price moves beyond the current spot price.

As the option moves from being deep out of money to near or at money, we see the rate of change of Delta increase, and with it we see Gamma rise. Once the rate of change of Delta flattens out, Gamma flattens out.

Gamma may be calculated using the Black–Scholes formula; the formal definition would be:

$$Gamma = \frac{\partial Delta}{\partial S} = \frac{N'(d_1)}{S\sigma\sqrt{T-t}}$$

where
S = Stock spot price
σ = Implied volatility
T = Time to maturity in years
t = Current time

$$N'(d_1) = \frac{1}{\sqrt{2\pi}} e^{-(d_1)^2/2}$$

$$d_1 = \frac{\ln\left(\frac{S}{K}\right) + \left(r + \frac{\sigma^2}{2}\right)(T-t)}{\sigma\sqrt{T-t}}$$

The denominator in the equation suggests an interesting relationship between Gamma, time to expiry and volatility.

ii Against time

The time to expiry relationship is examined in the two graphs below, for deep out of money options as well as for at and near money options. Can you see the relationship?

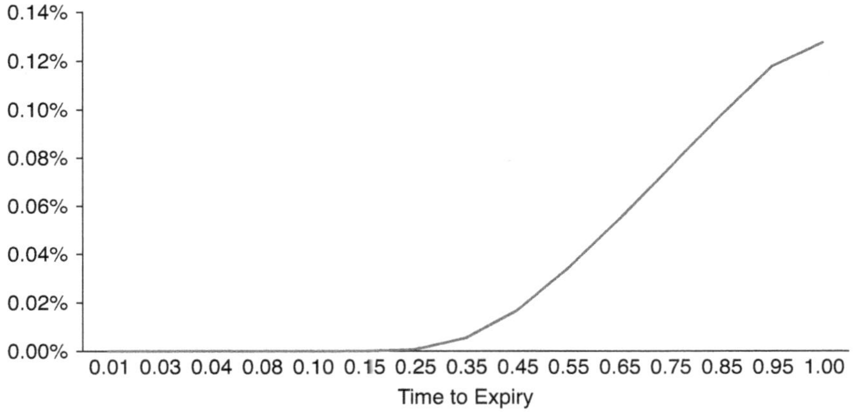

Figure 27 Gamma against time for deep out of money options
Source: FinanceTrainingCourse.com

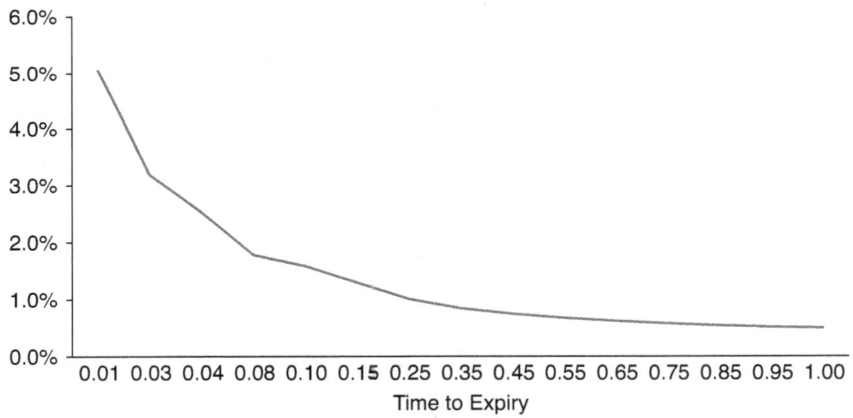

Figure 28 Gamma against time for at the money options
Source: FinanceTrainingCourse.com

In the figures above, time moves from right to left (from more to less). Gamma has a different reaction to changing time to expiry, depending on the moneyness of the option in question.

We now use Delta and Gamma plots to reinforce the relationship between the two.

The three panels above are used to dissect an at money call (Spot = 100, Strike = 100), an in money call (Spot = 110, Strike = 100) and a deep out of money call (Spot = 100, Strike = 200).

Notice how Delta declines as time to expiry for an at money call decreases, but rises to one for an in money call. For a deep out of money call on the other hand, it rises as time to expiry increases, though the level reached is not as high as that reached by the first two options.

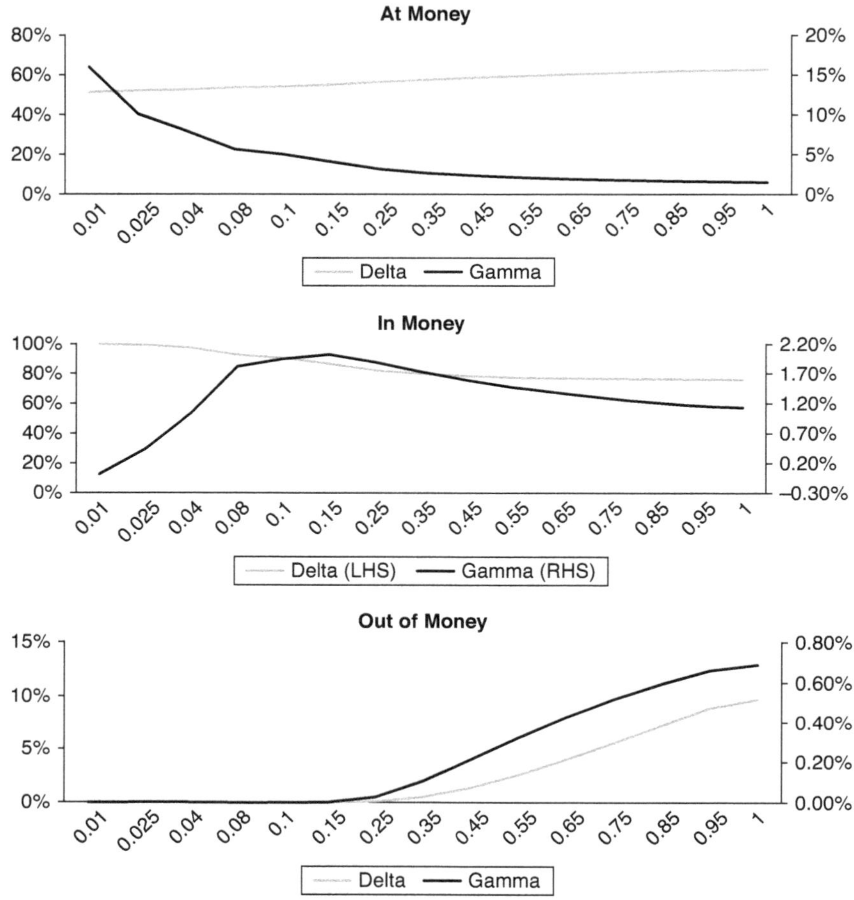

Figure 29 Delta and Gamma against time for in, at and out of money options
Source: FinanceTrainingCourse.com

For deep out of money options, Gamma declines as time to maturity is reduced. For at or near money options, Gamma increases as the option gets closer to expiry.

Practitioners including Taleb[3] recommend a more discrete way of calculating Gamma; by measuring the actual change in Delta that arises when the price of the underlying is changed. Here (dollar) Delta is also taken to be the discrete change in the value of the option for a change in the value of underlying; and not (hedge ratio) Delta as determined from the Black–Scholes formula.

1. Discrete Delta (x) = option Value (S_x)–option Value (S_0) where S_0 and S_x are the original and revised value of the underlying stock
2. The practical calculation of Gamma includes the calculation of up Gamma and down Gamma as follows:

Up Gamma (x_0) = (Discrete Delta (x_t) – Discrete Delta (x_0))/($x_t - x_0$) where $x_t > x_0$
Down Gamma (x_0) = (Discrete Delta (x_0) – Discrete Delta ($x_{t'}$))/($x_0 - x_{t'}$) where $x_{t'} < x_0$

Using Taleb's methodology and an example, we calculate up and down Gamma for options written on NVIDIA stock.

Let us consider a 30-day out of money European call option on NVIDIA stock. From ivolatility.com we obtained the following data for available options on 14 May 2014:

SYMBOL	EXCHANGE	DATE	PERIOD	STRIKE	OUT OF THE MONEY	CALL / PUT	IV	DELTA
NVDA	NASDAQ	14-May-2014	30	18.1	0	C	0.27	0.49204
NVDA	NASDAQ	14-May-2014	30	19.005	5	C	0.2734	0.26021
NVDA	NASDAQ	14-May-2014	30	19.91	10	C	0.2987	0.13058
NVDA	NASDAQ	14-May-2014	30	20.815	15	C	0.301	0.0516
NVDA	NASDAQ	14-May-2014	30	21.72	20	C	0.301	0.01689
NVDA	NASDAQ	14-May-2014	30	22.625	25	C	0.301	0.00472
NVDA	NASDAQ	14-May-2014	30	23.53	30	C	0.301	0.00114
NVDA	NASDAQ	14-May-2014	30	24.435	35	C	0.301	0.00024
NVDA	NASDAQ	14-May-2014	30	25.34	40	C	0.301	0.00005
NVDA	NASDAQ	14-May-2014	30	26.245	45	C	0.301	0.00001
NVDA	NASDAQ	14-	30	27.15	50	C	0.301	0

Continued

SYMBOL	EXCHANGE	DATE	PERIOD	STRIKE	OUT OF THE MONEY %	CALL / PUT	IV	DELTA
		May-2014						
NVDA	NASDAQ	14-May-2014	30	28.055	55	C	0.301	0
NVDA	NASDAQ	14-May-2014	30	28.96	60	C	0.2885	0

Figure 30 Implied volatilities: data for out of money call option on NVIDIA stock

Let us consider the 60% 30-day out of money call option with strike of US$28.96, spot price of US$18.1 and annualized volatility of 28.85%. The risk-free rate and dividend yield assumed in our calculations are 0.05% and 0% respectively. The value of the option works out at US$0.000000003.

Assume that the underlying stock price changes to US$22.1. The value of the option becomes US$0.0003291. Hence, an increase in the stock price led to a US$0.00033 change in the value of the option, the Delta. The following are Deltas calculated for changes in the underlying asset price (with respect to the original spot price) for the given option:

NVIDIA STOCK PRICE	DELTA
15.6	(0.00000)
16.1	(0.00000)
16.6	(0.00000)
17.1	(0.00000)
17.6	(0.00000)
18.1	-
18.6	0.00000
19.1	0.00000
19.6	0.00000

Continued

NVIDIA STOCK PRICE	DELTA
20.1	0.00000
20.6	0.00001
21.1	0.00003
21.6	0.00011
22.1	0.00033
22.6	0.00088
23.1	0.00218
23.6	0.00498
24.1	0.01058
24.6	0.02105
25.1	0.03935
25.6	0.06946
26.1	0.11624
26.6	0.18519
27.1	0.28201
27.6	0.41198
28.1	0.57942
28.6	0.78721
29.1	1.03647
29.6	1.32654
30.1	1.65513
30.6	2.01866
31.1	2.41271
31.6	2.83249
32.1	3.27323
32.6	3.73050

Figure 31 Discrete Deltas for deep out of money options on NVIDIA stock

In this discrete measurement, Gamma is calculated twice for each asset price. An up-Gamma is the change in the value of Delta, given the underlying asset price moves up by an incremental value; a down-Gamma is the change in the value of the Delta given that the underlying asset price moves down by an incremental value.

For example, the up-Gamma calculated at asset price US$25.1 for an increment of US$1 in the asset price is equal to the Delta calculated at asset price US$26.1 less the Delta calculated at asset price US$25.1, up-Gamma (25.1) = Delta (26.1) – Delta (25.1) = 0.11624–0.03935 = 0.0769.

Likewise, the down-Gamma calculated at asset price US$25.1 for a decrement of US$1 in the asset price is equal to the Delta calculated at asset price US$25.1 less the Delta calculated at asset price US$24.1, that is, down-Gamma (25.1) = Delta (25.1) – Delta (24.1) = 0.03935–0.01058 = 0.0288.

The up-Gamma and down-Gamma changes in Delta for a sample set of asset prices are given below:

NVIDIA STOCK PRICE	DELTA	UP GAMMA	DOWN GAMMA
15.6	(0.00000)	0.0000	0.0000
16.1	(0.00000)	0.0000	0.0000
16.6	(0.00000)	0.0000	0.0000
17.1	(0.00000)	0.0000	0.0000
17.6	(0.00000)	0.0000	0.0000
18.1	-	0.0000	0.0000
18.6	0.00000	0.0000	0.0000
19.1	0.00000	0.0000	0.0000
19.6	0.00000	0.0000	0.0000
20.1	0.00000	0.0000	0.0000
20.6	0.00001	0.0001	0.0000
21.1	0.00003	0.0003	0.0000
21.6	0.00011	0.0008	0.0001
22.1	0.00033	0.0018	0.0003
22.6	0.00088	0.0041	0.0008
23.1	0.00218	0.0084	0.0018
23.6	0.00498	0.0161	0.0041
24.1	0.01058	0.0288	0.0084

Continued

NVIDIA STOCK PRICE	DELTA	UP GAMMA	DOWN GAMMA
15.6	(0.00000)	0.0000	0.0000
16.1	(0.00000)	0.0000	0.0000
16.6	(0.00000)	0.0000	0.0000
17.1	(0.00000)	0.0000	0.0000
17.6	(0.00000)	0.0000	0.0000
18.1	-	0.0000	0.0000
18.6	0.00000	0.0000	0.0000
19.1	0.00000	0.0000	0.0000
19.6	0.00000	0.0000	0.0000
20.1	0.00000	0.0000	0.0000
20.6	0.00001	0.0001	0.0000
21.1	0.00003	0.0003	0.0000
21.6	0.00011	0.0008	0.0001
22.1	0.00033	0.0018	0.0003
22.6	0.00088	0.0041	0.0008
23.1	0.00218	0.0084	0.0018
23.6	0.00498	0.0161	0.0041
24.1	0.01058	0.0288	0.0084

Figure 32 Up-Gammas and down-Gammas for deep out of money options on NVIDIA stock

The difference between the up-Gamma and down-Gamma changes is depicted below:

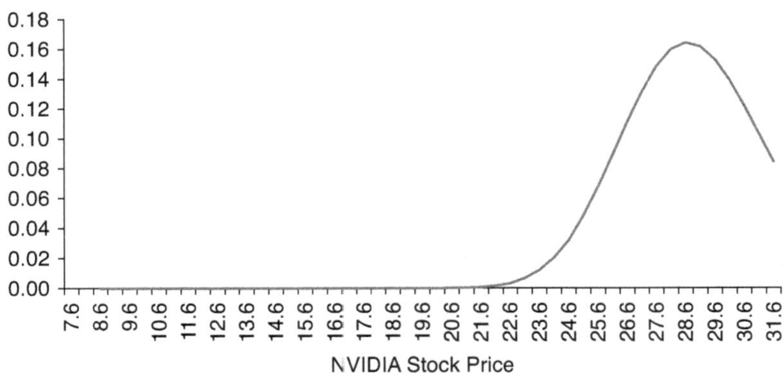

Figure 33 Difference between up-Gammas and down-Gammas for deep out of money options on NVIDIA stock

Source: FinanceTrainingCourse.com

We can see that the difference does not remain constant as the asset price changes. Hedging exactly for Gamma fails to account for the fact that changes in Delta are not constant across asset price changes.

Up-Gamma for a call option is always greater than down-Gamma. Do you think the same relationship holds true for put options, or will that be different? To improve your understanding go ahead and repeat the above exercise for a put option; plot the graph and see what happens.

iii Against volatility

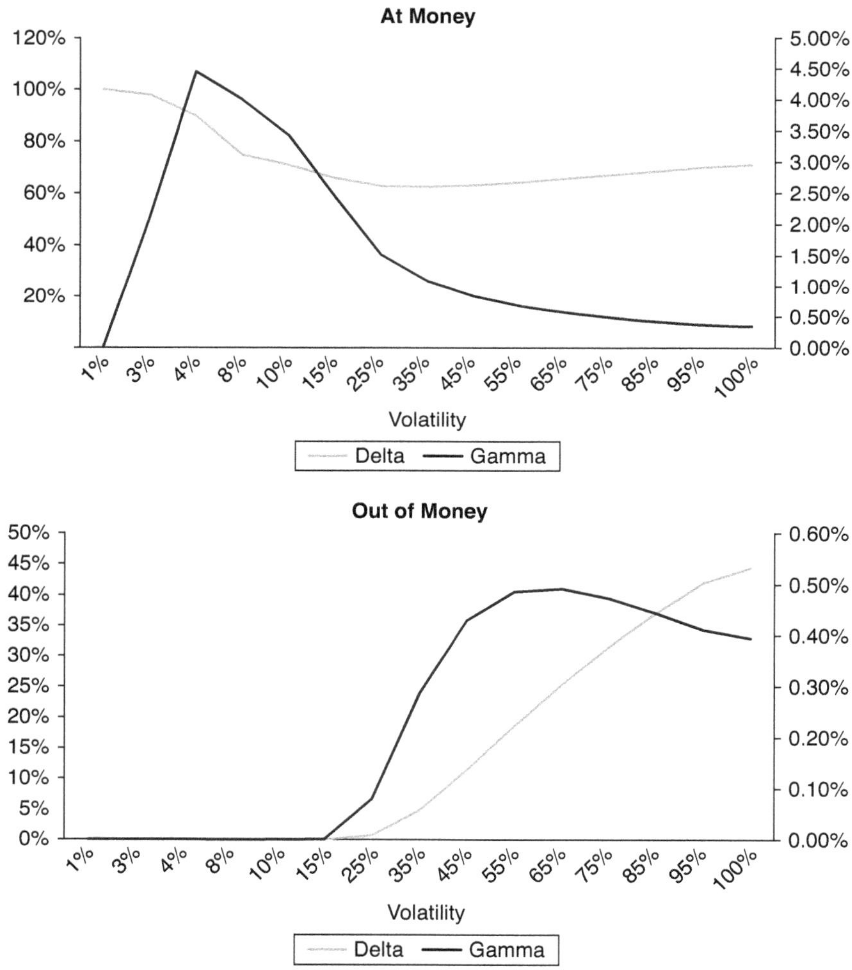

Figure 34 Delta, Gamma against volatility for at and out of money options
Source: FinanceTrainingCourse.com

For our last act, we plot Delta and Gamma against volatility and see a result which some people find counterintuitive.

For in, near or at money options, Delta actually falls with rising volatility. For some people, this is a surprising result – it is to be expected that with rising volatility the value of the option should go up (correct) because the range of values reachable by the underlying is higher (also correct) hence leading to a higher probability of exercise (incorrect). (Hint: Look up volatility drag.)

For deep out of money options, Delta rises with rising volatility. Gamma keeps pace initially but then runs out of steam as the rate of increase in Delta begins to flatten out.

To appreciate this behaviour you have to move away from the Greeks and look instead at exercise probabilities.

a The relationship between volatility, probability of exercise and price

Our next three plots show how the conditional probability of exercise $N(d_1)$, the unconditional probability of $S_t > X$, $N(d_2)$ and price behave and change for in, at and out of money European call options.

In the images beneath, price is measured using the right-hand scale, while the two probabilities are measured using the left-hand scale. For at, in and near money options, the two probabilities actually decline as volatility rises. This sounds counterintuitive when you consider that while the two probabilities are declining the price of the option is actually rising. For a deep out of money option, the trend is reversed. Once again, ask yourself why.

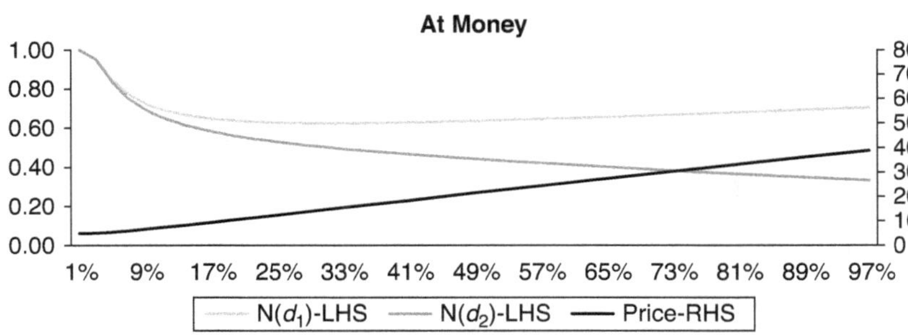

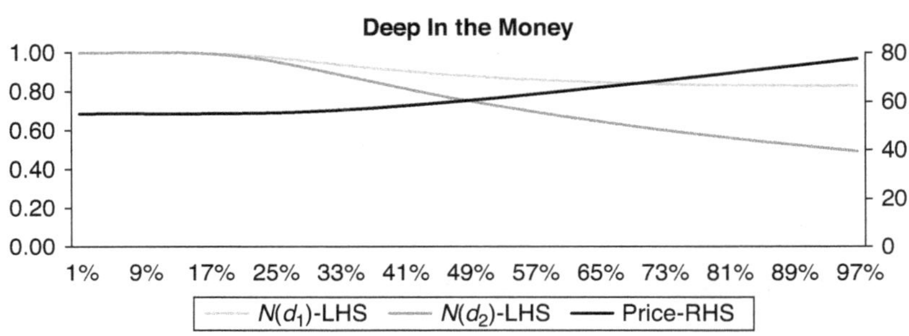

Continued

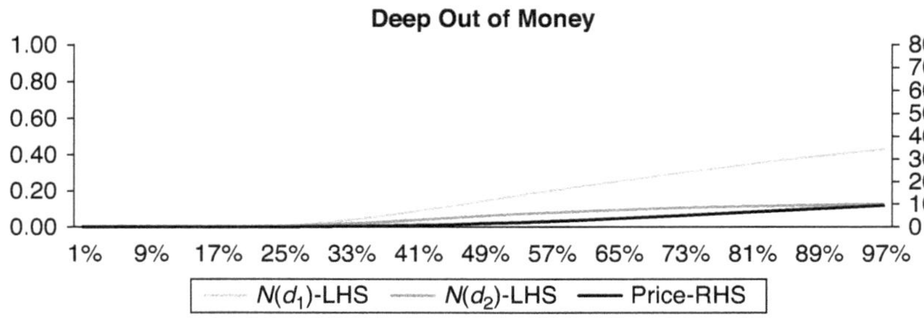

Figure 35 $N(d_1)$, $N(d_2)$ and price for at, deep in and deep out of money call options against volatility

Source: FinanceTrainingCourse.com

Appendix 1 Calculation Examples for At or Near Money Options

All options are assumed to be written on Barclays (BARC) Bank plc as of 3 March 2014. The underlying stock price is the closing price of US$247.83 on the same date. We assume a constant risk-free interest rate of 1%, zero dividends and time to expiry of 1 year for all options. All options are assumed to be European options unless stated otherwise.

1	**Parameters**	
2	Spot	247.83
3	Strike	247.83
4	Risk Free Rate	1%
5	Daily Vol	**1.7%**
6	Annualized Vol	31.84%
7	Time to Maturity	1
8	Notional	1
9	Annualized Vol	**31.8%**
10		

Figure 36 Base parameters used in the example

a Example 1 – Calculating Delta for a call option

The Delta for a call option is given by the following Black–Scholes formula:

$$Delta_{call} = \frac{\partial C}{\partial S} = N(d_1)$$

$$d_1 = \frac{\ln\left(\frac{S}{K}\right) + \left(r + \frac{\sigma^2}{2}\right)(T-t)}{\sigma\sqrt{T-t}}$$

where
S = Stock spot price
σ = Implied volatility
r = Risk-free rate
T = Time to maturity in years
t = Current time

We first calculate d_1

	A	B	C	D
17	d_1 -final	=((LN(Spot/Strike)+(Riskfree+0.5*Vol^2)*Time))/		
18	d_2 -final	(Vol*SQRT(Time))		

Figure 37 Calculation d_1 in Excel

	A	B
17	d_1 -final	0.1906
18	d_2 -final	0.1278
19	$N(d_1)$	=NORMSDIST(–B17)

Figure 38 Calculation of call Delta in Excel

Call Delta, $N(d_1)$ works out at 0.5756.

b Example 2 – Calculating Delta for a put option

We do a similar calculation for put Delta. The Delta for a put option is given by the formula:

$$Delta_{put} = \frac{\partial P}{\partial S} = N(d_1) - 1$$

$$d_1 = \frac{\ln\left(\frac{S}{K}\right) + \left(r + \frac{\sigma^2}{2}\right)(T-t)}{\sigma\sqrt{T-t}}$$

where
S = Stock spot price
σ = Implied volatility
r = Risk-free rate
q = Dividend yield rate
T = Time to maturity in years
t = Current time

And zero dividends mean the formula simplifies to:

$$Delta_{put} = \frac{\partial P}{\partial S} = N(d_1) - 1$$

In the above case, the value of Delta for a put option with the same parameters as above becomes 0.5657–1 = –0.4244.

What happens to the values of the two options Deltas (call and put) when we hold everything else constant but change the underlying stock price by US$1?

Parameters	
Spot	248.83
Strike	247.83
Risk Free Rate	1%
Daily Vol	**1.7%**
Annualized Vol	31.84%
Time to Maturity	1
Notional	1

Figure 39 Drivers of option prices – change in spot price

The value for the call option Delta increases by 0.0049, to stand at 0.5805, whereas the value for the put option Delta increases by 0.0049 to stand at –0.4195.

We repeat the process for varying spot prices. The result is depicted in the figure below:

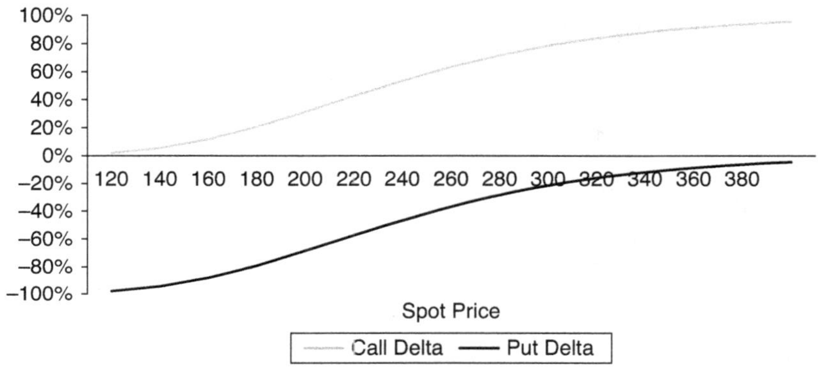

Figure 40 Call and put Delta against spot prices
Source: FinanceTrainingCourse.com

c Example 3 – Calculating Gamma

Gamma is given by the following Black–Scholes formula:

$$Gamma = \frac{\partial Delta}{\partial S} = \frac{N'(d_1)}{S\sigma\sqrt{T-t}}$$

$$N'(d_1) = e^{-\frac{(d_1)^2}{2}} * \frac{1}{\sqrt{2\pi}}$$

$$d_1 = \frac{\ln\left(\frac{S}{K}\right) + \left(r + \frac{\sigma^2}{2}\right)(T-t)}{\sigma\sqrt{T-t}}$$

where
S = Stock spot price
σ = Implied volatility
r = Risk-free rate
T = Time to maturity in years
t = Current time

We already have d_1, sigma and T from the examples above; all we need to do now is calculate $N'(d_1)$. Using the base parameters, this works out at 0.3918. We plug this value into the Gamma formula above. Because Gamma is a second-order rate of change with respect to change in the underlying, it is same for a call and put. The gamma works out at 0.0050.

d Example 4 – Calculating Vega

The value of Vega can be calculated using the following formula:

$$Vega = S\sqrt{T-t}N'(d_1)e^{-q(T-t)}$$

$$N'(d_1) = e^{-\frac{(d_1)^2}{2}} * \frac{1}{\sqrt{2\pi}}$$

$$d_1 = \frac{\ln\left(\frac{S}{K}\right) + \left(r + \frac{\sigma^2}{2}\right)(T-t)}{\sigma\sqrt{T-t}}$$

where
S = Stock spot price
σ = Implied volatility
r = Risk-free rate
ln = natural log
K = Strike price
q = Dividend yield rate
T = Time to maturity in years
t = Current time

Since we have assumed no dividends, the formula simplifies to:

$$Vega = S\sqrt{T-t}N'(d_1)$$

Alternatively, Vega could also be expressed as a function of Gamma.

$$v = \gamma S^2(T-t)\sigma$$

where
S = Stock spot price
σ = Implied volatility
T = Time to maturity in years
t = Current time
v = Vega
γ = Gamma.

We can use either of the two equations to calculate Vega. Like Gamma, the value of Vega is the same for both call and put options. For our example, it works out at 97.0901.

e Example 5 – Calculating Theta for a call option

The equation to calculate a call Theta is:

$$Theta_{call} = \frac{\partial C}{\partial (T-t)}$$

$$Theta_{call} = \frac{-SN'(d_1)\sigma e^{-q(T-t)}}{2\sqrt{T-t}} + qSN(d_1)e^{-q(T-t)} - rKN(d_2)e^{-r(T-t)}$$

Assuming zero dividends reduces the above formula to:

$$Theta_{call} = \frac{\partial C}{\partial (T-t)} = \frac{-SN'(d_1)\sigma}{2\sqrt{T-t}} - rKN(d_2)e^{-r(T-t)}$$

Using our base parameters, the Theta works out at 2.078.

f Example 6 – Calculating Theta for a put option:

The theta for a put option is calculated using the following formula:

$$Theta_{put} = \frac{\partial C}{\partial (T-t)} = \frac{-SN'(d_1)\sigma e^{-q(T-t)}}{2\sqrt{T-t}} - qSN(-d_1)e^{-q(T-t)} + rKN(-d_2)e^{-r(T-t)}$$

This simplifies to the following for zero dividends:

$$Theta_{put} = \frac{\partial C}{\partial (T-t)} = \frac{-SN'(d_1)\sigma}{2\sqrt{T-t}} + rKN(-d_2)e^{-r(T-t)}$$

The resultant theta value is –14.1052.

g Example 7 – Calculating Rho for a call option

The Rho for a European call option on stock that does not pay dividends is given by the following formula:

$$Rho_{call} = K(T-t)e^{-r(T-t)}N(d_2)$$

where
S = Stock spot price
σ = Implied volatility
r = Risk-free rate
T = Time to maturity in years
t = Current time

$$N'(d_1) = e^{-\frac{(d_1)^2}{2}} * \frac{1}{\sqrt{2\pi}}$$

$$d_1 = \frac{Ln\left(\frac{S}{K}\right) + \left(r + \frac{\sigma^2}{2}\right)(T-t)}{\sigma\sqrt{T-t}}$$

$$d_2 = d_1 - \sigma\sqrt{T-t}$$

In the above example d_2 works out at 0.1278, $N(d_2)$ equals 0.4492 and the value of Rho works out at 110.2068.

h Example 8 – Calculating Rho for a put option

The value of Rho for a European put option on a non-dividend paying stock is given by the formula:

$$Rho_{put} = -K(T-t)e^{-r(T-t)}N(-d_2)$$

In our example $N(-d_2) = 1 - N(d_2)$ and Rho = −135.1572.

A summary of results obtained using our base parameters for the five Greeks are as follows.

Greeks	Call	Put
Delta	0.5756	-0.4244
Gamma	0.0050	0.0050
Vega	97.09	97.09
Theta	-16.56	-14.11
Rho	110.21	-135.16

Figure 41 Example – summary of results

Appendix 2 Using Greeks

From Appendix 1 we have the following table of Greeks for our Barclays Bank plc call and put options. How can we put them to work?

Greeks	Call	Put
Delta	0.5756	-0.4244
Gamma	0.0050	0.0050
Vega	97.09	97.09
Theta	- 16.56	- 14.11
Rho	110.21	-135.16

Figure 42 Results of Greeks for call and put option example

For each Greek we will shock the variable in question and calculate the impact on the price of the option predicted by the Greek. We will call this approach the Delta Normal method.

We will also value the option using the Black–Scholes formula and the revised parameter input. The difference between this value and the original value will be the impact on option price. We will label this approach the Full Valuation approach.

If our numbers in the above tables are correct, the two approaches, Delta Normal **and** Full Valuation, should reconcile.

a Example 1 – Estimating Delta

The original parameters produced the following call and put prices:

	A	B	C	D	E
2	**Price of a Call**	**32.4400**		Spot	247.83
3	**Price of a Put**	**29.9740**		Strike	247.83
4				Risk Free Rate	1%
5	**Contracts**			Daily Vol	**1.7%**
6	Price of a Call	**32.44**		Annualized Vol	31.84%
7	Price of a Put	**29.97**		Time to Maturity	1
8	LC+LP - Long Straddle	62.41		Notional	1

Figure 43 Call and put valuation sheet

What happens to the call price and put price when we change the stock prices by US$1?

Method 1: Delta normal

The change in the price of a call option should be:

$$\Delta * \partial P$$

where
Δ is the Delta of the option calculated using the Black–Scholes formula
∂P is the unit change in price

Using the values of Delta from the table above, we get:

$$0.5756 \times 1 = 0.5756$$

Method 2: Full valuation

Using the Full Valuation approach, we simply update the spot price parameter in our Excel spreadsheet, and update the results, to get a new Full Valuation price of US$33.01 for a call option.

	BS Model Out Put	Parameters	
Price of a Call	**33.01807**	Spot	248.83
Price of a Put	**29.55212**	Strike	247.83
		Risk Free Rate	1%
Contracts		Daily Vol	**1.7%**
Price of a Call	**33.02**	Annualized Vol	31.84%
Price of a Put	**29.55**	Time to Maturity	1
LC+LP - Long Straddle	62.57	Notional	1
		Annualized Vol	**31.8%**

Figure 44 Values of call and put under revised spot price parameter
Source: FinanceTrainingCourse.com

The price of the call option has changed by:

$$33.01807 - 32.4400 = 0.57806$$

The results from the two methods, when it comes to the change in the price of a call option, are similar; there is a small positive error of 0.00246 = (0.57806 – 0.5756). This is due to the convexity of the option price. The difference is effectively the gamma effect.

b Example 2 – Estimating Gamma

To account for the error, we now include Gamma in our reconciliation mix.

Method 1: Delta normal

The approximation method for the change in option price now becomes:

$$\Delta * \partial P + \frac{\gamma * \partial P^2}{2}$$

where
γ is the Gamma of the option calculated using the Black–Scholes formula
Δ is the Delta of the option calculated using the Black–Scholes formula
∂P is the unit change in price

Using the above equation, the result of the calculation is:

$$0.5756 * 1 + \frac{0.005 * 1}{2} = 0.5781$$

Method 2: Full valuation

As mentioned earlier the Full Valuation change is 0.57806. The Delta Normal estimate is 0.5781. The error term has been reduced from 0.00246 to 0.00004.

An alternate approach to testing Gamma is to use it to calculate the change in Delta. Original Delta and Gamma values at inception prior to the price shock are:

Greeks	Call
Delta	0.5756
Gamma	0.0050

Figure 45 Delta and Gamma of a call option under original parameters
Source: FinanceTrainingCourse.com

Method 1: Delta normal

Theoretically speaking, the Delta value should become:

$$\Delta = \Delta_{old} + \gamma * \partial P$$

where
γ is the Gamma of the option calculated using the Black–Scholes formula
Δ_{old} is the Delta of the option calculated using the Black–Scholes formula
∂P is the unit change in price

$$\Delta = 0.5756 + 0.005*1 = 0.5806$$

Method 2: Full valuation

The full valuation approach recalculates the Greek, Delta (not the option price) using a revised parameter for the Spot price (US$248.83). The result for Delta is 0.5805. The error term, therefore, works out at 0.0001.

c Example 3 – Estimating Theta

The formula given below estimates the impact on option price if, together with the change in spot price, the time to maturity also changes:[4]

$$\Delta * \partial P + \frac{\gamma * \partial P^2}{2} + \theta h$$

γ is the Gamma of the option calculated using the Black–Scholes formula
Δ is the Delta of the option calculated using the Black–Scholes formula
∂P is the unit change in price
h is the marginal change in time to maturity in years
θ is the Theta of the option calculated using the Black–Scholes formula

However, to use Theta in the above equation, we have to first convert it to years. We have used the Actual by 360-day day-count convention[5] to do this, as shown below:

	G	H	I	J	K
16					1%
17	**Greeks**	**Call**	**Put**	**Unit**	**Change**
18	**Delta**	0.5756	-0.4244	Option Price	0.576
19	**Gamma**	0.0050	0.0050	Option Price	0.005
20	**Vega**	97.09	97.09	Option Price	0.971
21	**Theta**	- 16.56	- 14.11	Years	=H21/360

Figure 46 Value of theta (expressed in years) using the Black–Scholes formula

In our test for Theta below we will only focus on the change in the value of option on account of a change in the time to maturity, holding all other variables constant.

Method 1: Delta normal approach

The value of Theta for a one-day reduction in the time to maturity, holding all other variables constant, predicts a decline of 0.046 in the value of our call option.

Method 2: Full valuation

Our revised valuation parameters now show the option expiring a day before the original expiry.

	A	B	C	D	E
1		**BS Model Out Put**		**Parameters**	
2	**Price of a Call**	**32.39394**		Spot	247.83
3	**Price of a Put**	**29.93480**		Strike	247.83
4				Risk Free Rate	1%
5	**Contracts**			Daily Vol	**1.7%**
6	Price of a Call	**32.39**		Annualized Vol	31.84%
7	Price of a Put	**29.93**		Time to Maturity	0.997222222
8	LC+LP - Long Straddle	62.33		Notional	1

Figure 47 Value of call and put options under revised time to maturity parameter

The change in the value of the call option is

32.44400 – 32.39394 = –0.046

The full valuation result shows a result similar to that obtained using the Delta Normal approach.

d Example 4 – Estimating Vega

Method 1: Delta normal approach

The figure below shows the value of Vega calculated using the Black–Scholes formula with the original parameter values. Since we are considering a 1% change in volatility, the estimated change in the value of the call option is 97.0901 × 0.01 = 0.971.

	G	H	I	J	K
16					**1%**
17	**Greeks**	**Call**	**Put**	**Unit**	**Change**
18	**Delta**	0.5756	–0.4244	Option Price	0.576
19	**Gamma**	0.0050	0.0050	Option Price	0.005
20	**Vega**	97.09	97.09	Option Price	=H20*K16

Figure 48 Value of Vega (expressed in % shock) using the Black–Scholes formula

Method 2: Full valuation

Let us go to our option pricing example and see what happens when we increase volatility. Our new valuation parameters add 1% to the original value of implied volatility:

	A	B	C	D	E
1		BS Model Out Put		Parameters	
2	Price of a Call	33.41049		Spot	247.83
3	Price of a Put	30.94454		Strike	247.83
4				Risk Free Rate	1%
5	Contracts			Daily Vol	1.7%
6	Price of a Call	33.41		Annualized Vol	32.84%
7	Price of a Put	30.94		Time to Maturity	1
8	LC+LP - Long Straddle	64.36		Notional	1
9				Annualized Vol	32.8%

Figure 49 Value for call and put options under the revised volatility

The revised call option value based on the new volatility of 32.84% is 33.41049. Therefore, the change in the value of the call option because of this 1% change in the value of implied volatility is: 33.41049 – 32.44 = 0.9705.

e Example 5 – Estimating Rho

Method 1: Delta normal

Rho calculated using the Black–Scholes formula under the original assumptions is 110.21. Assume that the risk-free rate rises by 1%. The value of Rho suggests that the 1% increase in the risk-free rate will lead to a Rho × 0.01 = 110.21 × 0.01 = 1.102 increase in the value of the call option.

	G	H	I	J	K
16					1%
17	Greeks	Call	Put	Unit	Change
18	Delta	0.5756	-0.4244	Option Price	0.576
19	Gamma	0.0050	0.0050	Option Price	0.005
20	Vega	97.09	97.09	Option Price	0.971
21	Theta	–16.56	- 14.11	Years	–0.046
22	Rho	110.21	–135.16		=K16*H22

Figure 50 Value of Rho for a percentage change in interest rates, calculated using Black–Scholes formula

Method 2: Full valuation

The revised assumption uses a risk-free rate exactly 1% higher than the prior rate.

	A	B	C	D	E
1		**BS Model Out Put**		**Parameters**	
2	**Price of a Call**	**33.55170**		Spot	247.83
3	**Price of a Put**	**28.64434**		Strike	247.83
4				Risk Free Rate	2%
5	**Contracts**			Daily Vol	**1.7%**
6	Price of a Call	**33.55**		Annualized Vol	31.84%
7	Price of a Put	**28.64**		Time to Maturity	1
8	LC+LP - Long Straddle	62.20		Notional	1

Figure 51 Value of call and put options under revised risk-free rate

The change in the price of the call option is:

33.55 – 32.44 = 1.1

which is close to the one approximated using the Delta normal method.

f Example 6 – Estimating put option Greeks from call option Greeks using the put–call parity

As a final test, we use the put–call parity, the relationship that exists between call Greeks and put Greeks, to run a final reconciliation.

The relationship between Greeks of calls and puts is given below:

PUT-G	RELATION WITH CALL-GREEK
Delta	$\Delta put = \Delta call - e^{-q(T-t)}$
Gamma	$\gamma put = \gamma call$
Vega	$V put = V call$
Theta	$\theta put = \theta call + rKe^{-r(T-t)}$
Rho	$\rho put = \rho call - K(T-t)e^{-r(T-t)}$

Figure 52 Relationship between call Greeks and put Greeks

Method 1: Delta normal

The values of the Greeks for a call option are:

Greeks	**Call**
Delta	0.5756
Gamma	0.0050
Vega	97.09
Theta	– 16.56
Rho	110.21

Figure 53 Call Greeks calculated using the Black–Scholes formulas

Using the put–call parity relationship table, we calculate the value for Greeks for a put option.

PUT-GREEK	RELATION WITH CALL-GREEK	PUT-GREEK VALUE
Delta	$\Delta_{put} = 0.57558-1$	−0.4244
Gamma	$\gamma_{put} = \gamma_{call}$	0.005
Vega	$v_{put} = v_{call}$	97.0901
Theta	$\theta_{put} = -16.5588+0.01*247.83*e^{-0.01(1)}$	−14.1052
Rho	$\rho_{put} = 110.2068-247.83(1)e^{-0.01(1)}$	−135.1572

Figure 54 Put Greeks calculated using their relations with call Greeks

Method 2: Full valuation

Gamma and Vega are the same for both options, as mentioned earlier. We calculate the Delta, Theta and Rho of the put option using the Black–Scholes formula, and they are a match with the estimated results using the Delta Normal (put–call parity) methodology.

Greeks	Call	Put
Delta	0.5756	− 0.4244
Gamma	0.0050	0.0050
Vega	97.09	97.09
Theta	− 16.56	− 14.11
Rho	110.21	−135.16

Figure 55 Put Greeks calculated using Black–Scholes formulas

Likewise, given the value of put Greeks, the value of call option Greeks may be estimated using the put–call parity relationship mentioned above.

Part II

Delta Hedging

2
A Simulation Model for Delta Hedging – European Call Options

Delta hedging as a concept is covered within Black–Scholes–Merton pricing at a theoretical level (single-step or two-step binomial trees); however the actual implementation of a live Delta hedging program requires a bit more work.

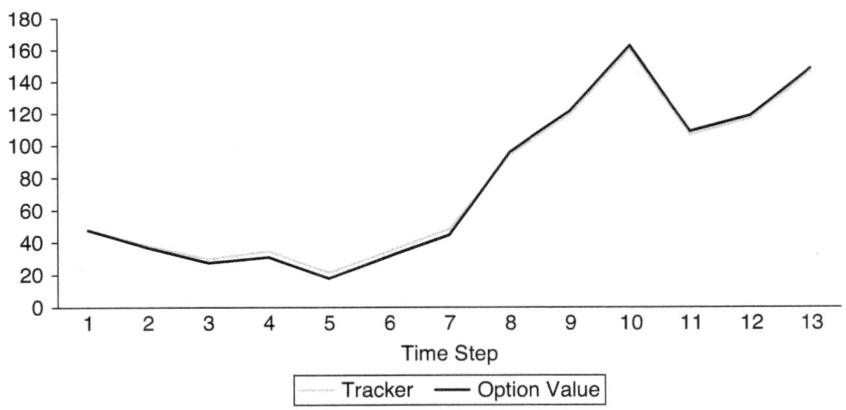

Figure 56 Delta hedging using Monte Carlo simulation
Source: FinanceTrainingCourse.com

Both Mark Broadie and John C. Hull have put together illustrative sheets that simulate the actual process of Delta hedging for a call option. As can be seen in the figure above, the basic Delta hedge model plots the values of the call option and the replicating or Delta hedge or tracker portfolio (vertical axis) against each time step (horizontal axis). This chapter will walk you through the basic model, and then extend the model to answer questions around profitability and model behaviour.

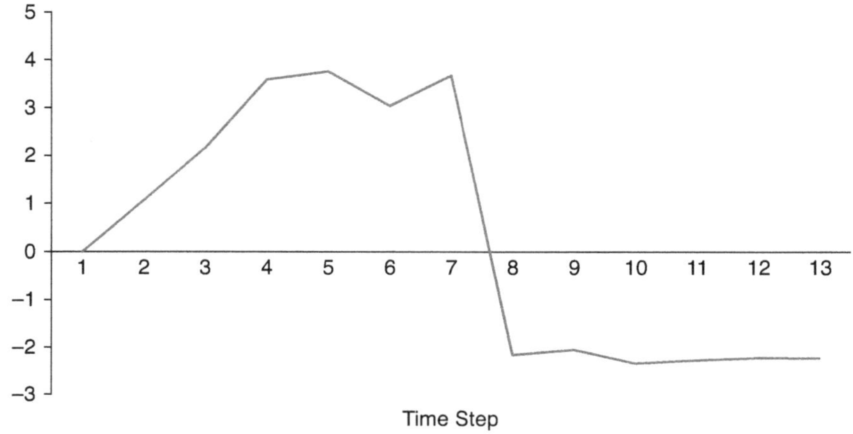

Figure 57 Tracking error between replicating portfolio and short option positions
Source: FinanceTrainingCourse.com

We will also track the error in the model (the difference between the option value and the replicating portfolio) and discuss its sources.

1 Setting the groundwork

We begin with Mark Broadie's method, which we will extend a bit when we evaluate profitability for the option book. The Hull approach is similar to the Broadie method, and if you are comfortable with either you will be fine.

					Replicating Portfolio		Replicating		Difference
Time	Time to	Stock		Option	Dollars	Total	Portfolio	Option	(port val -
step	expiration	price	d_1	delta	in stock	Borrowing	Value	Value	option val)

Figure 58 The baseline model and simulated values

The model simulates the underlying stock price and estimates the:

a. option Delta
b. replicating portfolio which comprises a long position in Delta x S (Spot price of stock) and a short position in Borrowing B, and
c. difference between the replicating portfolio and the option value.

2 Assumptions

For the purpose of our simulation, we start off with Barclays Bank plc, and assume that the bank will pay no dividends over the life of the option.

Figure 59 Barclays Bank price chart
Source: Google Finance.

We assume that the spot price is 242.5 and the daily volatility ranges between 2.5% and 5%. For the purpose of our illustration, the implied annualized volatility is assumed to be 40%, the risk-free interest rate is 1% and the time to maturity is one year.

Assumptions		
Spot		$242.50
Strike		$ 225.00
Model Volatility		40.000%
Time		1
Risk_Free		1%
Steps		12
Delta_T		0.083333333

Figure 60 Key assumptions
Source: FinanceTrainingCourse.com

Using the above assumptions, we simulate a path of the Barclays share price on a monthly basis over the next year. We assume that the recurring rebalancing period before the option Delta is evaluated and the replicating portfolio is rebalanced is one month. This approach gives us a price for each month for the next 12 months, and 12 rebalancing points.

3 Simulating the stock price

Using the discrete version of the Black–Scholes terminal price equation, we simulate the Barclays share price for the next 12 months.

$$S_t = S_0 e^{(\mu - \frac{1}{2}\sigma^2)t + \sigma\sqrt{t}z_t}$$

S_t = Terminal Spot Price at time t
S_0 = Current Spot Price at time 0
σ = Implied volatility
μ = Risk-free rate under the risk-neutral assumption
t = Time to expiry in years
z_t = Normally scaled random variable given in Excel as NORMSINV(RAND())

The result is given below. Your numbers, however, will not match those presented here, since the random seed used by the Excel RAND() function is different for every simulation.

TIME STEP	TIME TO EXPIRATION	STOCK PRICE
0	1.000	242.500
1	0.917	254.388
2	0.833	208.892
3	0.750	216.119
4	0.667	197.342
5	0.583	187.174
6	0.500	174.073
7	0.417	164.894
8	0.333	173.254
9	0.250	192.733
10	0.167	192.758
11	0.083	169.339
12	0.001	177.282

Figure 61 Simulated price series

While the first 11 time steps are equidistant, the 12th is slightly shorter. We have done this deliberately, in order to examine the option just before it expires. Hence in the "Time to Expiration' column for Time Step 12, you will see a value of 0.001 rather than 0.

The actual stock price simulation with the Black–Scholes terminal price discrete formula and the Excel implementation is shown below:

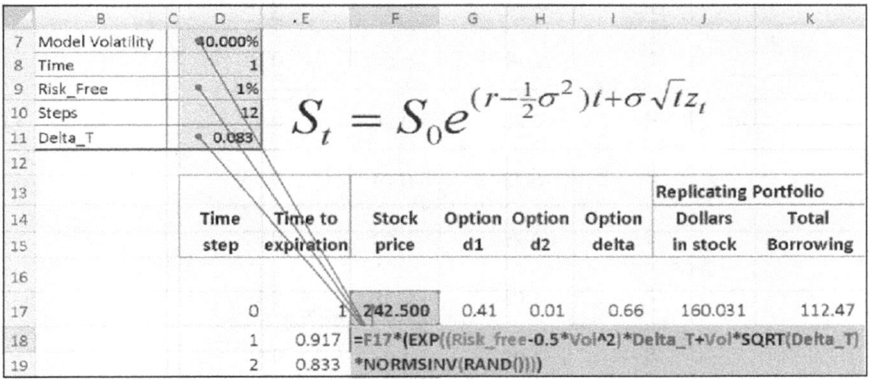

Figure 62 Excel implementation

4 Calculating Delta

The next step is to calculate the d_1, d_2 and Delta values based on the simulated stock prices at each step.

$$d_1 = \frac{\ln(S_0 / K) + (r - q + \sigma^2 / 2)T}{\sigma\sqrt{T}}$$

$$d_2 = d_1 - \sigma\sqrt{T}$$

where
ln = Natural log
S_0 = Spot price
K = Strike price
σ = Implied volatility
r = Risk-free rate
q = Dividend yield rate
T = Time to maturity in years

The value of d_1 and d_2 are given by the standard Black–Scholes model. Delta is $N(d_1)$, or in Excel NORMSDIST(d_1).

Time Step	Option d1	Option d2	Option Delta
0	0.41	0.01	0.66
1	0.54	0.15	0.70
2	0.00	–0.36	0.50
3	0.08	–0.27	0.53
4	–0.22	–0.54	0.41
5	–0.43	–0.74	0.33
6	–0.75	–1.03	0.23
7	–1.06	–1.32	0.14
8	–1.00	–1.23	0.16
9	–0.66	–0.86	0.25
10	–0.86	–1.02	0.20
11	–2.40	–2.51	0.01
12	–18.84	–18.85	0.00

Figure 63 d_1, d_2 and option Delta

5 Calculating total borrowing

Given the option Delta for each simulated stock price at each time step, the replicating portfolio's portion held in stock (Dollars in Stock) can now be calculated as Delta × *S*.

However, the second part of the replicating portfolio, total borrowing, requires a more involved calculation. At time zero when the option is written, total borrowing is given as the difference between Dollars in Stock (160.031) and the premium received from selling the option (47.56). This is given in the first cell of the "Total Borrowing" column at time zero (112.47). It is the second cell, at time one, where the calculation gets a little messy.

	REPLICATING PORTFOLIO	
TIME STEP	DOLLARS IN STOCK	TOTAL BORROWING
0	160.031	112.47
1	225.120	150.53
2	208.920	143.35
3	192.973	135.56
4	172.780	124.52
5	194.449	138.39
6	225.324	157.62
7	196.269	142.92
8	215.791	156.78
9	199.455	149.17
10	172.693	133.12
11	253.196	195.60
12	286.700	211.86

Figure 64 Replicating portfolio components

One way of dissecting this calculation is to take a quick look at the top few rows of our Delta hedge table and perform a step-by-step calculation that shows us how the total borrowing figure changes from one rebalancing period to the next. It is an essential step, without which you cannot decode the Delta hedging sheet.

					Replicating Portfolio		Replicating	
Time to expiration	Stock price	Option d1	Option d2	Option delta	Dollars in stock	Total Borrowing	Portfolio Value	Option Value
							Tracker	Option Val
1	242.500	0.41	0.01	0.66	160.031	112.47	47.56	47.56
0.917	283.592	0.82	0.44	0.79	225.120	150.53	74.59	76.00
0.833	272.396	0.73	0.36	0.77	208.920	143.35	65.57	65.67
0.750	261.917	0.63	0.29	0.74	192.973	135.56	57.42	56.09
0.667	249.638	0.50	0.18	0.69	172.780	124.52	48.26	45.48
0.583	261.057	0.66	0.35	0.74	194.449	138.39	56.06	51.75
0.500	276.851	0.89	0.61	0.81	225.324	157.62	67.70	62.14

Figure 65 Dissecting total borrowing

At time zero, the underlying stock is trading at US$242.5. Option Delta is 0.66.

We end up buying US$160.031 (66% of one share) of stock for the hedge. The purchase is funded by US$47.56 in option premium, and US$112.47 in borrowing. How does this balance change at Time Step 1?

At Time Step 1, the underlying stock has moved to 283.592.

Our 66% of one share is now worth 283.592/242.5 × 160.031, which translates into US$187 dollars and change.

In addition, option Delta has moved from 0.66 to 0.79, so we need to buy an incremental 13% of the underlying share at the new price, which is another US$38 dollars and change. The combined position after the new purchase is US$225.12.

So what is the incremental amount that was borrowed? US$38 dollars and change. How did we find the exact number? If you look above and review the calculation again, it is the difference between the new Delta and the old Delta multiplied by the new stock price. That is the new net incremental borrowing. When Delta and underlying prices fall, the formula will release funds. When they rise, the formula will require funds.

But there is one more step before the total borrowing calculation is complete. What about the previous balance borrowed? The balance that was borrowed at step zero. We owe accrued interest on it for one period at the one-period (time step) rate.

When you put all of this together, you end up with the formula used for calculating total borrowing balance at Time Step 1 in the Delta hedge sheet. The same process is used to calculate the total borrowing balance at Step 2, Step 3 and onwards.

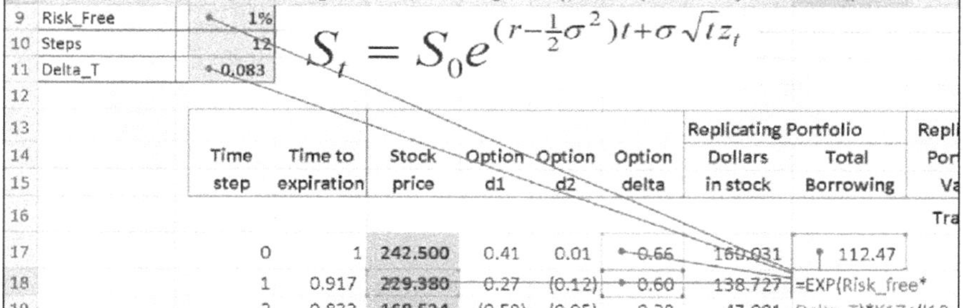

	B	C	D
9	Risk_Free		1%
10	Steps		12
11	Delta_T		0.083

$$S_t = S_0 e^{(r-\frac{1}{2}\sigma^2)t+\sigma\sqrt{t}z_t}$$

Time step	Time to expiration	Stock price	Option d1	Option d2	Option delta	Replicating Portfolio: Dollars in stock	Replicating Portfolio: Total Borrowing
0	1	242.500	0.41	0.01	0.66	160.031	112.47
1	0.917	229.380	0.27	(0.12)	0.60	138.727	=EXP(Risk_free*Delta_T)*K17+(I18-I17)*F18
2	0.833	168.524	(0.59)	(0.95)	0.28	47.001	
3	0.750	205.706	(0.06)	(0.41)	0.47	97.609	

Figure 66 Total borrowing at each time step

6 Putting it all together

Replicating portfolio value is Dollars in Stock (column J) less Total Borrowing (column K).

To calculate option value we use the standard Black–Scholes formula for a non-dividend paying stock.

$$c(S,t) = SN(d_1) - Ke^{-r(T-t)}N(d_2)$$

$$d_1 = \frac{\ln\left(\frac{S}{K}\right) + \left(r + \frac{\sigma^2}{2}\right)(T-t)}{\sigma\sqrt{T-t}}$$

$$d_2 = d_1 - \sigma\sqrt{T-t}$$

where
$c\ (S,t)$ = Call option value
S = Spot price
K = Strike price
σ = Implied volatility
r = Risk-free rate
ln = Natural log
$T–t$ = Time to maturity in years

The implementation is shared below:

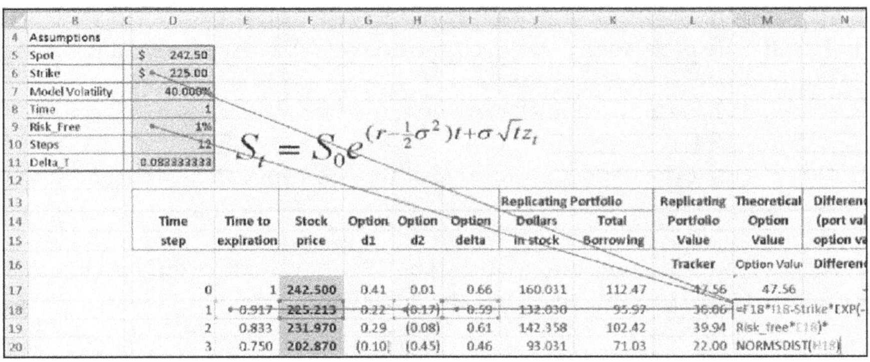

Assumptions	
Spot	$ 242.50
Strike	$ 225.00
Model Volatility	40.000%
Time	1
Risk_Free	1%
Steps	12
Delta_T	0.083333333

$$S_t = S_0 e^{(r-\frac{1}{2}\sigma^2)t+\sigma\sqrt{t}z_t}$$

Time step	Time to expiration	Stock price	Option d1	Option d2	Option delta	Replicating Portfolio Dollars in stock	Replicating Portfolio Total Borrowing	Replicating Portfolio Value	Theoretical Option Value	Differen (port val option va
								Tracker	Option Valu	Differen
0	1	242.500	0.41	0.01	0.66	160.031	112.47	47.56	47.56	
1	0.917	225.213	0.22	(0.17)	0.59	132.030	95.97	36.06	=F18*I18-Strike*EXP(-	
2	0.833	231.970	0.29	(0.08)	0.61	142.358	102.42	39.94	Risk_free*E18)*	
3	0.750	202.870	(0.10)	(0.45)	0.46	93.031	71.03	22.00	NORMSDIST(H18)	

Figure 67 Option value – Excel implementation

You can see now that while the replicating portfolio is doing a reasonable job of tracking the option value, there is a clear error in tracking, which moves up and down depending on how much in or out of money the option is.

Time step	Time to expiration	Stock price	Option d1	Option d2	Option delta	Dollars in stock	Total Borrowing	Portfolio Value	Option Value
								Tracker	Option Va
0	1	**242.500**	0.41	0.01	0.66	160.031	112.47	47.56	47.56
1	0.917	**220.343**	0.16	(0.22)	0.56	124.246	91.40	32.85	32.37
2	0.833	**212.253**	0.05	(0.32)	0.52	109.993	81.79	28.21	26.39
3	0.750	**263.454**	0.65	0.30	0.74	195.551	140.88	54.67	57.23
4	0.667	**276.479**	0.81	0.49	0.79	219.065	154.84	64.22	65.47
5	0.583	**280.026**	0.89	0.58	0.81	227.583	160.68	66.90	66.55
6	0.500	**245.745**	0.47	0.19	0.68	167.389	128.48	38.91	38.75
7	0.417	**219.079**	0.04	(0.22)	0.52	113.205	92.57	20.64	20.35
8	0.333	**231.169**	0.25	0.02	0.60	138.136	111.33	26.81	24.57
9	0.250	**260.328**	0.84	0.64	0.80	208.269	164.13	44.14	42.30
10	0.167	**231.231**	0.26	0.10	0.60	139.256	118.53	20.73	18.37
11	0.083	**221.665**	(0.06)	(0.18)	0.47	105.144	90.28	14.87	8.78
12	0.00100	**231.229**	2.17	2.15	0.98	227.723	208.40	19.33	6.25

Figure 68 The final picture
Source: FinanceTrainingCourse.com

7 Next steps, and questions

Now that the underlying simulation model is ready for Delta hedging, here is a list of questions that we would like to answer.

a. How would this hedging model change if the option contract was a put contract?
b. How do you calculate the P&L for this book? Do you actually end up making money in this business?
c. How does implied volatility impact profitability? How is that factored here?
d. To calculate profitability you need the dollar cost average price of purchase for the share. How is that calculated?
e. Once you have a P&L model, can you test how profitability behaves as you shorten the rebalancing period?
f. How do the other Greeks behave? Can we also hedge them using a similar approach?

Build the model in Excel, and then try and answer the above questions before we address them one by one in the chapters that follow.

3
Delta Hedging European Put Options

Previously we built a simple model in Excel that simulated an underlying price series and a step-by-step trace of a dynamic Delta hedging simulation model for a call option. Now we will modify and extend the model for a European put option. The basic approach remains the same, but a simple modification is required to make the sheet work for a European put contract.

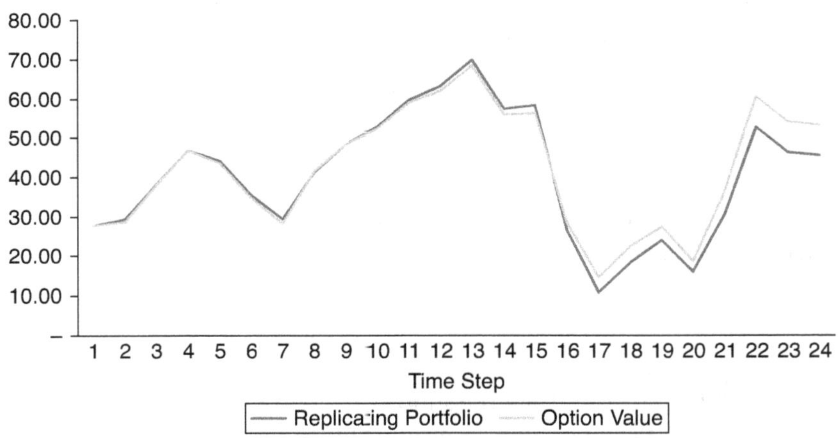

Figure 69 Put options – Monte Carlo simulation
Source: FinanceTrainingCourse.com

The end result will be a dynamic simulation graphical output showing the original option value and the replicating or tracker portfolio that is created to hedge it.

If you remember, our dynamic Delta hedging strategy for call options relied on going long (buying) Delta × S and financing this purchase by borrowing the difference between our purchase and the premium received for writing the option. This strategy defined the structure of our Monte Carlo simulation spreadsheet in Excel.

					Replicating Portfolio		Replicating		Difference
Time step	Time to expiration	Stock price	d1	Option delta	Dollars in stock	Total Borrowing	Portfolio Value	Option Value	(port val - option val)

Figure 70 The baseline model and simulated values for a European call option
Source: FinanceTrainingCourse.com

1 Tweaking the original Monte Carlo simulation model

How would you change this model to hedge a European put contract?

In a call option, the probability of exercise goes up as the underlying price goes up. But for a put option the opposite is true. For a call option, as the probability of exercise goes up we buy portions of the underlying to hedge our exposure and manage our dollar cost average purchase price.

For a put option we therefore short more of the underlying as the conditional probability of exercise goes up (the conditional probability is $N(d_1)$ for a call, $N(-d_1)$ for a put), and vice versa when the probability goes down.

For a call, we are short cash (i.e. we borrow it) to finance our purchases. For a put option, the short sale of the underlying generates cash, and we invest the proceeds for the duration that we remain short.

Therefore, the structure of our dynamic Delta hedging sheet for a European put contract changes and becomes:

					Delta Hedging using Replicated Portfolio for a Put Contract				
					Replicating Portfolio		Replicating		Difference
Time step	Time to expiration	Stock price	d1	Option delta	Dollars Shorted in stock	Total Lending	Portfolio Value	Option Value	(port val - option val)

Figure 71 Baseline model for European put options
Source: FinanceTrainingCourse.com

The only differences are:

a. in the replicating portfolio: where we are now short Delta × S and have lent (invested) the proceeds from the short sale
b. option Delta calculation: we are using $N(d_1) - 1$ rather than $N(d_1)$ as the option Delta for a put option.
c. financing cost is replaced by investment income on the proceeds of the short sales, invested for the duration of the option.

As in our earlier call option Delta hedging model, we still need to simulate the underlying stock price and estimate the:

a. option Delta for a put option linked to the underlying stock price
b. replicating portfolio, which comprises a short position in Delta × S (Spot price of stock) and a long position in lending/investment.
c. difference between the replicating portfolio and the option value to calculate tracking error (as plotted in the figure below).

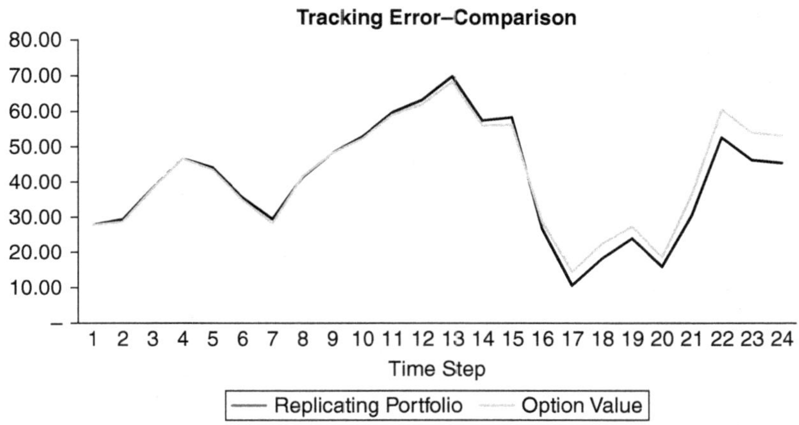

Figure 72 Put options – tracking error
Source: FinanceTrainingCourse.com

2 Assumptions

We use the shares of Barclays Bank to write our put, and assume that the bank will pay no dividends over the life of the option.

Figure 73 Barclays Bank price chart
Source: Google Finance.

We assume that the spot price is 242.5, the strike price is 225, the daily volatility ranges are between 2.5% and 5%. For our illustration, the implied annualized volatility is assumed to be 40%, the risk-free interest rate is 1% and the time to maturity is one year.

ASSUMPTIONS	VALUE	EXPLANATION
S	US$242.50	Stock spot price
K	US$225.00	Option strike price
T	1	Time to expiration in years
σ (sigma)	40%	Annualized stock volatility
r	1%	Annualized risk free interest rate
q	0%	Annualized expected stock return
N	24	Number of time steps
dt	0.042	Length of time step, delta t

Figure 74 Key assumptions

3 Simulating the underlying

Using the above assumptions, we simulate a path of Barclays share prices over the next year for 24 time steps using the discrete formulation of the Black–Scholes terminal price formula. For each value of the underlying stock price we also calculate d_1 using the Black–Scholes formula.

TIME STEP	TIME TO EXPIRATION	STOCK PRICE	d1
0	1	242.50	0.41
1	0.958	190.77	(0.20)
2	0.917	209.28	0.03
3	0.875	207.11	(0.01)
4	0.833	223.86	0.19
5	0.792	228.08	0.24
6	0.750	237.44	0.35
7	0.708	249.64	0.50
8	0.667	234.62	0.31
9	0.625	263.94	0.68

Continued

TIME STEP	TIME TO EXPIRATION	STOCK PRICE	d1
10	0.583	239.06	0.37
11	0.542	236.85	0.34
12	0.500	256.56	0.62
13	0.458	274.22	0.88
14	0.417	239.76	0.39
15	0.375	233.15	0.28
16	0.333	258.37	0.73
17	0.292	301.24	1.47
18	0.250	320.02	1.87
19	0.208	310.83	1.87
20	0.167	330.73	2.45
21	0.125	293.28	1.95
22	0.083	274.38	1.78
23	0.042	276.33	2.56
24	0.001	276.33	16.25

Figure 75 Put option – simulating the underlying stock price

The Excel implementation of the actual stock price simulation is shown below, and is the same as the approach used earlier for the call option Delta hedging example. The only difference is that our earlier Delta hedging sheet worked with a 12-step forecast. For the put option illustrated here, we are using a 24-step simulation. Generally, as the number of time steps increases, the tracking error between the replicating portfolio value and the option value decreases, as the portfolio is rebalanced more frequently. This, however, results in a higher cost to maintain the replicating portfolio. A balance, therefore, needs to be struck between accuracy and cost.

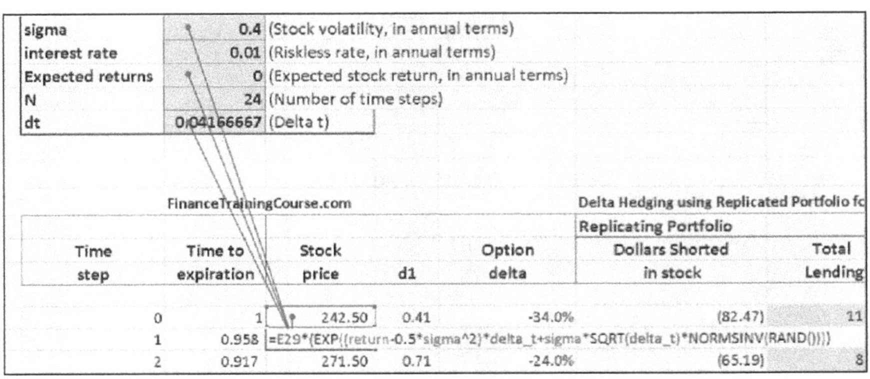

Figure 76 Simulating the underlying
Source: FinanceTrainingCourse.com

Armed with d_1 we can now calculate option Delta as well as the value of the replicating portfolio (–Delta × S + Total Lending).

TIME STEP	TIME TO EXPIRATION	STOCK PRICE	D1	OPTION DELTA	REPLICATING PORTFOLIO	
					Dollars Shorted in stock	Total Lending
0	1	242.50	0.41	–34.0%	(82.47)	110.29
1	0.958	208.47	0.03	–49.0%	(102.12)	141.56
2	0.917	179.80	(0.37)	–64.4%	(115.86)	169.40
3	0.875	189.19	(0.25)	–60.0%	(113.48)	161.05
4	0.833	180.52	(0.40)	–65.5%	(118.17)	171.00
5	0.792	189.54	(0.28)	–61.1%	(115.79)	162.79
6	0.750	196.83	(0.19)	–57.6%	(113.34)	155.96
7	0.708	196.00	(0.22)	–58.7%	(115.10)	158.26
8	0.667	177.65	(0.54)	–70.5%	(125.30)	179.30
9	0.625	170.57	(0.70)	–75.7%	(129.19)	188.25
10	0.583	163.87	(0.87)	–80.7%	(132.20)	196.42
11	0.542	166.77	(0.85)	–80.3%	(133.89)	195.85
12	0.500	176.91	(0.69)	–75.5%	(133.61)	187.51
13	0.458	187.33	(0.52)	–70.0%	(131.12)	177.24
14	0.417	189.75	(0.51)	–69.7%	(132.18)	176.67
15	0.375	198.31	(0.38)	–64.7%	(128.34)	166.95
16	0.333	176.69	(0.92)	–82.0%	(144.95)	197.61
17	0.292	179.77	(0.92)	–82.1%	(147.51)	197.73
18	0.250	181.06	(0.97)	–83.5%	(151.17)	200.41
19	0.208	174.88	(1.28)	–89.9%	(157.27)	211.76
20	0.167	191.71	(0.89)	–81.3%	(155.84)	195.28
21	0.125	178.23	(1.57)	–94.2%	(167.82)	218.29
22	0.083	164.52	(2.65)	–99.6%	(163.85)	227.33
23	0.042	171.55	(3.28)	–99.9%	(171.46)	228.03
24	0.001	180.74	(17.31)	–100.0%	(180.74)	228.22

Figure 77 Put option – completing the picture

4 Calculating the amount lent

The stocks shorted (i.e. 'Dollars Shorted in Stock' column) is calculated as Delta × S. The Total Lending calculation, however, requires some attention.

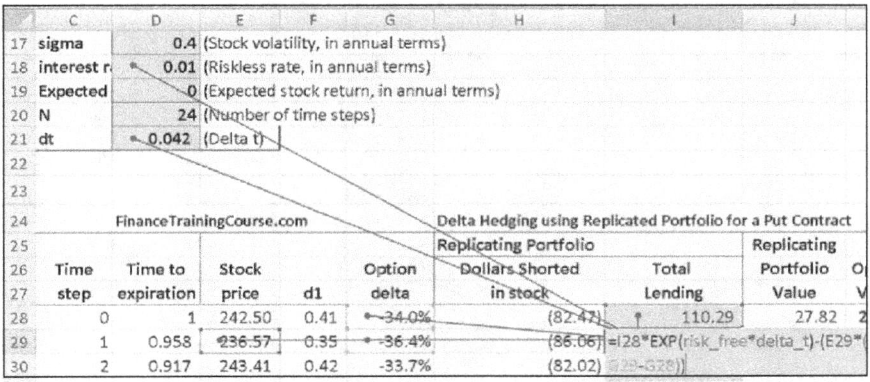

Figure 78 Put option – calculating the amount lent
Source: FinanceTrainingCourse.com

The calculation at Time Step 1 is simple. We receive US$27.82 in premium. Our short position generates US$82.47 in cash. The total cash available is 110.29. We immediately lend it at the risk-free rate. But what happens at Step 2? The price falls to US$236.57, and our Delta moves to –36.4% from –34.0%. Our short position increases from US$82.47 to US$86.06. Where does the approximately US$4 change come from?

The original balance at Time 1 has grown at the risk-free rate for the time step in question (one time step). However the change in stock is given by the change in Delta (G29 – G28) times the new underlying stock price. The way the formula is structured is such that it will release cash when the stock price rises (put Delta becomes less negative) and consume cash when prices decline (put Delta becomes more negative).

5 Putting the rest of the sheet together

The rest is exactly the same as our sheet for the European call option example. The replicating portfolio is given by (–Delta × S + Total Lending). The option value is calculated by the standard Black–Scholes put option premium calculation.

Time step	Time to expiration	Stock price	d1	Option delta	Replicating Portfolio Dollars Shorted in stock	Replicating Portfolio Total Lending	Replicating Portfolio Value	Option Value	Difference (port val - option val)	Interest Earned
										0.89
0	1	242.50	0.41	−34.0%	(82.47)	110.29	27.82	**27.82**	-	0.05
1	0.958	257.84	0.57	−28.5%	(73.47)	96.13	22.65	**22.34**	0.32	0.04
2	0.917	274.58	0.74	−23.1%	(63.44)	81.36	17.92	**17.32**	0.60	0.03
3	0.875	273.94	0.74	−23.1%	(63.21)	81.31	18.10	**16.77**	1.33	0.03
4	0.833	277.81	0.78	−21.7%	(60.25)	77.49	17.24	**15.19**	2.05	0.03
5	0.792	259.17	0.60	−27.5%	(71.30)	92.61	21.32	**19.01**	2.31	0.04
6	0.750	257.91	0.59	−27.8%	(71.68)	93.39	21.70	**18.57**	3.13	0.04
7	0.708	250.97	0.51	−30.4%	(76.21)	99.89	23.67	**19.78**	3.89	0.04
8	0.667	248.33	0.49	−31.4%	(77.86)	102.38	24.52	**19.75**	4.76	0.04
9	0.625	245.38	0.45	−32.6%	(79.89)	105.38	25.48	**19.82**	5.66	0.04
10	0.583	233.84	0.30	−38.3%	(89.52)	118.81	29.28	**22.99**	6.30	0.05
11	0.542	224.38	0.16	−43.8%	(98.26)	131.22	32.96	**25.93**	7.03	0.05
12	0.500	210.18	(0.08)	−53.3%	(111.94)	151.17	39.23	**31.86**	7.37	0.06
13	0.458	213.88	(0.03)	−51.4%	(109.91)	147.23	37.32	**28.96**	8.36	0.06
14	0.417	212.49	(0.08)	−53.0%	(112.71)	150.80	38.10	**28.68**	9.42	0.06
15	0.375	237.02	0.35	−36.3%	(86.06)	111.21	25.15	**16.62**	8.53	0.05
16	0.333	224.76	0.13	−45.0%	(101.18)	130.83	29.65	**20.39**	9.26	0.05
17	0.292	259.65	0.78	−21.6%	(56.18)	70.18	14.00	**7.73**	6.27	0.03
18	0.250	249.18	0.62	−26.7%	(66.45)	82.74	16.29	**9.00**	7.29	0.03
19	0.208	278.87	1.28	−10.1%	(28.05)	36.46	8.41	**2.62**	5.79	0.02
20	0.167	303.44	1.92	−2.7%	(8.26)	14.21	5.96	**0.55**	5.41	0.01
21	0.125	285.90	1.77	−3.8%	(10.89)	17.33	6.44	**0.65**	5.79	0.01
22	0.083	281.71	2.01	−2.2%	(6.24)	12.84	6.61	**0.28**	6.33	0.01
23	0.042	277.18	2.60	−0.5%	(1.29)	8.00	6.71	**0.03**	6.68	0.00
24	0.001	278.58	16.89	0.0%	-	6.71	6.71	**0.00**	6.71	0.00

Figure 79 Put option – total spreadsheet view

Source: FinanceTrainingCourse.com

4
Calculating Cash P&L for a Call Option

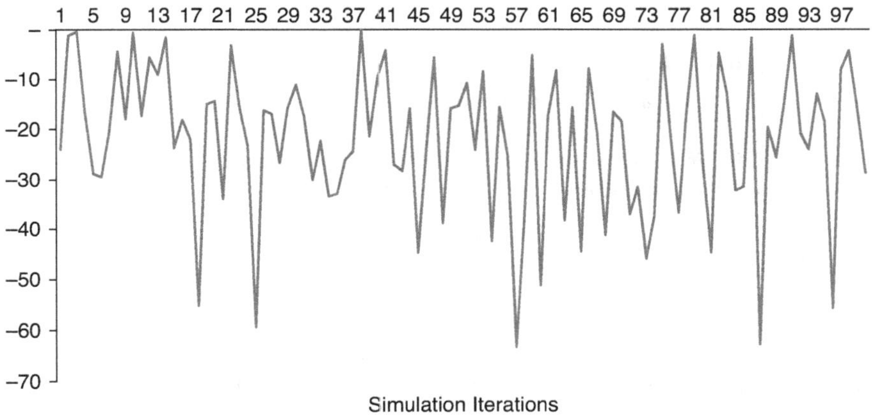

Figure 80 Trading losses on account of rebalancing
Source: FinanceTrainingCourse.com

The dynamic hedging spreadsheet for a European call option allowed us to do a step-by-step trace of a Delta hedging simulation. In this section, we will use the results from the simulation trace to calculate a cash accounting P&L for our hedging model, assuming the role of a call option writer.

One of the biggest intuitive challenges that arises in calculating hedge P&L is the question of double count. Do trading losses need to be calculated and accounted for separately, or are they already included in the cash results? What do you think? Is the above table correct or incorrect?

We are assuming that we have written a European call option on Barclays Bank where the current spot price is US$242.5 and the strike price is US$225. Time to expiry is one year and Barclays Bank is unlikely to pay a dividend during the life of the option.

Cash Accounting P&L		
Cash Inflow		
Premium Received	47.562	
Strike Price Received	225.000	
Gross Inflow		272.562
Cash out at Maturity		
Interest Paid	1.34	
Principal repaid	213.26	
Gross Outflow		214.60
Cash before trading losses		57.96
Trading Losses on Sale	(4.82)	
Net Cash after Trading Losses		53.14

Figure 81 Cash P&L for the writer for a call option that expires in the money
Source: FinanceTrainingCourse.com

1 Dissecting the P&L model

Our model uses a simplified cash-based approach to calculate P&L from our Delta hedging model. Our objective is to calculate P&L at option expiry for the option writer. Primary contributors to the model include:

Cash Accounting P&L		
Cash Inflow		
Premium Received	47.562	
Strike Price Received	-	
Gross Inflow		47.562
Cash out at Maturity		
Interest Paid	0.52	
Principal repaid	(10.59)	
Gross Outflow		(10.07)
Cash before trading losses		57.63
Trading Losses on Sale	(13.30)	
Net Cash after Trading Losses		44.32

Figure 82 Cash P&L for the writer for an option that expires out of money
Source: FinanceTrainingCourse.com

a. **Cash in**. receipts from the customer. Include premium received and the strike price if the option is exercised. If the option expires worthless, we only receive the premium.
b. **Cash out**. As explained earlier, to finance our hedge purchases we borrow money. We pay interest on this principal for the life of the hedge and return the principal at maturity.
c. **Trading losses**. As part of our strategy, we purchase the underlying as prices rise, and sell it when they fall By definition, this strategy will generate trading losses irrespective of whether the option expires worthless or in the money. Because we rebalance on a frequent basis, trading losses also consume cash. The question is, is that cash already accounted for, or do we need to account for it separately? Think about this question as you work through this note; the answer and how you reach it are important to build intuition about hedge P&L. We will come back to it before we conclude.

When we put the model in place, our final output should look something like this:

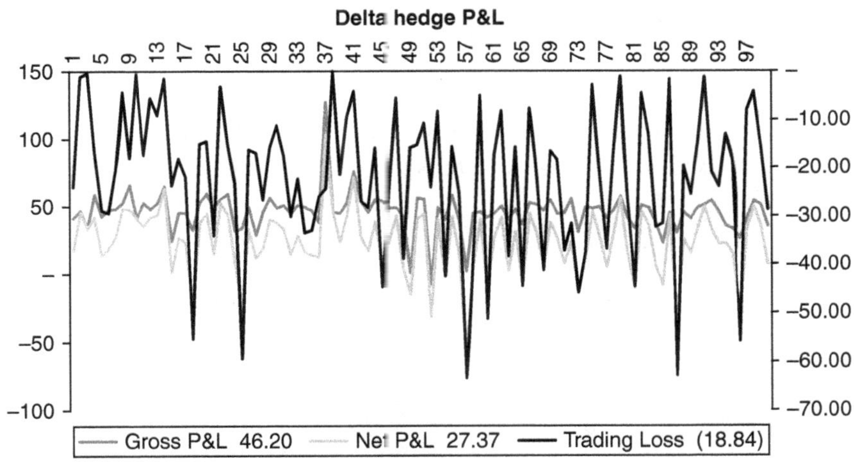

Figure 83 Gross P&L, net P&L, trading losses
Source: FinanceTrainingCourse.com

You can clearly see that the biggest contributor to our cash P&L uncertainty is trading loss. While this view gives us some indication of the variability in the P&L, it does not allow us to make any assumptions about the underlying distribution. For that, we need to build a histogram using the individual iteration data generated by our simulator.

The histogram above shows that the range of cash P&L for this specific option using 100 iterations and daily rebalancing is between –9.1 and a number higher than 9.0 (the horizontal access). The most common P&L figure is 0.9, and the midpoint of the P&L distribution lies between 0.0 and 0.9 (as determined by the cumulative probability density plot). The LHS of the

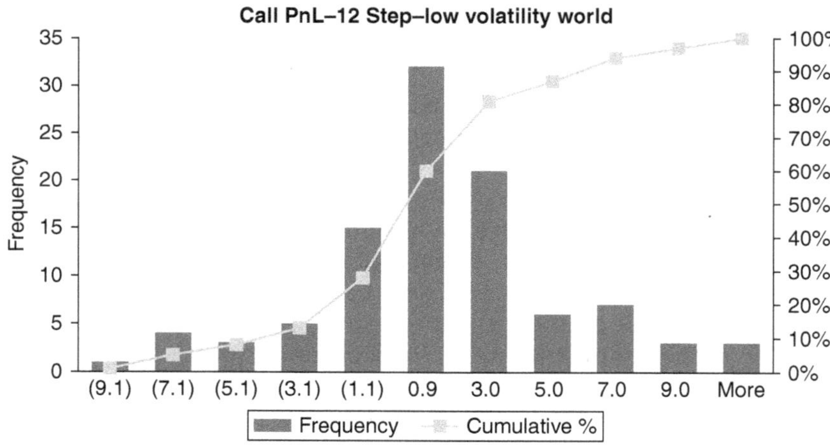

Figure 84 Histogram – cash P&L distribution across 100 iterations
Source: FinanceTrainingCourse.com

vertical axis shows the probability density, while the RHS shows the frequency count for a given bucket.

i Interest paid and principal borrowed for the hedge

The first step is to add two new columns to our Delta hedge model. These are:

1. Interest paid per period, and
2. Incremental amount borrowed per period.

Both elements have been calculated as part of the original sheet, and what we need to do is extract the relevant piece and dump the results in two new columns at the end.

TIME STEP	INTEREST PAID	INCREMENTAL AMOUNT BORROWED
0	0.09	112.47
1	0.08	(14.02)
2	0.08	(0.72)
3	0.11	35.33
4	0.07	(54.38)

Continued

TIME STEP	INTEREST PAID	INCREMENTAL AMOUNT BORROWED
5	0.09	23.64
6	0.10	17.53
7	0.08	(19.03)
8	0.06	(25.62)
9	0.05	(21.00)
10	0.02	(26.98)
11	0.02	1.50
12	(0.00)	(42.04)

Figure 85 Two new columns – interest paid and marginal borrowing

Incremental amount borrowed is included in the total borrowing figure. It is the difference between the two Deltas for the two time periods, multiplied by the new price of the underlying stock.

Time step	Time to expiry	Stock price	Option d1	Option d2	Option Delta	Replicating Portfolio		Replicating Portfolio Value	Option Value	Difference (replicating portfolio - option)	Interest Paid	Incremental Amount Borrowed
						Dollars in stock	Total Borrowing					
0	1.00	242.50	0.41	0.01	0.66	160.03	112.47	47.56	47.56	-	0.09	112.47
1	0.92	227.93	0.25	(0.13)	0.60	136.40	98.54	37.86	36.78	1.07	0.08	(14.02)
2	0.83	227.95	0.24	(0.12)	0.60	135.69	97.91	37.78	35.14	2.65	0.08	(0.72)
3	0.75	260.32	0.62	0.27	0.73	190.28	133.31	56.97	54.92	2.05	0.11	35.33
4	0.67	206.31	(0.08)	(0.41)	0.47	96.43	79.05	17.38	20.10	(2.73)	0.07	(54.38)
5	0.58	225.69	0.18	(0.12)	0.57	129.13	102.76	26.37	28.29	(1.92)	0.09	23.64
6	0.50	239.04	0.37	0.09	0.65	154.30	120.37	33.93	34.30	(0.38)	0.10	17.53
7	0.42	225.50	0.15	(0.10)	0.56	126.53	101.44	25.08	23.81	1.27	0.08	(19.03)
8	0.33	210.81	(0.15)	(0.38)	0.44	92.67	75.91	16.76	13.99	2.77	0.06	(25.62)
9	0.25	202.10	(0.42)	(0.62)	0.34	67.84	54.97	12.86	8.09	4.77	0.05	(21.00)
10	0.17	192.70	(0.86)	(1.02)	0.20	37.70	28.04	9.66	3.17	6.49	0.02	(26.98)
11	0.08	202.89	(0.83)	(0.95)	0.20	41.20	29.56	11.63	2.53	9.11	0.02	1.50
12	0.00	207.04	(20.79)	(20.80)	0.00	0.00	(12.45)	12.45	0.00	12.45	(0.00)	(42.04)

Figure 86 Calculating incremental borrowing

Interest paid per period is the interest accrued on the balance of the previous period. This is equal to the outstanding balance borrowed for the time step times the interest accrual factor. The interest accrual factor is EXP(Risk-free rate × Delta_*t*)–1.

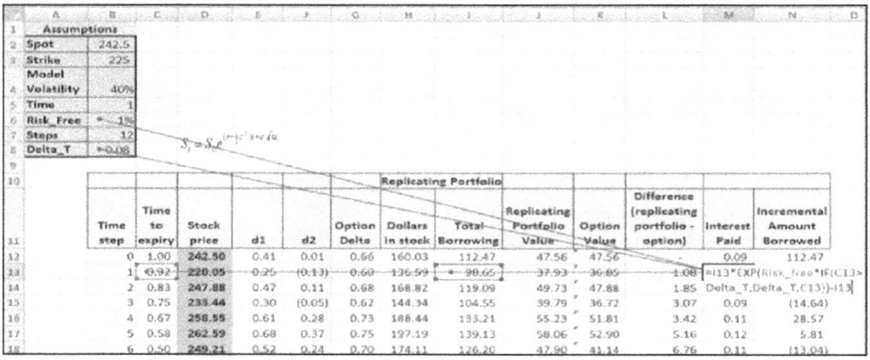

Assumptions	
Spot	242.5
Strike	225
Model Volatility	40%
Time	1
Risk_Free	1%
Steps	12
Delta_T	0.08

$S_t = S_0 e^{(r - \frac{1}{2}\sigma^2)t + \sigma\sqrt{t}u}$

Time step	Time to expiry	Stock price	d1	d2	Option Delta	Replicating Portfolio: Dollars in stock	Replicating Portfolio: Total Borrowing	Replicating Portfolio Value	Option Value	Difference (replicating portfolio - option)	Interest Paid	Incremental Amount Borrowed
0	1.00	242.50	0.41	0.01	0.66	160.03	112.47	47.56	47.56	-	0.09	112.47
1	0.92	220.05	0.25	(0.13)	0.60	136.59	98.65	37.93	36.85	1.08	=I13*EXP(Risk_free*IF(C13>Delta_T,Delta_T,C13))-I13	
2	0.83	247.88	0.47	0.11	0.68	168.82	119.09	49.73	47.88	1.85		
3	0.75	233.44	0.30	(0.05)	0.62	144.34	104.55	39.79	36.72	3.07	0.09	(14.64)
4	0.67	258.55	0.61	0.28	0.73	188.44	133.21	55.23	51.81	3.42	0.11	28.57
5	0.58	262.59	0.68	0.37	0.75	197.19	139.13	58.06	52.90	5.16	0.12	5.81
6	0.50	249.21	0.52	0.24	0.70	174.11	126.20	47.90	41.14	6.76	0.11	(13.04)

Figure 87 Calculating interest paid on borrowed cash

Note that Delta_*t* in the figure above has a condition attached to it. This is to account for the final time step being set fractionally less than Delta_*t*, as mentioned in Chapter 2.

ii Calculating the trading loss on account of selling low

The basic hedging strategy is to buy when Delta (or price) goes up, and sell when Delta (or price) goes down. Buy when prices rise; sell when they drop. The result is that as the underlying price seesaws, we end up buying high and selling low, rebalancing the portfolio in alignment with Delta but also generating trading losses.

Our calculation of trading losses has three components.

a. Calculate the number of incremental units purchased or sold as part of the required rebalancing (Unit Purchased column).
b. Then calculate the difference in price between the two rebalancing periods (Difference in Price column).
c. Finally identify all trades where a sale was made, and calculate the trading gain or loss (Loss on Sale column).

For this specific simulation, the trading loss is calculated as US$9.18, based on the above approach.

Trading Loss Calculation			
	1.00		9.18
Simulated	Units	Difference	Loss
Price	Sold/Purchase	in Price	on Sale
242.50	0.66		
223.68	(0.08)	(18.82)	1.52
192.49	(0.17)	(31.19)	5.21
222.74	0.15	30.25	-
202.65	(0.12)	(20.10)	2.41
201.10	(0.02)	(1.55)	0.04
244.62	0.25	43.53	-
250.34	0.04	5.72	-
281.50	0.15	31.15	-
276.01	0.01	(5.49)	-
315.88	0.11	39.87	-
306.98	0.01	(8.90)	-
364.59	0.00	57.60	-

Figure 88 Trading loss calculation
Source: FinanceTrainingCourse.com

iii Putting it all together

Now that we have all of the required P&L components together we hook them up with our Excel data table. We use our Monte Carlo bag of tricks to store the results of 100 iterations. Stored components include the Gross P&L (excluding trading losses), Net P&L (including trading losses), Interest Paid and Trading Loss on rebalancing sales.

Option P&L Simulation				
	47.77	28.05	1.22	(19.72)
	Gross P&L	Net P&L	Interest Paid	Trading Loss
	47.05	37.87	1.51	(9.18)
1	63.04	48.33	0.86	(14.71)
2	41.43	5.00	0.77	(36.44)
3	57.31	35.78	1.36	(21.54)
4	16.58	3.30	1.79	(13.29)
5	49.30	46.60	2.06	(2.70)
6	55.80	50.78	1.70	(5.02)
7	44.70	10.04	1.19	(34.65)
8	50.31	24.40	0.77	(25.91)
9	44.26	23.50	0.38	(20.76)
10	55.29	34.18	1.22	(21.11)

Figure 89 Storing the results

The final result is our Delta hedge P&L graph for a European call option.

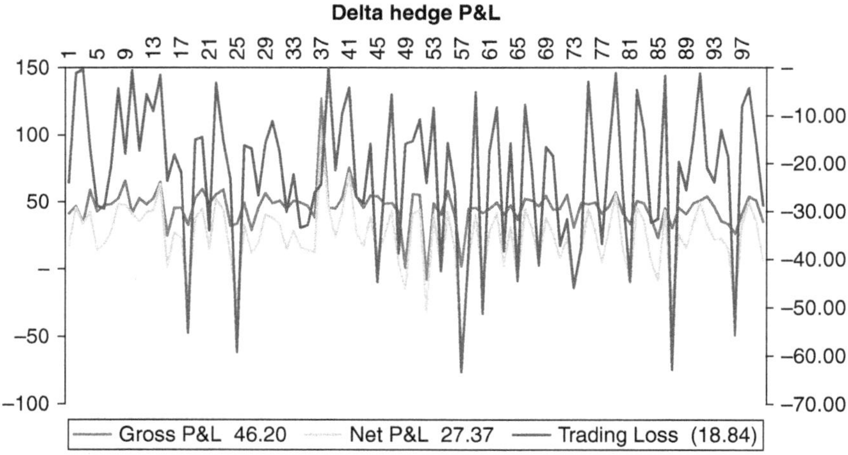

Figure 90 P&L graph
Source: FinanceTrainingCourse.com

In an earlier section, we plotted the histogram of the cash profit and loss from our Delta hedging simulation sheet. Here is what the trading gain loss distribution looks like from the same simulation.

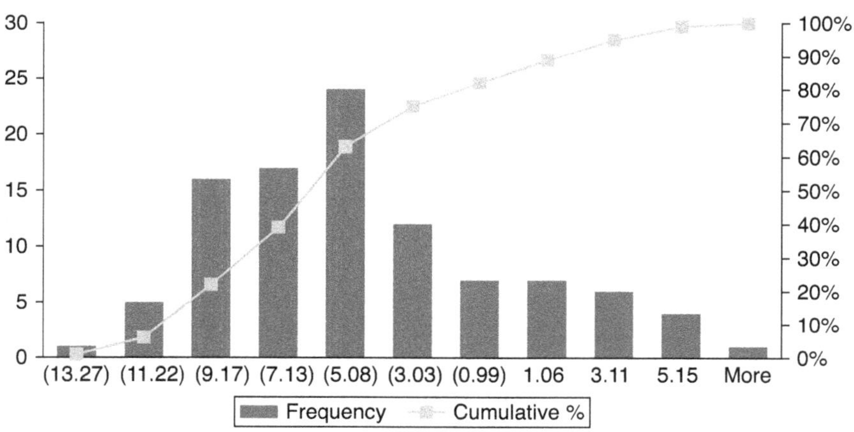

Figure 91 Trading gain/loss
Source: FinanceTrainingCourse.com

In an ideal world, where models work as expected, the actual cost (trading gain loss and interest expense paid) should average out to a number close to the premium charged for the option in question. In reality, however, if you priced yourself at the margin you would quickly go under, because there wouldn't be any margins to support losses incurred as a result of unexpected price movements and unanticipated market shocks.

The next time you are asked to calculate the premium for an option, take a look at the distribution below. Your best-case estimate is the expected value from the distribution below. Your worst case, depending on whether you are long or short, is one of the two extremes. In this instance we can see that the distribution is centred between 46 and 51, a range that includes our Black–Scholes premium of 47.56. Is that an accident? Or deliberate?

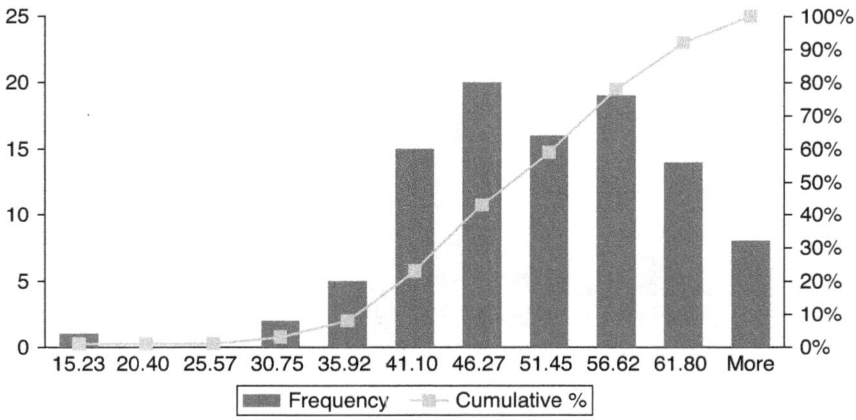

Figure 92 Cash P&L with premium
Source: FinanceTrainingCourse.com

To answer these questions, what we have to do is remove the premium income from our P&L calculation. In an ideal world, the P&L distribution should then be centred around zero, rather than 47 and change. The revised P&L distribution, post the change (no premium) is shared in the histogram below:

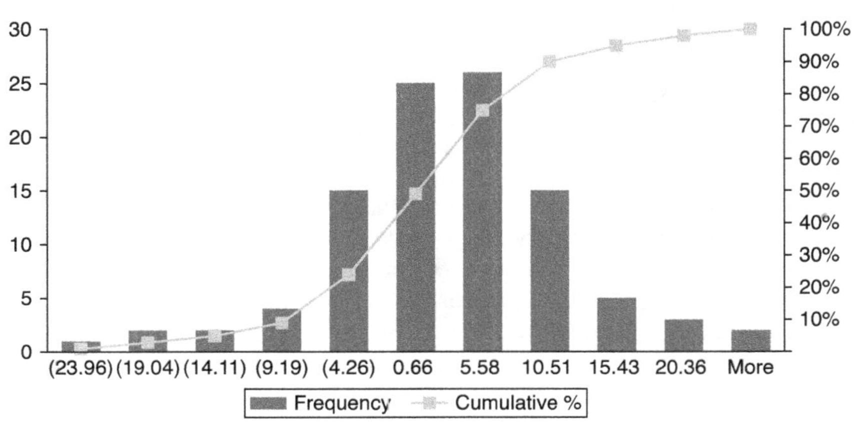

Figure 93 Cash P&L without premium
Source: FinanceTrainingCourse.com

We can see that with the revision of premium income, the P&L distribution is now centred on 0.08.

What kind of an impact does increasing or reducing volatility have? In our original high-volatility scenario that was used to generate the above histograms, we took implied volatility at 40%. When we drop it to 20%, the histogram shifts. Could you try and explain to your boss why that happens?

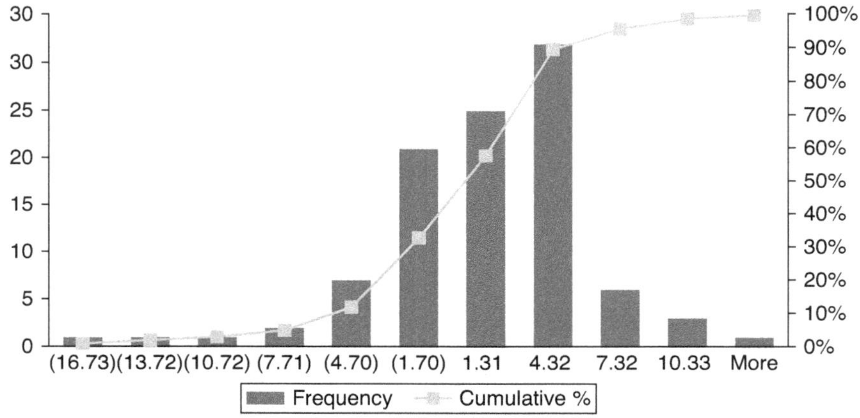

Figure 94 Cash P&L – low-volatility world: where is the centre now?
Source: FinanceTrainingCourse.com

2 The vexing question of trading gain (loss)

Now let's come back to the trading loss question. Do you have an answer? Should trading loss be included or excluded from the P&L calculation?

Sometimes you have to do things the wrong way before you can appreciate the correct answer.

The answer in this case lies with cash accounting. In our hedge P&L simulation, there is only one cash account. All trades hit that cash account. When you buy, you buy from the cash account; when you sell you sell into the cash account.

The balance of this cash account gets cleaned up at option expiry. If the option expires in the money, we use the sum proceeds from the premium and the payment of strike to pay off the principal borrowed. If the option expires worthless, the same logic still works; the principal borrowed number, our cash account, already includes the impact of trading gains or losses, and there is no need to adjust the final P&L figure for that amount.

Let's repeat this, for impact and clarity. Since we are calculating a cash P&L, the trading gain or loss is already included in the cash account figure. But then, why did we make the effort to calculate the gain/loss figure? Let's keep that as a question to be answered in a later chapter.

So the correct form for the cash accounting P&L is:

CASH ACCOUNTING P&L	
Cash Inflow	
Premium Received	47.56
Strike Price Received	225.00
Gross Inflow	272.56
Cash out at Maturity	
Interest Paid	1.95
Principal repaid	225.11
Gross Outflow	227.06
Net Cash Inflow	45.50
Trading Gain (Losses) on Sale	2.00

Figure 95 Accounting P&L – revised
Source: FinanceTrainingCourse.com

For clarity, you can still calculate the trading loss and present it, but it shouldn't impact your net cash figure. If you still have doubts, remember the test that you ran earlier; when you modified the dynamic hedging simulation to run a fully funded scenario (premium received is zero) what results came up? Where was the premium distribution centred? If it was centred around zero without incorporating trading gains/losses, you have your answer.

3 Next steps, and questions

Once you have the basic model figured out, here are many interesting questions that follow:

a. How would you extend this model for P&L calculations for a European put option?

b. How would you incorporate the impact of implied volatility?
c. Of transaction costs? And non-risk-free interest rates? Jumps and dividends?
d. How would profitability (cash P&L) change if you shortened the time step and the rebalancing period? Or extended it?
e. What does the distribution of profits suggest about the risk inherent in the underlying business?
f. Is this the most effective way of hedging options?
g. What about the risk embedded in other Greeks? How is that managed and hedged? How does that impact P&L?

5
Calculating Cash P&L for a Put Option

Our cash P&L model for a European put option is a mirror image of our cash P&L for a European call option model. The difference arises from how we hedge a put versus how we hedge a call.

To hedge a put option we short Delta units of the underlying and invest the proceeds in a risk-free security, essentially generating excess cash in addition to the premium received. Both amounts are invested in an interest-earning instrument.

If a put is exercised at maturity, we receive the underlying security on which the put option is written, and close our short position. In exchange, we deliver the strike price in cash to the buyer of the put option (or the seller of the underlying security when the put option is exercised).

To model our P&L, we will assume writing a European put option on Barclays Bank where the current spot price is US$242.5 (the 5 June 2014 stock price) and the strike price is US$225. Time to expiry is one year. For simplicity, we will assume that Barclays Bank will not pay a dividend during the life of the option.

1 Dissecting the P&L model

As mentioned above, primary contributors to our put cash P&L model include:

a. **Cash in.** Includes premium received, interest received on investment for the life of the hedge, and the proceeds from the short sale of the underlying position.
b. **Cash out.** The excess cash generated from the short sales grows to the amount we have to pay to the customer if the put option is exercised. If the option expires worthless, no payment is made.
c. **Trading gains.** As part of our strategy, we sell the underlying as prices rise, and purchase it when they fall. Earlier we discussed that trading P&L is separated only for presentation purposes. The amount is already included in the cash account.

Cash Accounting P&L		
Cash Inflow		
Premium Received	27.823	
Interest Earned	1.595	
Sales Proceeds from short sales	232.750	
Gross Inflow		**262.168**
Cash out at Maturity		
Strike Paid	225.000	
Gross Outflow		**225.000**
Net Cash inflow		**37.168**
Trading Gain (Losses) on Closing short position		**0.514**

Figure 96 Cash P&L for the writer for a put option that expires in the money
Source: FinanceTrainingCourse.com

i Interest paid and principal borrowed for the hedge

The first step is to add two new columns to our Delta hedge model. These are:

1. Interest received per period, and
2. Incremental amount invested/lent per period

Cash Out flow on Maturity	
Interest Earned	**Principal Amount Lent**
0.09	110.29
0.11	22.83
0.11	4.01
0.13	18.48
0.16	33.86
0.17	14.43
0.18	10.73
0.15	(31.41)
0.16	10.34
0.18	24.62
0.15	(43.07)
0.09	(65.24)
0.00	117.33
1.69	**227.19**
Total Lending	**228.88**

Figure 97 Two new columns – interest received and marginal investment
Source: FinanceTrainingCourse.com

The principal amount lent is included in the total investment figure; it is the difference between two Deltas for the two time periods times the new price of the underlying stock.

Time step	Time to expiry	Stock price	d1	d2	Option Delta	Dollars shorted in stock	Total Lending	Replicating Portfolio Value	Option Value	(replicating portfolio - option)	Interest Earned	Principal Amount Lent
0	1.00	242.50	0.41	0.01	(0.34)	(82.47)	110.29	27.82	27.82	-	0.09	110.29
1	0.92	283.80	0.82	0.44	(0.21)	(58.36)	72.23	13.87	15.31	(1.44)	0.06	=(G14-G13)*-D14
2	0.83	307.92	1.06	0.70	(0.14)	(44.19)	53.16	8.97	9.83	(0.86)	0.04	(19.12)
3	0.75	344.86	1.43	1.08	(0.08)	(26.45)	30.17	3.71	4.77	(1.06)	0.03	(23.04)
4	0.67	343.44	1.48	1.15	(0.07)	(23.91)	27.76	3.85	3.95	(0.10)	0.02	(2.43)

Figure 98 Calculating incremental investment

Source: FinanceTrainingCourse.com

The interest received per period is the interest accrued on the balance of the previous period, which is the outstanding investment times the interest accrual factor. The interest accrual factor is EXP(Risk-free rate × Delta_*t*)–1.

Assumptions	
Spot	242.5
Strike	225.0
Model Volatility	40%
Time	1
Risk_Free	1%
Steps	12
Delta_T	0.08

Time step	Time to expiry	Stock price	d1	d2	Option Delta	Replicating Portfolio: Dollars shorted in stock	Replicating Portfolio: Total Lending	Replicating Portfolio Value	Option Value	Difference (replicating portfolio - option)	Cash In/Out fl on Maturity: Interest Earned	Princ Amo Len
0	1.00	242.50	0.41	0.01	(0.34)	(82.47)	110.29	27.82	27.82	-	0.09	110
1	0.92	250.78	0.50	0.12	(0.31)	(77.49)	102.59	25.10	23.71	1.39	Risk_free*IF(	
2	0.83	213.61	0.06	(0.30)	(0.47)	(101.43)	138.10	36.67	36.62	0.05	C14>Delta_T,	
3	0.75	225.56	0.20	(0.14)	(0.42)	(94.72)	125.83	31.11	29.75	1.36	Delta_T,C14))-	
4	0.67	213.25	0.02	(0.31)	(0.49)	(104.97)	141.35	36.39	33.75	2.64	I14	

Figure 99 Calculating interest received on the investment

Source: FinanceTrainingCourse.com

Note that Delta_*t* in the figure above has a condition attached to it. This is to account for the final time step being set at fractionally less than Delta_*t*, as mentioned in Chapter 2.

ii Calculating the trading gain/loss

How does the hedge actually work for the put option? As prices go up, the put is less likely to be exercised, and the put Delta ($N(d_1)-1$) comes down, requiring us to reduce our short exposure. As prices decline, the conditional likelihood of the put being exercised ($N(-d_1)$) goes up, and so does our requirement for short selling the underlying security. Unlike the call, in this specific instance we are selling short when prices begin to drop and covering (closing our short position) when they begin to rise.

The result is that as the underlying price seesaws, we end up short selling when prices begin to decline, and close the short sale position when they start to rise, rebalancing the portfolio in alignment with Delta, but also generating trading losses on a consistent basis.

Our calculation of trading gains/losses therefore has the following components.

When the put option is exercised:

1. the client delivers the security. We use the security received to close our short position.
2. the proceeds from the short sale plus accrued interest (our cash balance) on that amount is used to pay the strike price to the client.
3. the difference between our cash balance and the strike price is our profit.

When the put option is not exercised:

1. ideally the short position is either not created or has already been closed before the expiry of the put option. But since we only close the short position as prices rise (and we have a short position) there is a trading loss on closing the short position. The trading loss is already reflected in our cash balance.
2. the premium plus interest earned should ideally be sufficient to cover our trading loss, on account of (1) above.

For both instances we can run a test for model validation by excluding the premium component from our P&L calculation. If our model is correct, the distribution of P&L with out premium should be centered around zero. We will do that as soon as we have a plot from our P&L simulation.

Our calculation of trading gain/ loss includes the following components:

a. Calculate the number of incremental units purchased (**covering the short position**) or sold (**creating the short position**) as part of the required rebalancing (Unit Short Sold/Purchased column).
b. Calculate the incremental value of the short position which is the units short sold times the simulated price (Incremental Short Position column).
c. Calculate the total cost of the short position which is the total cost from the prior period less the short sale cost from positions that are closed in the prior period + cost of any incremental short sales for the current period (Cost of Short Position column).
d. Calculate the total units in the portfolio, which is the sum of the prior number of units plus the current incremental number of units determined in (a) above (Remaining Units column).
e. Determine the unit cost of short sales, that is the total cost of the short position divided by the total units remaining in the hedge portfolio.
f. Finally, identify all trades where a purchase was made to close the position and calculate the value of the purchase (Cost of Closing Short Sale Position column) and the cost of the short sale position (Sale Proceeds column) to determine the trading gain or loss (Gain/Loss column).

For this specific simulation, the trading loss is calculated as US$50.242 based on the above approach.

Gain (Loss) on Closing a Short Position								
Total units sold & purchased	-						Gain (Loss)	- 50.242
Simulated Price	Units Sold Short/Purchased to close	Incremental Short position	Cost of Short Position	Remaining Units	Unit Cost of Sales	Sale Proceeds	Cost of Closing Short Position	Gain/Loss
320.4000	(0.4216)	(135.0717)	(135.0717)	(0.4216)	320.4000	-	-	-
400.2567	0.2377	-	(135.0717)	(0.1839)	320.4000	76.1612	95.1437	(18.9825)
486.0989	0.1266	-	(58.9104)	(0.0573)	320.4000	40.5586	61.5340	(20.9754)
464.9640	(0.0111)	(5.1766)	(23.5285)	(0.0684)	343.9267	-	-	-
468.7530	0.0123	-	(23.5285)	(0.0561)	343.9267	4.2416	5.7811	(1.5395)
447.7289	(0.0116)	(5.1936)	(24.4804)	(0.0677)	361.7181	-	-	-
472.4167	0.0335	-	(24.4804)	(0.0342)	361.7181	12.1070	15.8122	(3.7052)
457.4020	(0.0003)	(0.1454)	(12.5188)	(0.0345)	362.5992	-	-	-
469.5805	0.0185	-	(12.5188)	(0.0160)	362.5992	6.7097	8.6893	(1.9796)
553.3964	0.0157	-	(5.8092)	(0.0003)	362.5992	5.7067	8.7096	(3.0028)
562.7640	0.0003	-	(0.1024)	(0.0000)	362.5992	0.0994	0.1543	(0.0549)
596.1198	0.0000	-	(0.0030)	(0.0000)	362.5992	0.0030	0.0049	(0.0019)
620.0856	0.0000	-	(0.0000)		362.5992	0.0000	0.0000	(0.0000)

Figure 100 Trading gains calculation
Source: FinanceTrainingCourse.com

iii Putting it all together

Now that we have all of the required P&L components together, we hook them up with our Excel data table to store the results of 100 iterations. The stored components include Gross P&L (excluding trading losses), Net P&L (including trading losses), Interest Paid and Trading loss on rebalancing sales.

OPTION P&L SIMULATION				
Average	39.45	161.41	1.63	–24.81
Simulated Run	Net P&L	Proceeds from	Interest earned	Gain (Loss)
	29.23	–10.64	0.27	–50.24
1	26.70	–14.17	1.27	–53.77
2	32.22	310.78	1.84	–14.85
3	46.08	5.63	0.85	–33.97
4	54.54	332.69	2.25	–6.03
5	40.80	318.81	2.39	0.02
6	34.98	314.09	1.28	–36.78
7	33.54	–6.67	0.61	–46.27
8	45.41	323.33	2.49	1.35
9	49.90	328.21	2.08	–3.15
10	28.39	–13.32	2.11	–52.92

Figure 101 Storing the results – extract
Source: FinanceTrainingCourse.com

The final result is our Delta Hedge P&L graph for a European call option.

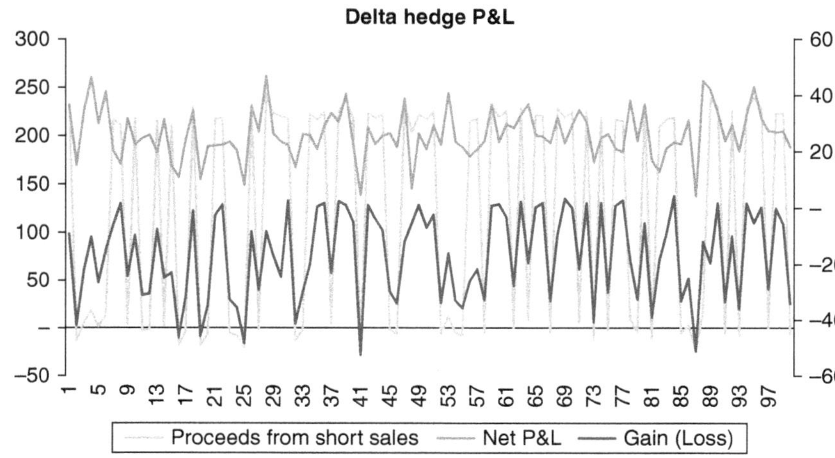

Figure 102 P&L graph
Source: FinanceTrainingCourse.com

The P&L distributions for a put option are shown below. These include an instance that includes the premium, as well as an instance that excludes the premium (see our discussion on P&L in the previous chapter on P&L for call options.

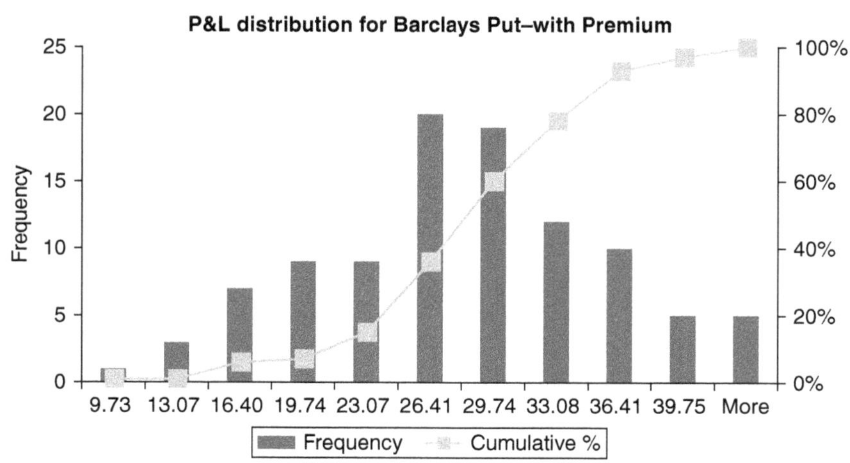

Figure 103 Histogram – distribution of P&L with premium
Source: FinanceTrainingCourse.com

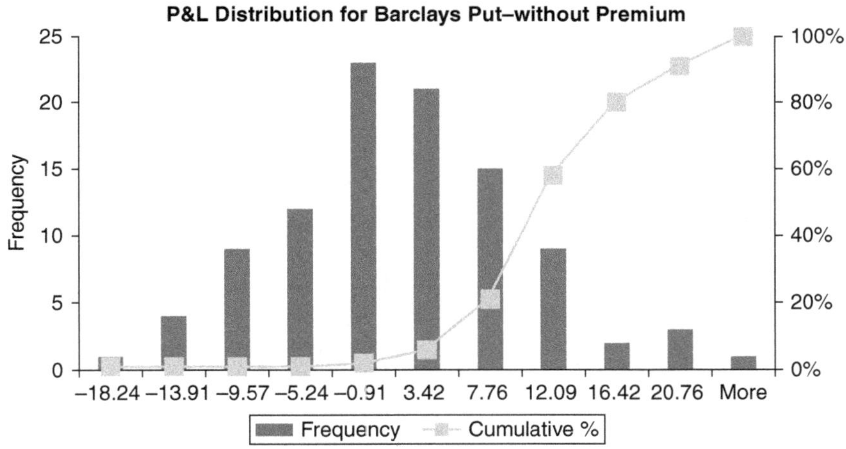

Figure 104 Histogram – distribution of P&L without premium
Source: FinanceTrainingCourse.com

The correct form for the cash accounting P&L excludes the trading gain/loss amount based on our discussion in the previous chapter; since we are working with a cash account, the cash balance already includes the trading gain/loss component. A separate adjustment would be a double count. The P&L template is presented below:

CASH ACCOUNTING P&L	
Cash Inflow	
Premium Received	27.823
Interest Earned	1.700
Sales Proceeds from short sales	224.855
Gross Inflow	254.378
Cash out at Maturity	
Strike Paid	225.000
Gross Outflow	225.000
Net Cash inflow	29.378
Trading Gain (Losses) on Closing short position	2.020

Figure 105 Correct P&L

Part III
Building Surfaces in Excel

6
Understanding Volatility

1 The many flavours of volatility

In the option pricing world, volatility comes in many flavours. When you first download the price series for an underlying security and calculate the daily returns for the entire review period, the volatility estimate you generate is called empirical or historical volatility. It gives you an indication of how much prices have moved in the historical period you have just analysed, and, were history to repeat itself, are likely to move. But if your review period is five years, a five-year average volatility estimate is really not going to help you price a 90-day option or estimate the price risk associated with the underlying security. On the other hand, if you are looking for a distribution of volatility to get an indication of the range that volatility is likely to extend to – trailing volatility – a moving average of volatility is a great tool.

However, the problem with trailing volatility is that it still relies on historical or empirical data. What we really need is a market-consistent estimate of volatility that can be used to match (calibrate) market-based option prices. Enter implied volatility. Pick an option, use its currently quoted price, plug in the Black–Scholes equation, and solve for the value of volatility that would lead to that price. At any given point in time, the historical volatility is our best estimate of what has happened in the past, whereas the implied volatility is our estimate of the level of volatility at which a market participant is willing to trade (buy or sell) his position. If volatility levels are higher than average, they are likely to revert to the mean, and at this level I, as a trader, I would rather sell options than buy. If volatility levels are at historical lows, they are likely to rise higher and, again as a trader, at those levels I would rather buy options than sell.

The challenge here is that implied volatility levels change based on the moneyness of the options in question. For a simple call option on stock, the implied volatility level moves up and down depending on how in or out of money our call option is. For example, the two figures below show plots of implied volatilities by moneyness for MRK and NVDA options that will expire in 30 days. The plot, given its shape, is popularly known as volatility smile.

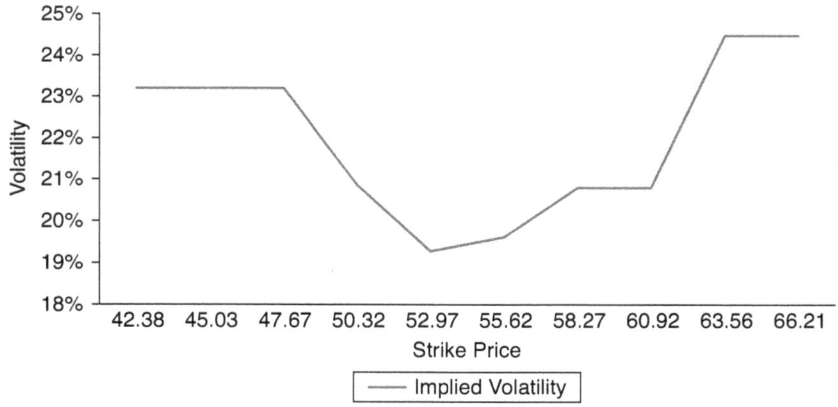

Figure 106 MRK volatility smile
Source: FinanceTrainingCourse.com

The data on ivolatility.com presents implied volatilities for at and out of money put and call options. In an arbitrage-free world, the implied volatilities for put and call options with similar expiries and strikes would be the same. So, to derive the volatility smile, we have assumed that implied volatilities for out of money puts will be the same as implied volatilities for in the money calls.

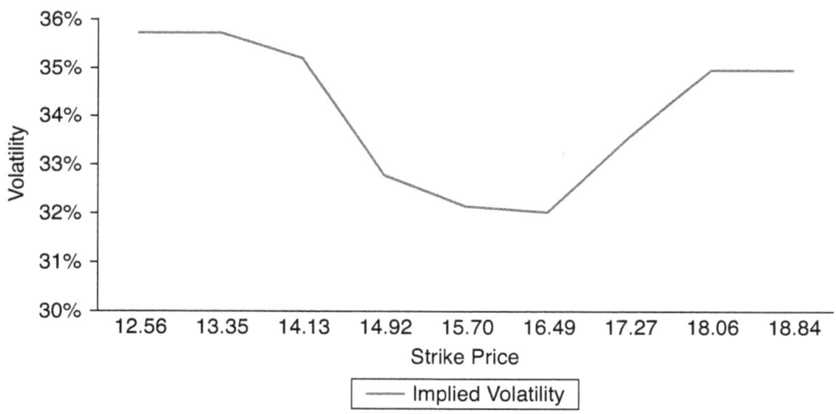

Figure 107 NVDA volatility smile
Source: FinanceTrainingCourse.com

If you were a novice or naive option trader unaware of the smile, and you used implied volatility levels inferred by at the money options to price your out of money positions, your active option trader status would not survive beyond a few trades.

However, volatility smile is not the only twist in this game. If we shift our focus from 30-day options (call options) to longer, 36-month, options, we get a somewhat different shape when we plot implied volatilities for MRK and NVDA. In both images, we see that implied volatilities for lower strike prices are higher than implied volatilities for higher strike prices. This shape is known as reverse skew.

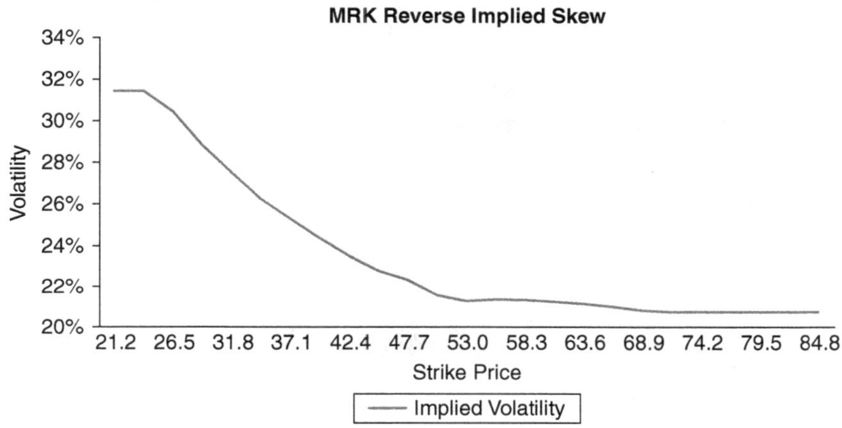

Figure 108 Reverse skew for 36-month MRK call options
Source: FinanceTrainingCourse.com

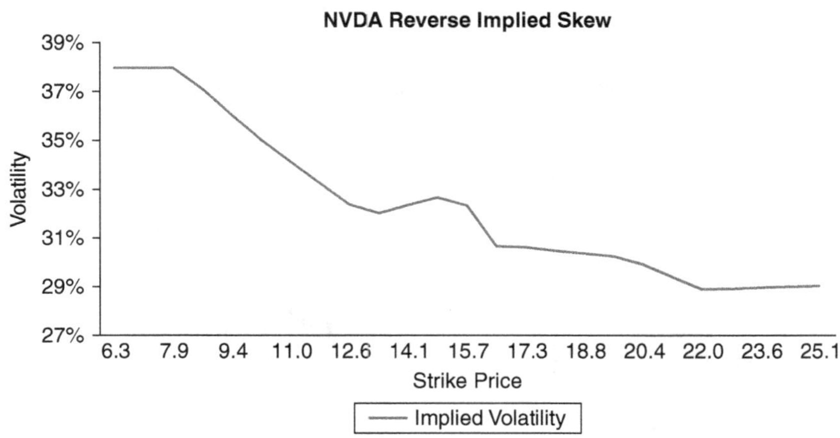

Figure 109 Reverse skew for 36-month NVDA call options
Source: FinanceTrainingCourse.com

2 Enter volatility surface

A crude conclusion after reviewing the four images above is that if you decided to model market-consistent implied volatility behaviour, you would need to factor in moneyness (strike prices) as well as maturity (expiry). Enter volatility surface.

A volatility surface plots market-consistent volatilities across moneyness (strike prices) and maturity (time to expiry). Within the surface, market-consistent volatilities are referred to as local volatilities. Rather than backing out or solving for volatility by applying the Black–Scholes model in reverse to at the money options, local volatilities use implied volatilities and a one-factor Black–Scholes model to derive local volatility values across the surface.

The end result, when applied to the entire universe of Barclays and NVDIA call options respectively, is something along the lines of the two figures that follow.

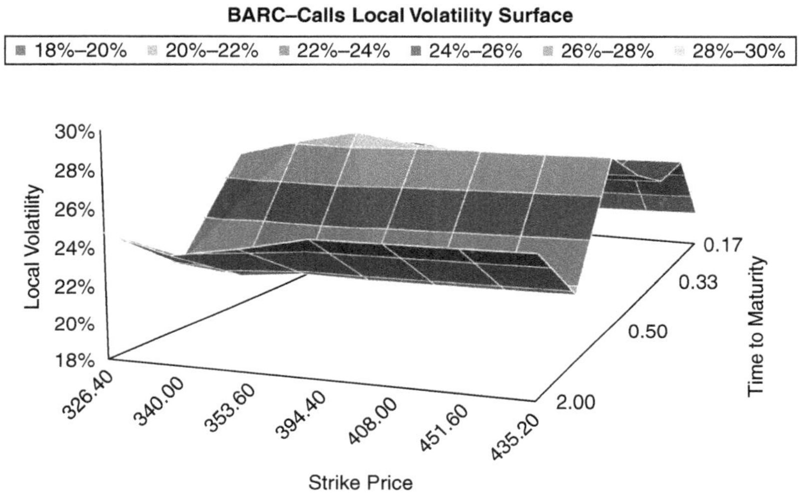

Figure 110 BARC call options – volatility surface
Source: FinanceTrainingCourse.com

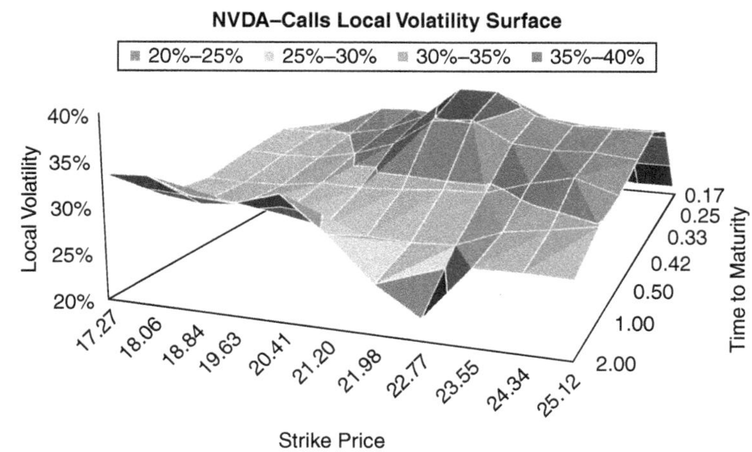

Figure 111 NVDA call options – volatility surface
Source: FinanceTrainingCourse.com

Klaus Schmitz quotes Ricardo Rebanato (1999) in his PhD thesis at Oxford on local volatilities:

> Implied volatility is the wrong number to put into wrong formulae to obtain the correct price. Local volatility on the other hand has the distinct advantage of being logically consistent. It is a volatility function which produces, via the Black-Scholes equation, prices which agree with those of the exchange traded options.[1]

And just in case you were wondering what the fuss is about, as well as to get a minor unpleasantness out of the way, here is the discrete form of the equation that Schmitz and Rebanato are referring to in the above statement:

$$\sigma_L^2(K,T) = \frac{\sigma^2 + 2\sigma(T-t)\left(\frac{\Delta\sigma}{\Delta T} + (r-D)K\frac{\Delta\sigma}{\Delta K}\right)}{\left(1+Kd\frac{\Delta\sigma}{\Delta K}\sqrt{(T-t)}\right)^2 + \sigma K^2(T-t)\left(\left(\frac{\Delta^2\sigma}{\Delta K^2}\right) - d\left(\frac{\Delta\sigma}{\Delta K}\right)^2\sqrt{(T-t)}\right)}$$

where
σ_L = Local volatility
K = Strike price
σ = Implied volatility
$\Delta\sigma$ = Change in implied volatility
ΔK = Change in strike prices
ΔT = Change in time
$\Delta^2\sigma/\Delta K^2$ = Second finite difference of sigma with respect to strike prices
T = Time to expiry
t = Current time
D = Dividend rate
r = Risk-free rate
S = Stock spot price

$$d = \frac{\ln\left(\frac{S}{K}\right) + \left(r + \frac{\sigma^2}{2}\right)(T-t)}{\sigma\sqrt{T-t}}$$

3 The difference between implied and local volatilities

While we introduced the concept of implied and local volatilities earlier, we have not yet differentiated between the two volatilities. In this section, we will try and shed some (albeit not a lot of) light on this topic.

i Implied volatilities

An implied volatility estimate is essentially a reverse solution for the value of sigma (volatility) given a price for a call or put option using the Black–Scholes equation. A generalized treatment assumes the same value of implied volatility using the Black–Scholes equation for all strike prices (K) and expiries

(T) for a given underlying security. More importantly, it is a price-quoting convention that allows market participants to communicate their assessments and expectations with respect to expected future realized volatility. By definition as well as design, it is not a model-pricing parameter.

In earlier chapters, when we spoke about the impact of rising volatility on deep out of money options and showed a range of option prices across different strikes, they all used a single implied volatility estimate. The problem with this single volatility assumption is that such a model cannot accommodate documented volatility smiles and skews.

ii Local volatilities

A local volatility model calculates the volatilities for different combination of strike prices (K) and expiries (T). It does this in a market-consistent no-arbitrage manner. This means that for a given date, time and underlying spot price combination, local volatilities are calculated in such a fashion that the resultant option prices match market prices. This assumes that we treat market prices as correct and arbitrage-free, and wish to calibrate our volatility model using basic liquid securities. Such a calibrated model (using basic securities) can then be used to 'correctly' price illiquid exotic derivatives. A volatility surface represents such a generalized calibrated model. It creates a surface that makes it possible to generalize a 'local' volatility value for all combinations of strike prices and expiries, something a simplified implied volatility model cannot deliver.

Derman and Kani trees and Dupire's formula (see below) are two approaches that we commonly see in this space. Dupire's formula is the approach that we introduced in building volatility surfaces, and the approach that we will use in the following sections to produce our volatility surface. The continuous form of the formulas is given below:

$$\sigma_L^2(K,T)=\frac{\sigma^2+2\sigma(T-t)\left(\frac{\delta\sigma}{\delta T}+(r-D)K\frac{\delta\sigma}{\delta K}\right)}{\left(1+Kd\frac{\delta\sigma}{\delta K}\sqrt{(T-t)}\right)^2+\sigma K^2(T-t)\left(\left(\frac{\delta^2\sigma}{\delta K^2}\right)-d\left(\frac{\delta\sigma}{\delta K}\right)^2\sqrt{(T-t)}\right)}$$

where

σ_L = Local volatility

σ = Implied volatility

K = Strike price

T = Time to expiry

T = Current date

D = Dividend rate

r = Risk-free rate

S = Stock spot price

$$d=\frac{\ln\left(\frac{S}{K}\right)+\left(r+\frac{\sigma^2}{2}\right)(T-t)}{\sigma\sqrt{T-t}}$$

And now for a visual summary in English that is easier to understand for ordinary mortals. Sometimes a picture is worth a thousand words; in this instance, we will use four pictures.. The first three figures plot implied volatilities and local volatilities for two-year, one-year and three-month NVIDIA call options respectively for a given date, spot and time to maturity. The two variables in each of the plots are volatility and strike prices.

The three plots show three different relationships between implied and local volatilities. The three relationships are only a small sample of the options universe on NVIDIA shares. The fourth shows the completed volatility surface for NVIDIA, incorporating the universe of these relationships.

If you are still reeling, here is a hint. **Market consistent. Arbitrage free.** Think about it before proceeding to the next chapter. And now without further ado we present the four pictures.

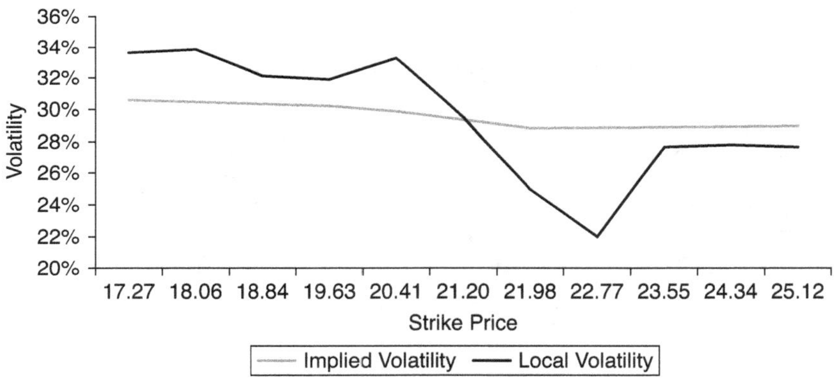

Figure 112 NVDA local versus implied volatilities – two-year maturity options
Source: FinanceTrainingCourse.com

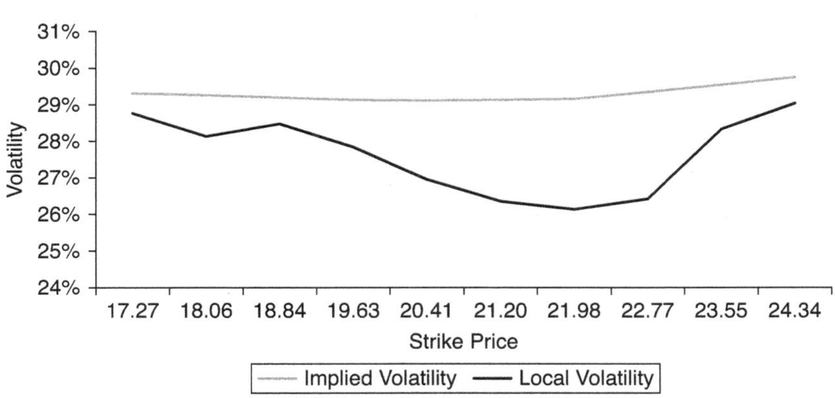

Figure 113 NVDA local versus implied volatilities – one-year maturity options
Source: FinanceTrainingCourse.com

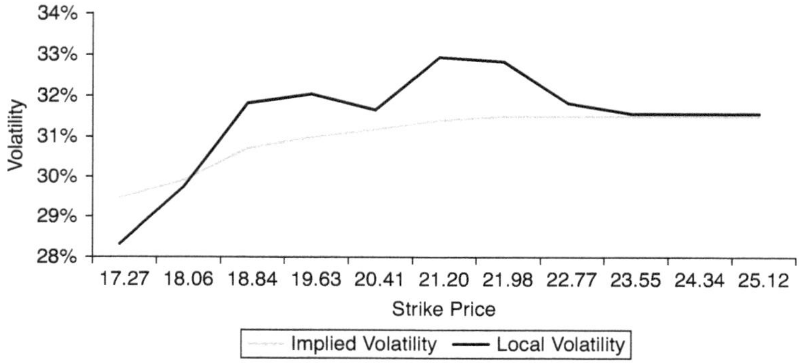

Figure 114 NVDA local versus implied volatilities – three-month maturity options
Source: FinanceTrainingCourse.com

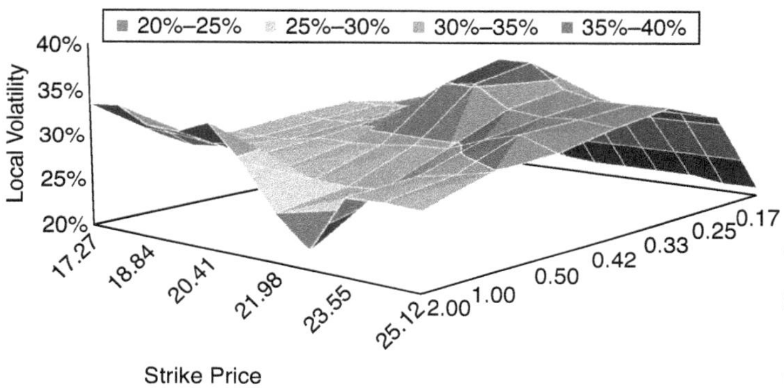

Figure 115 NVDA local volatility surface
Source: FinanceTrainingCourse.com

7
Building Volatility Surfaces

1 Creating the implied volatility dataset

Downloaded implied volatility datasets from volatility data sources generally include the following information:

symbol	exchange	date	period	strike	out-of-the-money %	call/put	iv	delta
NVDA	NASDAQ	05/15/14	30	7.2	60	P	0.3056	-
NVDA	NASDAQ	05/15/14	30	8.1	55	P	0.3056	-
NVDA	NASDAQ	05/15/14	30	9	50	P	0.3056	-
NVDA	NASDAQ	05/15/14	30	9.9	45	P	0.3056	-
NVDA	NASDAQ	05/15/14	30	10.8	40	P	0.3058	-
NVDA	NASDAQ	05/15/14	30	11.7	35	P	0.3264	-
NVDA	NASDAQ	05/15/14	30	12.6	30	P	0.3264	- 0.00
NVDA	NASDAQ	05/15/14	30	13.5	25	P	0.3264	- 0.00
NVDA	NASDAQ	05/15/14	30	14.4	20	P	0.3264	- 0.01
NVDA	NASDAQ	05/15/14	30	15.3	15	P	0.3264	- 0.04
NVDA	NASDAQ	05/15/14	30	16.2	10	P	0.2984	- 0.11
NVDA	NASDAQ	05/15/14	30	17.1	5	P	0.2721	- 0.26
NVDA	NASDAQ	05/15/14	30	18	0	P	0.2687	- 0.51
NVDA	NASDAQ	05/15/14	30	18	0	C	0.2757	0.49
NVDA	NASDAQ	05/15/14	30	18.9	5	C	0.2799	0.27
NVDA	NASDAQ	05/15/14	30	19.8	10	C	0.2986	0.13
NVDA	NASDAQ	05/15/14	30	20.7	15	C	0.3176	0.06
NVDA	NASDAQ	05/15/14	30	21.6	20	C	0.3189	0.02
NVDA	NASDAQ	05/15/14	30	22.5	25	C	0.3189	0.01
NVDA	NASDAQ	05/15/14	30	23.4	30	C	0.3189	0.00
NVDA	NASDAQ	05/15/14	30	24.3	35	C	0.3189	0.00

Figure 116 Raw implied volatility dataset
Source: ivolatility.com.

For a quarterly sample data snapshot on a daily basis, it is not uncommon to end up with a few thousand rows. But to build a volatility surface, we need a much smaller focus. One option is to cut the dataset by Maturity (expiry, T) and Strikes (K) as shown below. Options are sorted using date and period filters, and we get all combinations of implied volatilities by strikes for a given expiry date.

symbol	exchange	date	period	strike	out-of-the-money %	call/put	iv	delta
NVDA	NASDAQ	05/15/14	30	18	0	C	27.6%	0.49
NVDA	NASDAQ	05/15/14	30	18.9	5	C	28.0%	0.27
NVDA	NASDAQ	05/15/14	30	19.8	10	C	29.9%	0.13
NVDA	NASDAQ	05/15/14	30	20.7	15	C	31.8%	0.06
NVDA	NASDAQ	05/15/14	30	21.6	20	C	31.9%	0.02
NVDA	NASDAQ	05/15/14	60	18	0	C	27.2%	0.51
NVDA	NASDAQ	05/15/14	60	18.9	5	C	27.0%	0.33
NVDA	NASDAQ	05/15/14	60	19.8	10	C	27.4%	0.20
NVDA	NASDAQ	05/15/14	60	20.7	15	C	28.2%	0.11
NVDA	NASDAQ	05/15/14	60	21.6	20	C	28.5%	0.06

Figure 117 Volatility surface data cut – option 1

A second possible cut is to focus on all possible implied volatility values by expiry dates for a given strike price. This is the approach that we will opt for in our model-building exercise in Excel.

symbol	exchange	date	period	strike	out-of-the-money %	call/put	iv	delta
NVDA	NASDAQ	12/31/13	30	16.02	0	C	22.7%	0.51
NVDA	NASDAQ	12/31/13	60	16.02	0	C	27.7%	0.52
NVDA	NASDAQ	12/31/13	90	16.02	0	C	27.4%	0.52
NVDA	NASDAQ	12/31/13	120	16.02	0	C	27.9%	0.52
NVDA	NASDAQ	12/31/13	150	16.02	0	C	28.2%	0.53
NVDA	NASDAQ	12/31/13	180	16.02	0	C	28.5%	0.53
NVDA	NASDAQ	12/31/13	360	16.02	0	C	29.3%	0.54
NVDA	NASDAQ	12/31/13	720	16.02	0	C	30.1%	0.56
NVDA	NASDAQ	12/31/13	1080	16.02	0	C	30.1%	0.58

Figure 118 Volatility surface data cut – option 2

We use the filter option in Excel to select a given date, and then sort the dataset by maturity and by strike combination. The result on your sheet should look something like the following panel:

symbol	exchange	date	period	strike	out-of-the-money %	call/put	iv	delta
NVDA	NASDAQ	01/31/14	30	15.7	0	C	32.2%	0.51
NVDA	NASDAQ	01/31/14	60	15.7	0	C	29.3%	0.51
NVDA	NASDAQ	01/31/14	90	15.7	0	C	29.1%	0.52
NVDA	NASDAQ	01/31/14	120	15.7	0	C	29.5%	0.52
NVDA	NASDAQ	01/31/14	150	15.7	0	C	29.7%	0.52
NVDA	NASDAQ	01/31/14	180	15.7	0	C	29.8%	0.53
NVDA	NASDAQ	01/31/14	360	15.7	0	C	29.9%	0.54
NVDA	NASDAQ	01/31/14	720	15.7	0	C	30.6%	0.56
NVDA	NASDAQ	01/31/14	1080	15.7	0	C	30.6%	0.58
NVDA	NASDAQ	01/31/14	30	16.485	5	C	32.0%	0.30
NVDA	NASDAQ	01/31/14	60	16.485	5	C	29.1%	0.35
NVDA	NASDAQ	01/31/14	90	16.485	5	C	28.9%	0.38
NVDA	NASDAQ	01/31/14	120	16.485	5	C	29.3%	0.40
NVDA	NASDAQ	01/31/14	150	16.485	5	C	29.4%	0.42
NVDA	NASDAQ	01/31/14	180	16.485	5	C	29.4%	0.43
NVDA	NASDAQ	01/31/14	360	16.485	5	C	29.6%	0.47
NVDA	NASDAQ	01/31/14	720	16.485	5	C	30.6%	0.52
NVDA	NASDAQ	01/31/14	1080	16.485	5	C	30.6%	0.54

Figure 119 Volatility surface data cut – option 2 revisited

The date yields nine maturity buckets, which are then translated into yearly figures by dividing each of them by 360 (the assumption here is that there are 360 days in a year).

BUCKETS	EXPIRY	YEARLY
1	30	0.08
2	60	0.17
3	90	0.25
4	120	0.33
5	150	0.42
6	180	0.50
7	360	1.00
8	720	2.00
9	1,080	3.00

Figure 120 Volatility surface data cut – maturity buckets

On 31 January 2014, there are 13 available strike prices for call options on NVIDIA.

COUNT	STRIKES
1	15.70
2	16.49
3	17.27
4	18.06
5	18.84
6	19.63
7	20.41
8	21.20
9	21.98
10	22.77
11	23.55
12	24.34
13	25.12

Figure 121 Volatility surface data cut – available strikes

When we use the combination of maturity buckets and strike prices, we get a grid of implied volatilities.

Implied Volatilities									
	Maturities								
Strikes	0.08	0.17	0.25	0.33	0.42	0.50	1.00	2.00	3.00
15.70									
16.49									
17.27									
18.06									
18.84									
19.63									
20.41									
21.20									
21.98									
22.77									
23.55									
24.34									
25.12									

Figure 122 Implied volatility blank grid for volatility surface

Our final step is to fill in the grid, based on implied volatility data from our data source. The final grid produced below becomes the starting point in our next section.

Implied Volatilities									
	Maturities								
Strikes	0.08	0.17	0.25	0.33	0.42	0.50	1.00	2.00	3.00
15.70	32.15%	29.34%	29.13%	29.52%	29.70%	29.76%	29.88%	30.62%	30.62%
16.49	32.03%	29.11%	28.88%	29.26%	29.43%	29.44%	29.56%	30.63%	30.63%
17.27	33.57%	29.25%	28.96%	29.25%	29.34%	29.26%	29.32%	30.59%	30.59%
18.06	34.97%	29.72%	29.41%	29.45%	29.41%	29.28%	29.26%	30.46%	30.46%
18.84	34.97%	30.73%	30.21%	29.93%	29.71%	29.46%	29.20%	30.34%	30.34%
19.63	34.97%	30.96%	30.48%	30.19%	29.94%	29.65%	29.14%	30.22%	30.22%
20.41	34.97%	30.98%	30.67%	30.63%	30.43%	29.99%	29.12%	29.89%	29.89%
21.20	34.97%	30.98%	30.90%	31.19%	31.04%	30.40%	29.14%	29.38%	29.38%
21.98	34.97%	30.98%	31.00%	31.42%	31.32%	30.66%	29.16%	28.88%	28.88%
22.77	34.97%	30.98%	31.00%	31.43%	31.38%	30.83%	29.35%	28.90%	28.90%
23.55	34.97%	30.98%	31.00%	31.43%	31.45%	31.06%	29.55%	28.94%	28.94%
24.34	35.16%	30.98%	31.00%	31.43%	31.49%	31.21%	29.75%	28.98%	28.98%
25.12	35.16%	30.98%	31.00%	31.43%	31.49%	31.21%	29.92%	29.01%	29.01%

Figure 123 Volatility surface – implied volatilities from source data

This is the raw implied volatility data provided by our data provider. If we plot a surface with these volatilities it will be relatively flat, as seen below:

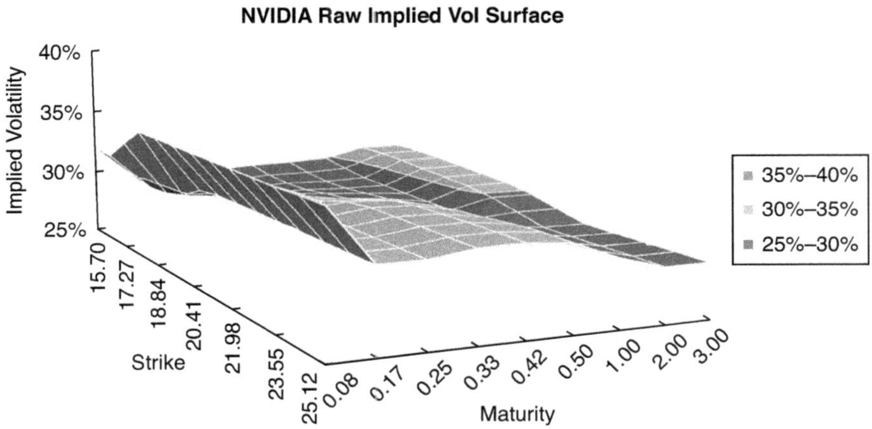

Figure 124 Sample raw implied volatility surface before calculation of local volatilities
Source: FinanceTrainingCourse.com.

2 Building local volatility surfaces in Excel

We now have everything required to build the volatility surface for NVIDIA in Excel.

1. We have the implied volatility data for NVIDIA as of 31 January 2014:

		Implied Volatilities Maturities								
		0.08	0.17	0.25	0.33	0.42	0.50	1.00	2.00	3.00
Strikes	**15.70**	32.15%	29.34%	29.13%	29.52%	29.70%	29.76%	29.88%	30.62%	30.62%
	16.49	32.03%	29.11%	28.88%	29.26%	29.43%	29.44%	29.56%	30.63%	30.63%
	17.27	33.57%	29.25%	28.96%	29.25%	29.34%	29.26%	29.32%	30.59%	30.59%
	18.06	34.97%	29.72%	29.41%	29.45%	29.41%	29.28%	29.26%	30.46%	30.46%
	18.84	34.97%	30.73%	30.21%	29.93%	29.71%	29.46%	29.20%	30.34%	30.34%
	19.63	34.97%	30.96%	30.48%	30.19%	29.94%	29.65%	29.14%	30.22%	30.22%
	20.41	34.97%	30.98%	30.67%	30.63%	30.43%	29.99%	29.12%	29.89%	29.89%
	21.20	34.97%	30.98%	30.90%	31.19%	31.04%	30.40%	29.14%	29.38%	29.38%
	21.98	34.97%	30.98%	31.00%	31.42%	31.32%	30.66%	29.16%	28.88%	28.88%
	22.77	34.97%	30.98%	31.00%	31.43%	31.38%	30.83%	29.35%	28.90%	28.90%
	23.55	34.97%	30.98%	31.00%	31.43%	31.45%	31.06%	29.55%	28.94%	28.94%
	24.34	35.16%	30.98%	31.00%	31.43%	31.49%	31.21%	29.75%	28.98%	28.98%
	25.12	35.16%	30.98%	31.00%	31.43%	31.49%	31.21%	29.92%	29.01%	29.01%

Figure 125 Implied volatility data from ivolatility.com, cleaned up and structured for surface plot

2. We have Dupire's formula for calculating local volatilities from implied volatilities:

$$\sigma_L^2(K,T)=\frac{\sigma^2+2\sigma(T-t)\left(\frac{\delta\sigma}{\delta T}+(r-D)K\frac{\delta\sigma}{\delta K}\right)}{\left(1+Kd\frac{\delta\sigma}{\delta K}\sqrt{(T-t)}\right)^2+\sigma K^2(T-t)\left(\left(\frac{\delta^2\sigma}{\delta K^2}\right)-d\left(\frac{\delta\sigma}{\delta K}\right)^2\sqrt{(T-t)}\right)}$$

where
σ_L = Local volatility
σ = Implied volatility
K = Strike price
T = Time to expiry
T = Current date
D = Dividend rate
r = Risk-free rate
S = Stock spot price

$$d=\frac{\ln\left(\frac{S}{K}\right)+\left(r+\frac{\sigma^2}{2}\right)(T-t)}{\sigma\sqrt{T-t}}$$

3. Using the continuous form of Dupire's equation, we create a discrete variation for usage in our spreadsheet:

$$\sigma_L^2(K,T)=\frac{\sigma^2+2\sigma(T-t)\left(\frac{\Delta\sigma}{\Delta T}+(r-D)K\frac{\Delta\sigma}{\Delta K}\right)}{\left(1+Kd\frac{\Delta\sigma}{\Delta K}\sqrt{(T-t)}\right)^2+\sigma K^2(T-t)\left(\left(\frac{\Delta^2\sigma}{\Delta K^2}\right)-d\left(\frac{\Delta\sigma}{\Delta K}\right)^2\sqrt{(T-t)}\right)}$$

where
σ_L = Local volatility
K = Strike price
σ = Implied volatility
$\Delta\sigma$ = Change in implied volatility
ΔK = Change in strike prices
ΔT = Change in time
$\Delta^2\sigma/\Delta K^2$ = Second finite difference of sigma with respect to strike prices
T = Time to expiry
t = Current time
D = Dividend rate
r = Risk-free rate
S = Stock spot price

$$d = \frac{\ln\left(\frac{S}{K}\right) + \left(r + \frac{\sigma^2}{2}\right)(T-t)}{\sigma\sqrt{T-t}}$$

4. In order to calculate sigma's first-order derivative with respect to time (strike price) in the equation, we use the finite backward difference approximation:

$$f(x_i)'' = \frac{f(x_i) + f(x_{i-1})}{h}$$

where
$f(x_i)$ = value of implied volatility at time to maturity i
h = difference between time periods *i* and *i*–1 if the first-order derivative is with respect to time, or the difference in strike at times *i* and *i*–1 if with respect to strike.

5. In order to calculate sigma's second-order derivative with respect to the strike price K in the equation above, we use the finite backward difference approximation:

$$f(x_i)'' = \frac{f(x_{i-2}) - 2f(x_{i-1}) + f(x_i)}{h^2}$$

where
$f(x_i)$ = value of implied volatility at time to maturity *i*
h^2 = (difference in the two strike prices between periods *i* and *i*–2)^2

6. All that is left now is to follow the process for calculating local volatilities.

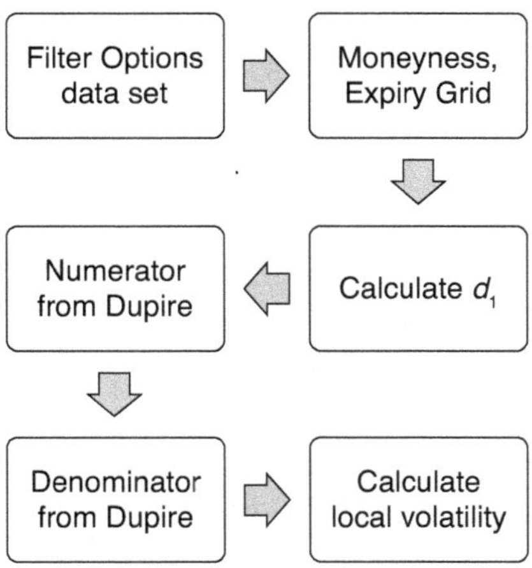

Figure 126 Volatility surface in Excel – a six-step process

Four steps remain of the original list. Let's go through them one by one. We will build multiple grids using the same template as that used for implied volatilities in the earlier section.

a Step 1 – Calculating d

The first grid calculates d using the formula shown below; this is the same d_1 that we use for pricing European options in the Black–Scholes–Merton model.

$$d = \frac{\ln\left(\frac{S}{K}\right) + \left(r + \frac{\sigma^2}{2}\right)(T - t)}{\sigma\sqrt{T - t}}$$

The Excel implementation of the formula is given below.

```
fx  =(LN(spot/$B30)+(risk_free+C12^2/2)*(C$29))/(C12*SQRT(C$29))
```

Figure 127 Calculating *d* in Excel

A common spreadsheet error is the incorrect anchoring (using the F4 key) of strike prices (the B column) or maturities (the 29th row) in the implementation below, or missing the anchoring completely.

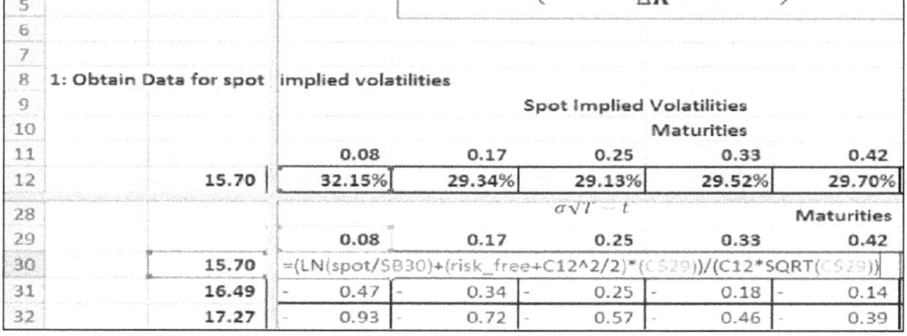

Figure 128 d_1 Excel implementation in strike by expiry grid

Once that is done, it is a simple copy–paste of the original formula across the remaining cells in the grid.

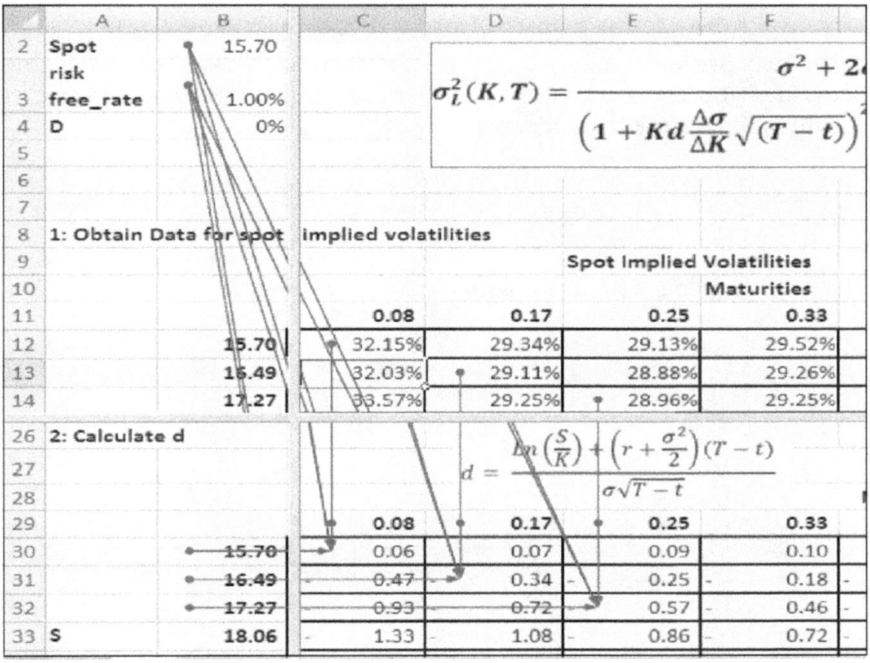

Figure 129 Anchoring the correct cell in the Excel strike by maturity grid
Source: FinanceTrainingCourse.com

The final result looks like the grid below:

	d								
	Maturities								
Strikes	0.08	0.17	0.25	0.33	0.42	0.50	1.00	2.00	3.00
15.70	0.06	0.07	0.09	0.10	0.12	0.13	0.18	0.26	0.32
16.49	−0.47	−0.34	−0.25	−0.18	−0.14	−0.11	0.02	0.15	0.23
17.27	−0.93	−0.72	−0.57	−0.46	−0.39	−0.33	−0.14	0.04	0.14
18.06	−1.33	−1.08	−0.86	−0.72	−0.62	−0.55	−0.30	−0.06	0.06
18.84	−1.75	−1.38	−1.11	−0.95	−0.83	−0.75	−0.44	−0.16	−0.03
19.63	−2.15	−1.69	−1.37	−1.17	−1.04	−0.94	−0.59	−0.26	−0.11
20.41	−2.54	−2.00	−1.62	−1.38	−1.22	−1.11	−0.72	−0.36	−0.19
21.20	−2.91	−2.30	−1.85	−1.56	−1.38	−1.27	−0.85	−0.47	0.28
21.98	−3.27	−2.58	−2.08	−1.75	−1.54	−1.42	−0.97	−0.57	0.36
22.77	−3.62	−2.86	−2.30	−1.94	−1.71	−1.57	−1.09	−0.66	0.43
23.55	−3.96	−3.13	−2.52	−2.13	−1.88	−1.71	−1.19	−0.74	0.50
24.34	−4.26	−3.39	−2.73	−2.31	−2.03	−1.85	−1.29	−0.82	0.56
25.12	−4.57	−3.64	−2.94	−2.48	−2.19	−2.00	−1.39	−0.89	0.62

Figure 130 d_1 Excel grid

b Step 2 – Calculating the first- and second-order rates of change

Using finite differences, we now calculate our two first-order and one second-order rates of change used in Dupire's formula. We use the same sequence of steps to create three more grids – one each for each rate of change.

The two first-order rates of change are sigma with respect to changing maturities, and sigma with respect to changing strikes. An extract of Dupire's formula showing the first-order rates of change is given below:

$$\frac{\Delta\sigma}{\Delta T}+(r-D)K\frac{\Delta\sigma}{\Delta K}$$

The Excel implementations for both are shown below:

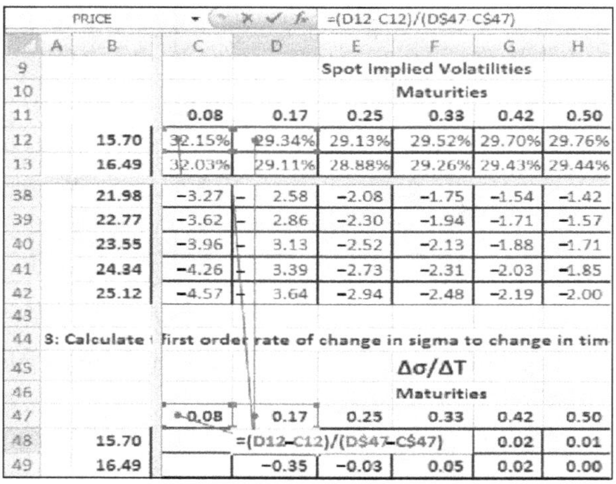

PRICE =(D12-C12)/(D$47-C$47)

	A	B	C	D	E	F	G	H
9					Spot Implied Volatilities			
10						Maturities		
11			0.08	0.17	0.25	0.33	0.42	0.50
12		15.70	32.15%	29.34%	29.13%	29.52%	29.70%	29.76%
13		16.49	32.03%	29.11%	28.88%	29.26%	29.43%	29.44%
38		21.98	−3.27	– 2.58	−2.08	−1.75	−1.54	−1.42
39		22.77	−3.62	– 2.86	−2.30	−1.94	−1.71	−1.57
40		23.55	−3.96	– 3.13	−2.52	−2.13	−1.88	−1.71
41		24.34	−4.26	– 3.39	−2.73	−2.31	−2.03	−1.85
42		25.12	−4.57	– 3.64	−2.94	−2.48	−2.19	−2.00
43								
44	3: Calculate first order rate of change in sigma to change in tim							
45						Δσ/ΔT		
46						Maturities		
47			0.08	0.17	0.25	0.33	0.42	0.50
48		15.70		=(D12-C12)/(D$47-C$47)			0.02	0.01
49		16.49		−0.35	−0.03	0.05	0.02	0.00

Figure 131 First-order rate of change – Sigma by time

Notice the empty first column (C). This is because you need two results to calculate the first-order difference.

Here again the first row is empty, as you need two results to calculate the first-order difference.

The second-order rate of change (sigma with respect to strike) is used in the denominator of the discrete presentation of Dupire's formula. An extract from the denominator showing the second-order rate of change is shown below:

$$\sigma K^2(T-t)\left(\left(\frac{\Delta^2\sigma}{\Delta K^2}\right)-d\left(\frac{\Delta\sigma}{\Delta K}\right)^2\sqrt{(T-t)}\right)$$

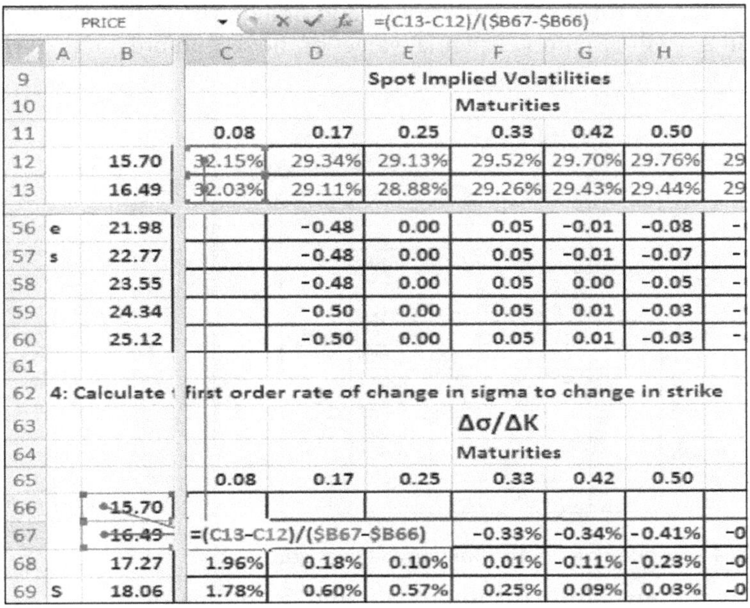

PRICE =(C13-C12)/($B67-$B66)

	A	B	C	D	E	F	G	H	
9					Spot Implied Volatilities				
10						Maturities			
11			0.08	0.17	0.25	0.33	0.42	0.50	
12		15.70	32.15%	29.34%	29.13%	29.52%	29.70%	29.76%	29
13		16.49	32.03%	29.11%	28.88%	29.26%	29.43%	29.44%	29
56	e	21.98		-0.48	0.00	0.05	-0.01	-0.08	-
57	s	22.77		-0.48	0.00	0.05	-0.01	-0.07	-
58		23.55		-0.48	0.00	0.05	0.00	-0.05	-
59		24.34		-0.50	0.00	0.05	0.01	-0.03	-
60		25.12		-0.50	0.00	0.05	0.01	-0.03	-
61									
62	4: Calculate first order rate of change in sigma to change in strike								
63						Δσ/ΔK			
64						Maturities			
65			0.08	0.17	0.25	0.33	0.42	0.50	
66		15.70							
67		16.49	=(C13-C12)/($B67-$B66)			-0.33%	-0.34%	-0.41%	-0
68		17.27	1.96%	0.18%	0.10%	0.01%	-0.11%	-0.23%	-0
69	S	18.06	1.78%	0.60%	0.57%	0.25%	0.09%	0.03%	-0

Figure 132 First-order rate of change – Sigma by strike

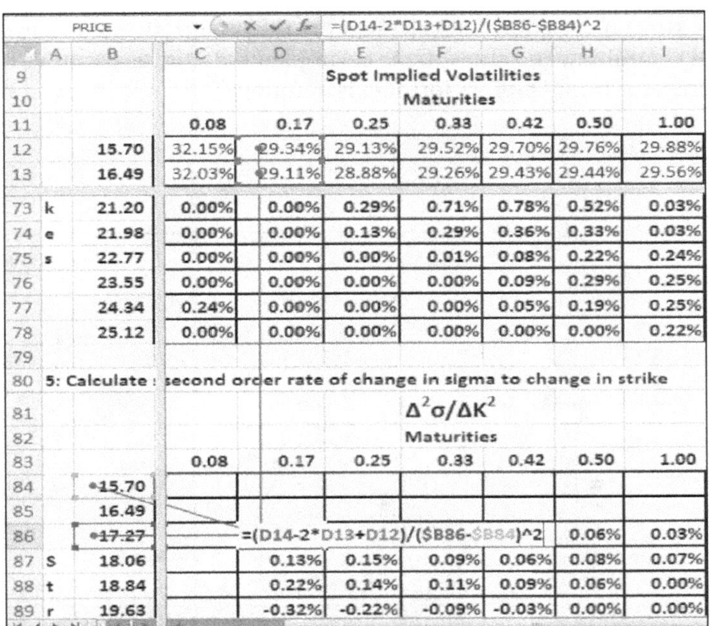

PRICE =(D14-2*D13+D12)/($B86-$B84)^2

	A	B	C	D	E	F	G	H	I
9					Spot Implied Volatilities				
10						Maturities			
11			0.08	0.17	0.25	0.33	0.42	0.50	1.00
12		15.70	32.15%	29.34%	29.13%	29.52%	29.70%	29.76%	29.88%
13		16.49	32.03%	29.11%	28.88%	29.26%	29.43%	29.44%	29.56%
73	k	21.20	0.00%	0.00%	0.29%	0.71%	0.78%	0.52%	0.03%
74	e	21.98	0.00%	0.00%	0.13%	0.29%	0.36%	0.33%	0.03%
75	s	22.77	0.00%	0.00%	0.00%	0.01%	0.08%	0.22%	0.24%
76		23.55	0.00%	0.00%	0.00%	0.00%	0.09%	0.29%	0.25%
77		24.34	0.24%	0.00%	0.00%	0.00%	0.05%	0.19%	0.25%
78		25.12	0.00%	0.00%	0.00%	0.00%	0.00%	0.00%	0.22%
79									
80	5: Calculate second order rate of change in sigma to change in strike								
81						$\Delta^2\sigma/\Delta K^2$			
82						Maturities			
83			0.08	0.17	0.25	0.33	0.42	0.50	1.00
84		15.70							
85		16.49							
86		17.27		=(D14-2*D13+D12)/($B86-$B84)^2				0.06%	0.03%
87	S	18.06		0.13%	0.15%	0.09%	0.06%	0.08%	0.07%
88	t	18.84		0.22%	0.14%	0.11%	0.09%	0.06%	0.00%
89	r	19.63		-0.32%	-0.22%	-0.09%	-0.03%	0.00%	0.00%

Edit

Figure 133 Second-order rate of change – Sigma by strike – using finite differences

Since you need three values for the second-order change, the first two rows (84 and 85) will be empty. The final values of the second-order rate of change in the grid are shown below:

	$\Delta^2\sigma/\Delta K^2$								
	Maturities								
Strikes	0.08	0.17	0.25	0.33	0.42	0.50	1.00	2.00	3.00
15.70									
16.49									
17.27		0.15%	0.13%	0.10%	0.07%	0.06%	0.03%	−0.02%	−0.02%
18.06		0.13%	0.15%	0.09%	0.06%	0.08%	0.07%	−0.04%	−0.04%
18.84		0.22%	0.14%	0.11%	0.09%	0.06%	0.00%	0.00%	0.00%
19.63		−0.32%	−0.22%	−0.09%	−0.03%	0.00%	0.00%	0.00%	0.00%
20.41		−0.09%	−0.03%	0.07%	0.11%	0.06%	0.02%	−0.09%	−0.09%
21.20		−0.01%	0.02%	0.05%	0.05%	0.03%	0.02%	−0.07%	−0.07%
21.98		0.00%	−0.05%	−0.13%	−0.13%	−0.06%	0.00%	0.00%	0.00%
22.77		0.00%	−0.04%	−0.09%	−0.09%	−0.04%	0.07%	0.21%	0.21%
23.55		0.00%	0.00%	0.00%	0.00%	0.02%	0.00%	0.01%	0.01%
24.34		0.00%	0.00%	0.00%	−0.01%	−0.03%	0.00%	0.00%	0.00%
25.12		0.00%	0.00%	0.00%	−0.02%	−0.06%	−0.01%	0.00%	0.00%

Figure 134 Second-order finite differences – final grid

c Step 3 – Calculating the numerator and denominator

All that is left now is to calculate the numerator and denominator in the grid using Dupire's formula, and we are done. We use the same sequence of steps to create three more grids that calculate the numerator, the denominator and the local volatilities, and show the Excel implementation as we move forward. The numerator from Dupire's formula is as follows:

$$\sigma^2+2\sigma(T-t)\left(\frac{\Delta\sigma}{\Delta T}+(r-D)K\frac{\Delta\sigma}{\Delta K}\right)$$

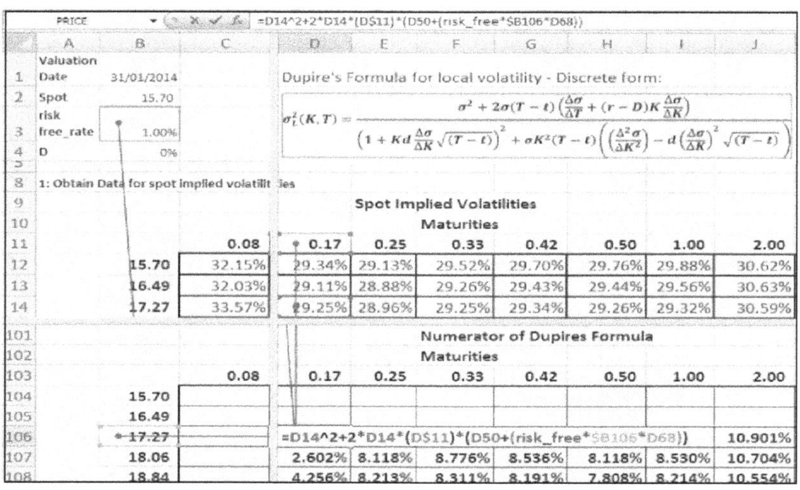

Figure 135 Dupire's formula – numerator calculation in Excel grid
Source: FinanceTrainingCourse.com

where cells D50 and D68 in the formula above reference the relevant first-order rates of change of sigma with respect to time and strike from the respective grids.

The denominator of Dupire's is reproduced below:

$$\left(1+Kd\frac{\Delta\sigma}{\Delta K}\sqrt{(T-t)}\right)^2+\sigma K^2(T-t)\left(\left(\frac{\Delta^2\sigma}{\Delta K^2}\right)-d\left(\frac{\Delta\sigma}{\Delta K}\right)^2\sqrt{(T-t)}\right)$$

PRICE =(1+$B126*D32*D68*SQRT(D$123))^2+D14*($B126^2)*D$123*(D86-D32*(D68^2)*SQRT(D$123))

	A	B	C	D	E	F	G	H	I	J	K	L
115		24.34		4.418%	9.647%	10.960%	10.108%	8.706%	7.150%	7.520%	8.420%	
116		25.12		4.418%	9.647%	10.960%	10.105%	8.692%	7.441%	7.371%	8.433%	
117												
118	7: Calculate the Denominator of Dupire's formula											
119						$\left(1+Kd\frac{\Delta\sigma}{\Delta K}\sqrt{(T-t)}\right)^2+\sigma K^2(T-t)\left(\left(\frac{\Delta^2\sigma}{\Delta K^2}\right)-d\left(\frac{\Delta\sigma}{\Delta K}\right)^2\sqrt{(T-t)}\right)$						
120												
121						Denominator						
122						Maturities						
123			0.08	0.17	0.25	0.33	0.42	0.50	1.00	2.00	3.00	
124		15.70										
125		16.49										
126		17.27		=(1+$B126*D32*D68*SQRT(D$123))^2+D14*($B126^2)*D$123*(D86-D32*(D68^2)*SQRT(D$123))								
127		18.06		0.9290	0.9493	0.9896	1.0131	1.0352	1.0779	0.9328	0.8854	

Figure 136 Dupire's formula – denominator calculation in Excel grid
Source: FinanceTrainingCourse.com

where cells D14, D32, D68 and D86 refer to the relevant entries in the implied volatility, d, the first-order rate of change with respect to strike, and the second-order rate of change with respect to strike grids.

8: Result - Calculate Local Volatilities

					Local Volatilities	
					Maturities	
		0.08	0.17	0.25	0.33	0.42	0
Strikes	15.70						
	16.49						
	17.27		=SQRT(D106/D126)		29.93%	29.25%	28.
	18.06		16.74%	29.24%	29.78%	29.03%	28.
	18.84		23.25%	31.32%	30.08%	29.13%	28.
	19.63		23.20%	31.54%	30.95%	30.05%	28.
	20.41		21.87%	31.15%	32.92%	31.64%	28.
	21.20		21.59%	32.44%	36.87%	34.81%	28.

Figure 137 Local volatility calculations in Excel grid
Source: FinanceTrainingCourse.com

where cells D106 and D126 refer to the relevant entries in the Dupire's formula numerator and denominator grids.

The final step leaves us with a grid of local volatilities that vary by Strike prices and Maturities.

	Local Volatilities								
	Maturities								
Strikes	0.08	0.17	0.25	0.33	0.42	0.50	1.00	2.00	3.00
15.70									
16.49									
17.27		18.69%	27.82%	29.93%	29.25%	28.15%	28.76%	33.66%	31.52%
18.06		16.74%	29.24%	29.78%	29.03%	28.00%	28.13%	33.87%	32.28%
18.84		23.25%	31.32%	30.08%	29.13%	28.10%	28.48%	32.13%	30.02%
19.63		23.20%	31.54%	30.95%	30.05%	28.75%	27.84%	31.89%	29.96%
20.41		21.87%	31.15%	32.92%	31.64%	28.66%	26.95%	33.29%	34.42%
21.20		21.59%	32.44%	36.87%	34.81%	28.87%	26.35%	29.52%	31.32%
21.98		21.57%	32.34%	36.82%	35.24%	29.30%	26.14%	24.98%	25.86%
22.77		21.57%	31.32%	34.05%	32.79%	29.42%	26.42%	21.99%	20.77%
23.55		21.57%	31.06%	33.14%	32.33%	30.88%	28.33%	27.70%	28.71%
24.34		21.02%	31.06%	33.11%	32.48%	31.96%	29.04%	27.82%	29.37%
25.12		21.02%	31.06%	33.11%	32.00%	30.41%	29.89%	27.69%	29.68%

Figure 138 Local volatility surface grid – final results
Source: FinanceTrainingCourse.com

d Step 4 – Plotting the surface

Select the local volatility grid that you have just created. In your Excel toolbar:

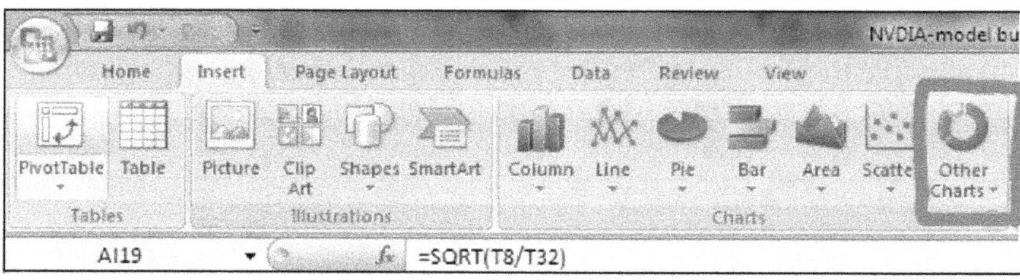

Figure 139 3D surface charts in Excel – step 1
***Source:* FinanceTrainingCourse.com**

1. Click on Insert
2. Pick Other Charts
3. Click on 3D Surface

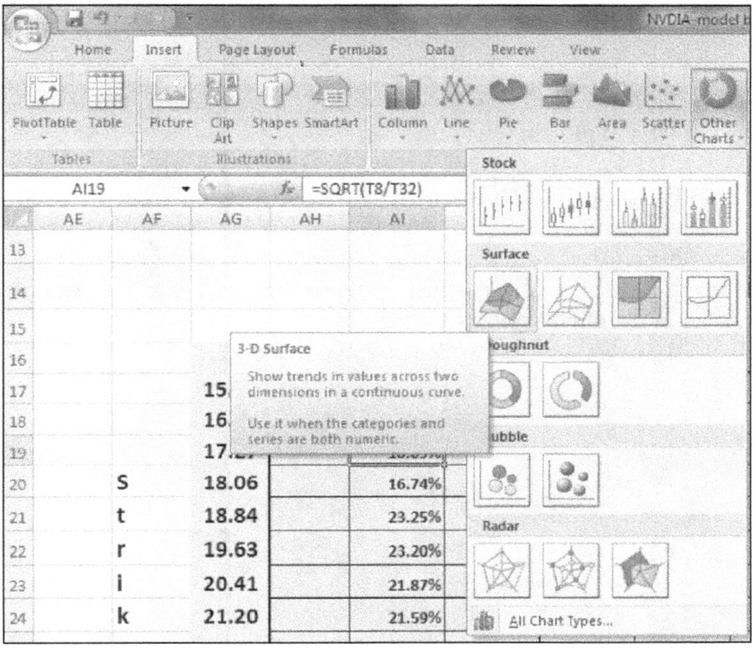

Figure 140 3D surface charts in Excel – step 2
Source: FinanceTrainingCourse.com

That's it. Done. Your local volatility 3D surface chart is ready for review and presentation:

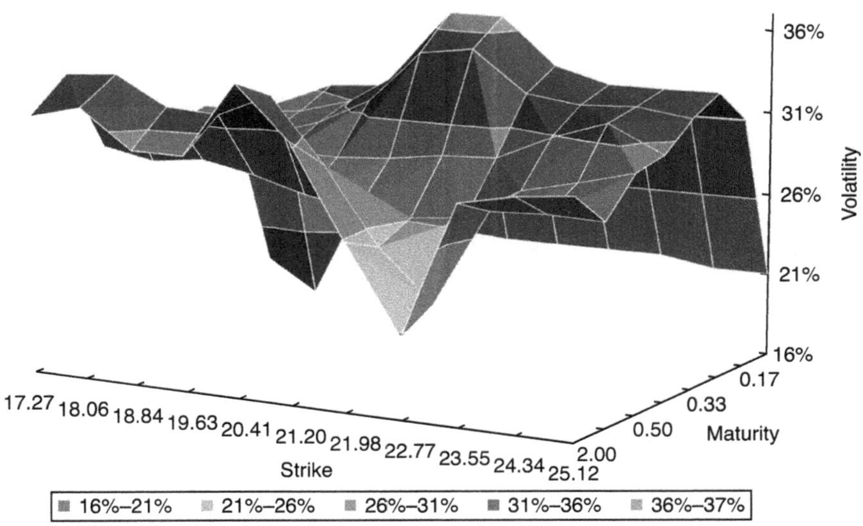

Figure 141 Local volatility surface in Excel – final results

3 Next steps, and questions

While we can all take a bow for completing the volatility surface plot in a tool like Excel, the real work has only just started. Here is a list of questions that you should start exploring:

1. How do you interpret the volatility surface diagram above?
2. How do you go about putting it to work?
3. How does that usage change when you want to use the surface for pricing and market calibration versus using the surface for risk management?
4. What about implied forward volatilities?
5. How do they relate to the work you have just done?

8
Forward Implied Volatilities

For path-dependent and forward starting options, it is important to assess Vega, the sensitivity of the option's value to changes in volatility, and in particular to assess these sensitivities for forward buckets. A first step in this process is to determine how forward volatilities for these forward buckets are calculated from the spot volatilities implied in current market option prices.

The procedure for determining these forward implied volatilities is similar to the procedure used for determining forward rates from spot prices. Given the spot rates for a zero coupon security maturing at time 1 and a zero coupon security maturing at time 2, (where time 1 < time 2), it is possible, through bootstrapping, to calculate the forward rate for the period between time 1 and time 2. Similarly given the spot implied volatilities for the periods t_0 to t_1 ($\sigma_{t0,\,t1}$) and t_0 to t_2 ($\sigma_{t0,\,t2}$) respectively, it is possible to infer the expected volatility between t_1 and t_2 ($\sigma_{t1,\,t2}$). This volatility is the forward implied volatility (also known as the forward-forward volatility) for the period $[t_1, t_2]$.

In *Dynamic Hedging*, Taleb presents the formula[1] for computing the annualized forward implied volatility for the period between $[t_{n-\alpha}, t_n]$, that is, $\sigma_{tn-\alpha,tn}$, as follows:

$$\sigma_{tn-\alpha,tn} = \sqrt{\frac{\sigma^2_{t0,tn}(t_n - t_0) - \sigma^2_{t0,tn-\alpha}(t_{n-\alpha} - t_0)}{(t_n - t_{n-\alpha})}}$$

where

$\sigma_{t0,tn}$ is the annualized spot implied volatility for the period t_0 to t_n for options expiring at time t_n

$\sigma_{t0,tn-\alpha}$ is the annualized spot implied volatility for the period t_0 to $t_{n-\alpha}$ for options expiring at time $t_{n-\alpha}$

This formula accounts for unequal non-overlapping time steps, in line with how spot implied volatilities and options prices are quoted in the market.

For example, let us consider the following annualized spot implied volatilities for at the money call options of strike US$272 on Barclays stock (BARC) for 31 January 2014 obtained from ivolatility.com.

Symbol	Period (i.e. option expiry) (t_0,t_n)	Spot Implied volatilities $(\sigma_{t0,tn})$
BARC	30	31.84%
BARC	60	27.45%
BARC	90	26.64%
BARC	120	26.27%
BARC	150	26.16%
BARC	180	26.25%
BARC	360	26.01%
BARC	720	26.08%
BARC	1080	26.13%

Figure 142 Spot implied volatilities for at the money call options on Barclays stock

where t_0 is time 0.

Using the data provided, first calculate the annualized variance for the periods (t_0,t_n), that is, $\sigma^2_{t0,tn}$.

PRICE =C15^2

	A	B	C	D
14	t_n	$t_{n-\alpha},t_n$	$\sigma_{t0,tn}$	$\sigma^2_{t0,tn}$
15	30	0-30	31.84%	=C15^2
16	60	30-60	27.45%	7.54%
17	90	60-90	26.64%	7.10%

Figure 143 Calculating annualized variance

Then calculate the annualized forward variance for the period $[t_{n-\alpha}, t_n]$, $\sigma^2_{tn-\alpha,tn}$. For the first period, 0–30, the forward variance will be the same as the spot variance. For later periods, 30–60, 60–90, 90–120, ... 360–720 and 720–1080, the forward variance will be calculated using Taleb's formula, as follows:

$$\sigma^2_{tn-\alpha,tn} = \frac{\sigma^2_{t0,tn}(t_n - t_0) - \sigma^2_{t0,tn-\alpha}(t_{n-\alpha} - t_0)}{(t_n - t_{n-\alpha})}$$

PRICE =(A16*D16-D15*A15)/(A16-A15)

	A	B	C	D	E	
14	t_n	$t_{n-\alpha},t_n$	$\sigma_{t0,tn}$	$\sigma^2_{t0,tn}$	$\sigma^2_{tn-\alpha,tn}$	$\sigma_{tn-\alpha,tn}$
15	30	0-30	31.84%	10.14%	10.14%	
16	60	30-60	27.45%	7.54%	=(A16*D16-D15*A15)/(A16-A15)	
17	90	60-90	26.64%	7.10%	6.22%	

Figure 144 Excel implementation of implied forward volatility

The square root of this forward variance will be the annualized forward implied volatility for the period $[t_{n-\alpha}, t_n]$:

PRICE =SQRT(E16)

	A	B	C	D	E	F
14	t_n	$t_{n-\alpha},t_n$	$\sigma_{t0,tn}$	$\sigma^2_{t0,tn}$	$\sigma^2_{tn-\alpha,tn}$	$\sigma_{tn-\alpha,tn}$
15	30	0-30	31.84%	10.14%	10.14%	31.84%
16	60	30-60	27.45%	7.54%	4.93%	=SQRT(E16)
17	90	60-90	26.64%	7.10%	6.22%	24.94%

Figure 145 Implied forward volatility final steps
Source: FinanceTrainingCourse.com

For the entire dataset, the forward implied volatilities are as follows:

t_n	$t_{n-\alpha},t_n$	$\sigma_{t0,tn}$	$\sigma^2_{t0,tn}$	$\sigma^2_{tn-\alpha,tn}$	$\sigma_{tn-\alpha,tn}$
30	0–30	31.84%	10.14%	10.14%	31.84%
60	30–60	27.45%	7.54%	4.93%	22.21%
90	60–90	26.64%	7.10%	6.22%	24.94%
120	90–120	26.27%	6.90%	6.31%	25.13%
150	120–150	26.16%	6.84%	6.61%	25.72%
180	150–180	26.25%	6.89%	7.13%	26.70%
360	180–360	26.01%	6.77%	6.64%	25.77%
720	360–720	26.08%	6.80%	6.84%	26.15%
1080	720–1080	26.13%	6.83%	6.88%	26.23%

Figure 146 Forward Implied volatilities derived
Source: FinanceTrainingCourse.com

The graphical plot of the spot and forward implied volatilities is given below:

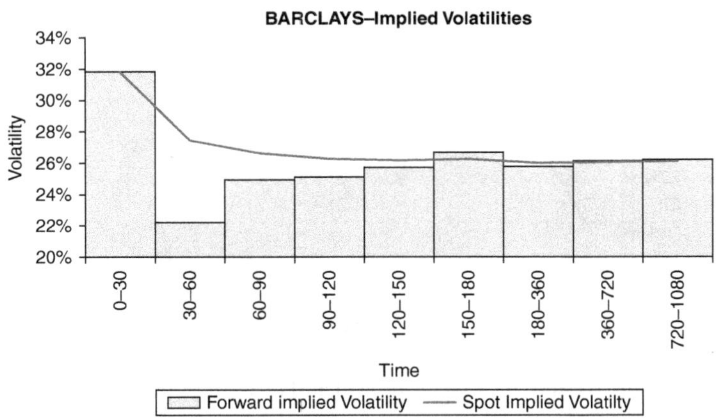

Figure 147 Plot of forward implied volatilities against spot implied volatilities
Source: FinanceTrainingCourse.com

Forward implied volatility between two points is the 'local volatility' between (S, t) and $(S, t + \Delta t)$. The generalization of this formula gives Dupire–Derman–Kani's local volatility, which is a function of time to expiry and option moneyness.

1 Comparing local, implied and forward volatilities

Since we spent a fair bit of time with NVIDIA options in earlier chapters while charting the local volatility surface for NVIDIA, it would be instructive to see how the forward implied volatility for NVIDIA option plots when put through Taleb's implied forward volatility formula.

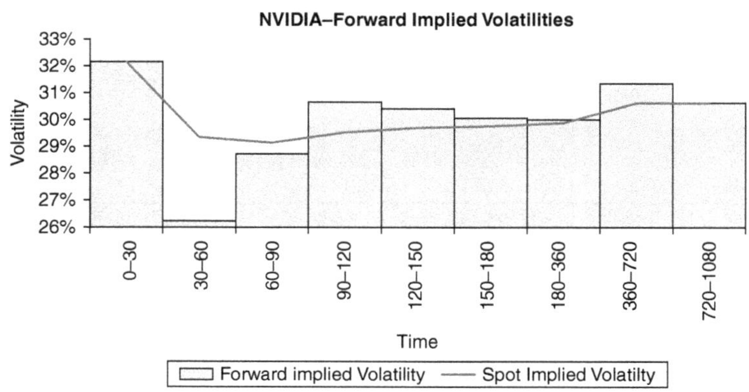

Figure 148 Forward implied volatilities NVIDIA
Source: FinanceTrainingCourse.com

The implied forward volatilities will change for every series of option expiries for a given strike price. It is also useful to compare all three volatilities (implied, local and forward) on the same grid for the same series of options.

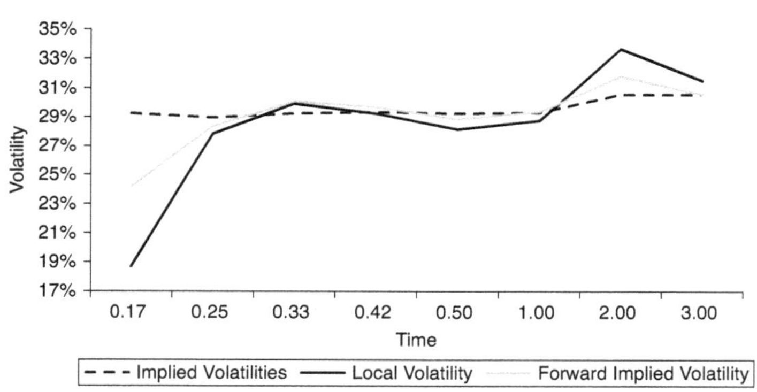

Figure 149 Comparison of local, spot implied and forward implied volatilities
Source: FinanceTrainingCourse.com

We would have expected to see convergence between local volatilities and implied forward volatilities, and the plot above shows some tracking between these two volatility numbers. The raw implied volatility data is relatively flat when compared to the other two volatility estimates.

Part IV

Hedging Higher-Order Greeks

9
Vega, Volga and Vanna

1 Vega

Vega is the change in the value of the option with respect to a change in volatility.

Within the Greeks, Vega's importance rises given both the degree of misunderstanding relating to the behaviour of volatility, and the impact that changes in volatility have on option prices. In earlier chapters we saw that:

a. implied volatility is not constant.
b. deep out of money options react very differently to changes in implied volatility. and
c. volatility ends up behaving as a function of time to expiry and moneyness. We used implied volatility surfaces to plot the behaviour of volatility across these two dimensions.

In this chapter, we will take a deeper look at Vega and its two associated derivatives, as well as examining Vega's relationship with Gamma. As part of this exploration process, we will introduce the concept of Shadow Gamma, Volga and Vanna – instances of what we could call cross Greeks. We have spent sufficient time with the concept of surface plots, and now we will add a new dimension, the underlying asset price, to our surface plots.

The equation for calculating Vega is given by:

$$Vega = S\sqrt{T-t}N'(d_1)e^{-q(T-t)}$$

$$N'(d_1) = \frac{1}{\sqrt{2\pi}}e^{-(d_1)^2/2}$$

$$d_1 = \frac{\ln\left(\frac{S}{K}\right) + \left(r + \frac{\sigma^2}{2}\right)(T-t)}{\sigma\sqrt{T-t}}$$

where
S = Stock spot price
σ = Implied volatility
r = Risk-free rate
T = Time to maturity in years
t = Current time
q = Dividend rate

As we assume no dividends, the formula simplifies to:

$$Vega = S\sqrt{T-t}N'(d_1)$$

Alternatively, Vega could also be expressed as a function of Gamma.[1] Gamma for an option on a non-dividend-paying stock is given by:

$$Gamma = \frac{\partial Delta}{\partial S} = \frac{N'(d_1)}{\sigma\sqrt{T-t}}$$

which implies:

$$Vega = Gamma \times S^2 \times (T-t) \times \sigma$$

where
We can use either of the two equations to calculate Vega. As with Gamma, the value of Vega is the same for both call and put options.

2 Vanna

Vanna, a second-order cross Greek, can be defined as:[2]

- $\partial v/\partial s$ – the change in Vega because of a change in underlying price
- $\partial \Delta/\partial \sigma$ – the change in Delta because of a change in volatility
- $\partial^2 P/\partial \sigma \partial A$ – the second derivative of option value with respect to a joint move in volatility and underlying asset price.

In the Black–Scholes model, Vanna is calculated using the following equation:

$$vanna = e^{-qt}\sqrt{T-t}N'(d_1)\left(\frac{d_2}{\sigma}\right)$$

where
S = Stock spot price
σ = Implied volatility
r = Risk-free rate
T = Time to maturity in years

t = Current time
q = Dividend rate

$$N'(d_1) = \frac{1}{\sqrt{2\pi}} e^{-(d_1)^2/2}$$

$$d_1 = \frac{\ln\left(\frac{S}{K}\right) + \left(r - q + \frac{\sigma^2}{2}\right)(T-t)}{\sigma\sqrt{T-t}}$$

The assumption of zero dividends simplifies the above equation to:

$$vanna = \sqrt{T-t}N'(d_1)\left(\frac{d_2}{\sigma}\right)$$

3 Volga

Volga, or Volatility Gamma, determines the rate of change in Vega on account of a unit change in volatility. This is similar to the relationship that convexity has with duration and Gamma with Delta. It can be defined as:[3]

- $\partial V/\partial\sigma$ – the change in Vega because of a change in volatility
- $\partial^2 P/\partial\sigma^2$ – the second derivative of option value with respect to volatility

$$volga = e^{-qt}\sqrt{T-t}N'(d_1)\left(\frac{d_1 d_2}{\sigma}\right)$$

where
S = Stock spot price
σ = Implied volatility
r = Risk-free rate
T = Time to maturity in years
t = Current time
q = Dividend rate

$$N'(d_1) = \frac{1}{\sqrt{2\pi}} e^{-(d_1)^2/2}$$

$$d_1 = \frac{\ln\left(\frac{S}{K}\right) + \left(r - q + \frac{\sigma^2}{2}\right)(T-t)}{\sigma\sqrt{T-t}}$$

$$d_2 = d_1 - \sigma\sqrt{T-t}$$

The assumption of zero dividends simplifies the above equation to:

$$volga = \sqrt{T-t}N'(d_1)\left(\frac{d_1 d_2}{\sigma}\right)$$

It is also possible to express both Vanna and Volga in terms of Vega.

We now know that for an option on a non-dividend-paying stock:

$$Vega = S\sqrt{T-t}N'(d_1)$$

$$Vanna = \sqrt{T-t}N'(d_1)\left(\frac{d_2}{\sigma}\right)$$

$$Volga = \sqrt{T-t}N'(d_1)\left(\frac{d_1 d_2}{\sigma}\right)$$

Vanna can be expressed in terms of Vega as follows:

$$Vanna = Vega\frac{(d_2)}{S\sigma}$$

Similarly, Volga can be expressed in terms of Vega as follows:

$$Volga = Vega\left(\frac{d_1 d_2}{S\sigma}\right)$$

The formulas for Vega, Vanna and Volga above indicate a direct linkage with time; unlike Gamma, which peaks with a reduction in time for an at the money option, for Vega, Volga and Vanna it is an increase in time that gives the volatility an opportunity to impact option value. The volatility Greeks will decline as time to expiry comes closer to zero. This creates different choices that need to be balanced when we try to hedge Gamma and Vega together.

4 Plotting Vega and Gamma

i Against strike

The plot below calculates values of Vega and Gamma for an option against changing strike prices. In this specific case the current spot price lies between 270 and 280 (at and near money), which is where Vega peaks. Despite the fact that we have a different scale for measuring Vega and Gamma, the interesting thing in the graph below is the similarity in shape of the two Greeks.

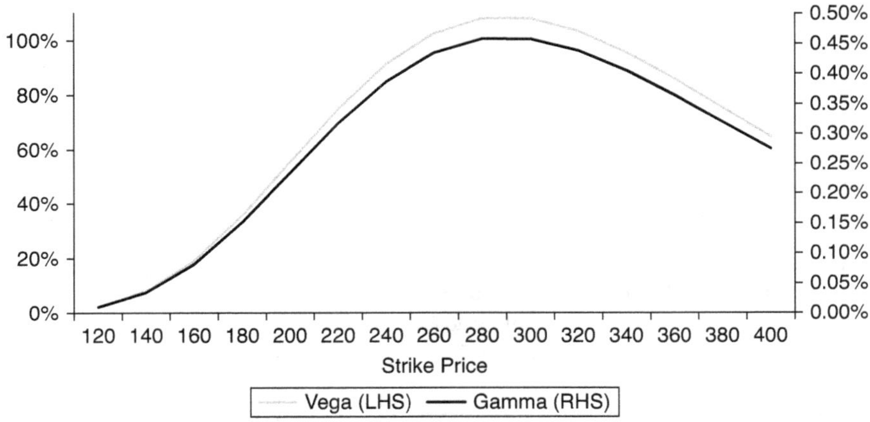

Figure 150 Vega and Gamma for options on Barclays stock with varying strikes
Source: FinanceTrainingCourse.com

ii Against time

It is when we plot Vega against changing expiry for deep out of money options and at money options that we see a difference emerging in the relationship between Vega and Gamma. For deep out of money options, reducing time to maturity reduces both Vega and Gamma.

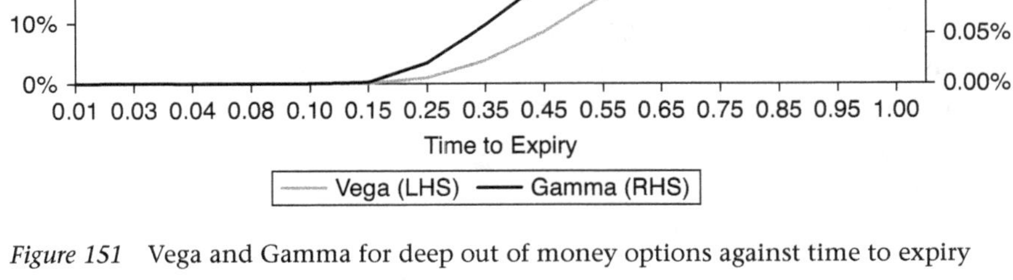

Figure 151 Vega and Gamma for deep out of money options against time to expiry
Source: FinanceTrainingCourse.com

However, for at the money options, the impacts of time on Vega and Gamma are exactly opposite; Vega rises as we increase time to expiry, whereas Gamma rises as we decrease time to expiry.

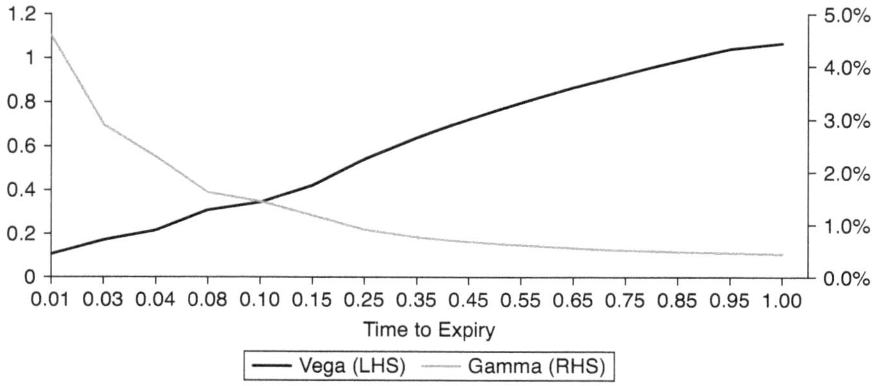

Figure 152 Vega and Gamma for at the money options against time to expiry
Source: FinanceTrainingCourse.com

5 Shadow Gamma – including the impact of volatility changes

In the Gamma calculation (as discussed in Chapter 1), a change in Delta is due to a change in the underlying asset price. A change in that asset price suggests a change in volatility (and possibly other price elements as well). Meanwhile, a static Gamma calculation assumes that volatility remains unchanged. Therefore, there needs to be an adjustment in the Gamma measure that considers that the underlying asset price volatility has changed. Taleb[4] suggests the calculation of the Shadow Gamma measure, which adjusts the basic Gamma measure by calculating the changes in Delta taking volatility changes into account as well as price changes.

The revised Delta measure used in the calculation of the Shadow Gamma is the difference between the value of the option considering both a price change and revised volatility level, and the original value of the option at the original spot and volatility level. In our example (this is a continuation of the example first introduced in Chapter 1) using options on NVIDIA, we have increase volatility by 5%, so that it is now 33.85%. The results for the revised Delta are given below for a sample set of asset prices:

NVIDIA STOCK PRICE	DELTA	DELTA-HIGHER VOL	DELTA DIFFERENCE
15.6	(0.00000)	(0.0000)	0.0000
16.1	(0.00000)	(0.0000)	0.0000
16.6	(0.00000)	(0.0000)	0.0000
17.1	(0.00000)	0.0000	0.0000
17.6	(0.00000)	0.0000	0.0000

Continued

NVIDIA STOCK PRICE	DELTA	DELTA - HIGHER VOL	DELTA DIFFERENCE
18.1	-	0.0000	0.0000
18.6	0.00000	0.0000	0.0000
19.1	0.00000	0.0000	0.0000
19.6	0.00000	0.0000	0.0000
20.1	0.00000	0.0001	0.0000
20.6	0.00001	0.0001	0.0001
21.1	0.00003	0.0004	0.0004
21.6	0.00011	0.0009	0.0008
22.1	0.00033	0.0021	0.0018
22.6	0.00088	0.0045	0.0036
23.1	0.00218	0.0089	0.0067
23.6	0.00498	0.0168	0.0118
24.1	0.01058	0.0301	0.0195
24.6	0.02105	0.0513	0.0303
25.1	0.03935	0.0838	0.0444
25.6	0.06946	0.1312	0.0618
26.1	0.11624	0.1978	0.0816
26.6	0.18519	0.2877	0.1025
27.1	0.28201	0.4050	0.1230
27.6	0.41198	0.5531	0.1411
28.1	0.57942	0.7346	0.1552
28.6	0.78721	0.9512	0.1640
29.1	1.03647	1.2032	0.1667
29.6	1.32654	1.4901	0.1635
30.1	1.65513	1.8101	0.1549
30.6	2.01866	2.1608	0.1421
31.1	2.41271	2.5390	0.1263
31.6	2.83249	2.9416	0.1091
32.1	3.27323	3.3648	0.0916
32.6	3.73050	3.8054	0.0749

Figure 153 Original Delta and revised Delta using a higher volatilities assumption

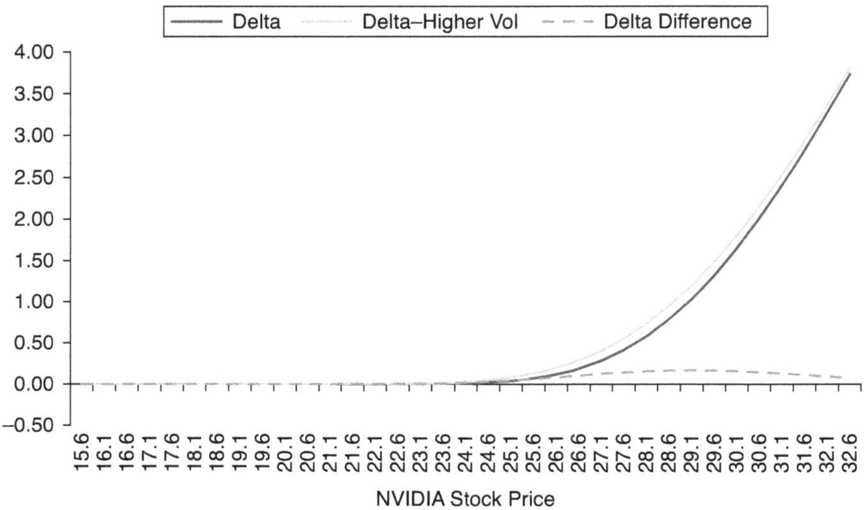

Figure 154 Comparison of original Delta, revised Delta and their difference
Source: FinanceTrainingCourse.com

The Shadow Gamma is calculated as follows for a given stock price point, B, such that A > B < C where A is a stock price less than B, and C is a stock price greater than B:

Shadow up – Gamma (B) = (Delta (C, revised vol) – Delta (B, original vol))/(C–B), where the underlying asset price is assumed to go up to C from B.
Shadow down – Gamma (B) = (Delta (B, original vol) – Delta (A, revised vol))/(B–A), where the underlying asset price is assumed to go down to A from B.

For example, the up-Gamma calculated at asset price US$25.1 for an increment of US$1 in the asset price is equal to the Delta using the revised volatility calculated at asset price US$26.1 less the Delta using the original volatility calculated at asset price US$25.1; that is, shadow up-Gamma (25.1) = [Delta_higher vol (26.1) – Delta (25.1)]/(26.1 – 25.1) = 0.1978 – 0.03935 = 0.1585.

Likewise, the down-Gamma calculated at asset price US$25.1 for a decrement of US$1 in the asset price is equal to the Delta using the original volatility calculated at asset price US$25.1 less the Delta using the revised volatility calculated at asset price US$24.1; that is, down-Gamma (25.1) = [Delta (25.1) – Delta_higher vol (24.1)]/(25.1 – 24.1) = 0.03935 – 0.0301 = 0.0093.

The Gammas and Shadow Gammas for a sample set of asset prices are given below:

NVIDIA STOCK PRICE	UP-GAMMA	DOWN-GAMMA	SHADOW UP GAMMA	SHADOW DOWN GAMMA
15.6	0.0000	0.0000	0.0000	(0.0000)
16.1	0.0000	0.0000	0.0000	(0.0000)
16.6	0.0000	0.0000	0.0000	(0.0000)
17.1	0.0000	0.0000	0.0000	(0.0000)
17.6	0.0000	0.0000	0.0000	(0.0000)
18.1	0.0000	0.0000	0.0000	(0.0000)
18.6	0.0000	0.0000	0.0000	(0.0000)
19.1	0.0000	0.0000	0.0001	(0.0000)
19.6	0.0000	0.0000	0.0001	(0.0000)
20.1	0.0000	0.0000	0.0004	(0.0000)
20.6	0.0001	0.0000	0.0009	(0.0000)
21.1	0.0003	0.0000	0.0021	(0.0000)
21.6	0.0008	0.0001	0.0043	(0.0000)
22.1	0.0018	0.0003	0.0086	(0.0001)
22.6	0.0041	0.0008	0.0159	(0.0000)
23.1	0.0084	0.0018	0.0279	0.0001
23.6	0.0161	0.0041	0.0463	0.0005
24.1	0.0288	0.0084	0.0732	0.0017
24.6	0.0484	0.0161	0.1102	0.0043
25.1	0.0769	0.0288	0.1585	0.0093
25.6	0.1157	0.0484	0.2183	0.0181
26.1	0.1658	0.0769	0.2888	0.0324
26.6	0.2268	0.1157	0.3679	0.0539
27.1	0.2974	0.1658	0.4526	0.0842
27.6	0.3752	0.2268	0.5392	0.1242
28.1	0.4570	0.2974	0.6238	0.1744
28.6	0.5393	0.3752	0.7029	0.2341
29.1	0.6187	0.4570	0.7736	0.3018
29.6	0.6921	0.5393	0.8342	0.3754
30.1	0.7576	0.6187	0.8839	0.4519
30.6	0.8138	0.6921	0.9229	0.5286
31.1	0.8605	0.7576	0.9521	0.6026
31.6	0.8980	0.8138	0.9729	0.6717

Figure 155 Gammas and shadow Gammas – example

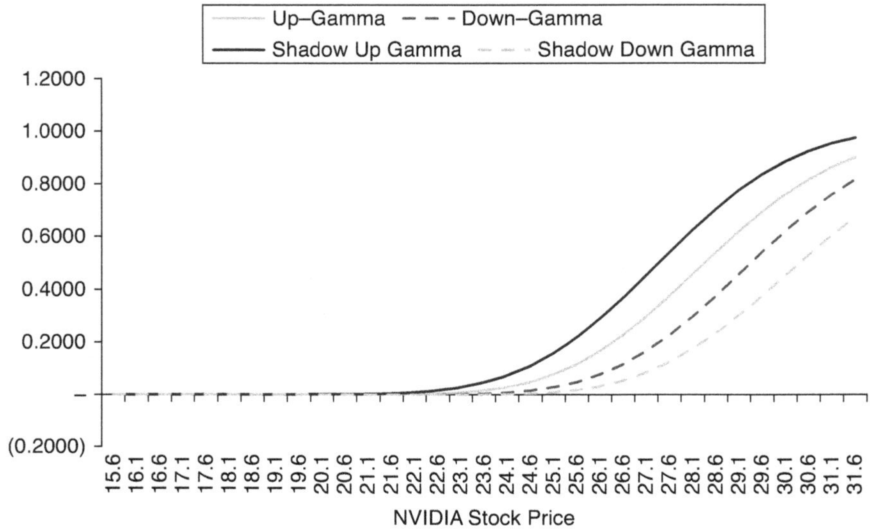

Figure 156 Gammas and shadow Gammas – plotted

The up-Gamma at a stock price of US$28.6 forecasts a change in Delta of 0.5393 if the underlying price increases by US$1. The shadow up-Gamma, however, suggests that the forecast of the change in Delta taking into account volatility is 0.9512. An exact Gamma hedge that does not factor in volatility means that the portion of the position that is unhedged and exposed to risk when volatility levels change could be larger than expected.

6 Vega, Gamma, Vanna and Volga surfaces

Since we have expressed volatility as a surface, when we review Vega we also view it as a surface. From an analysis point of view, there are four dimensions:

- Maturity or Expiry
- Strike prices
- Implied volatility and Vega
- Underlying asset prices

Since we are limited to three dimensions by Excel, we first pick:

- Maturity or Expiry
- Strike prices
- Implied volatility and Vega.

We then do a second iteration of plots, using a constant strike and changing underlying asset prices. To incorporate the impact of all four dimensions in one chart, we would need to use simulated asset prices using the Monte Carlo simulation. The problem with such a simplified approach is that we assume that both the original implied volatilities and the volatility surface specified as input to the model still remain valid for the new simulated prices. But a more appropriate approach would be to recalibrate the implied volatilities for each simulated price.

Essentially, in the surfaces plotted we see the same curves that we have seen so far in two dimensions put across against changing strikes (or spots) and maturities. In previous surface plots, we plotted implied volatility; in the plots that follow, we replace implied volatility with our estimates for Vega, Vanna, Volga and Gamma respectively.

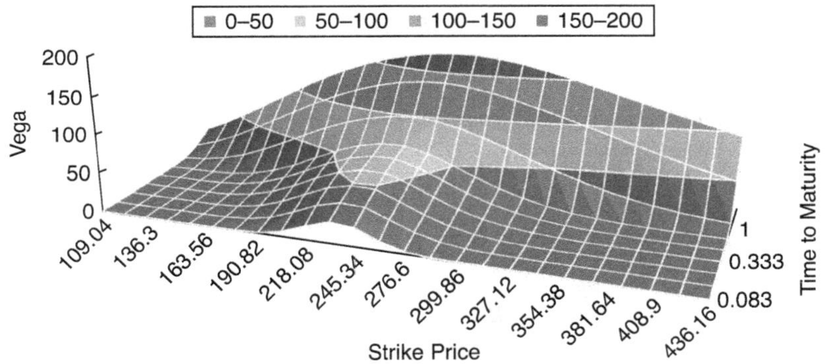

Figure 157 Vega surface plotted against time to expiry and strike prices
Source: FinanceTrainingCourse.com

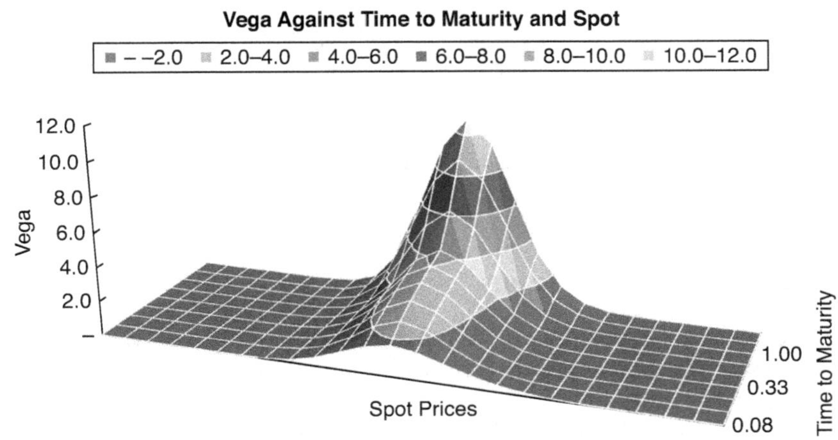

Figure 158 Vega surface plotted against time to expiry and spot prices
Source: FinanceTrainingCourse.com

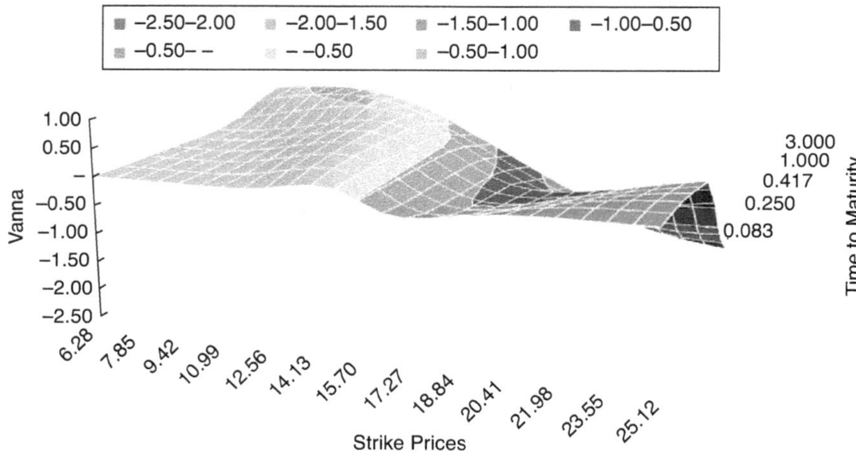

Figure 159 Vanna surface plotted against time to expiry and strike prices
Source: FinanceTrainingCourse.com

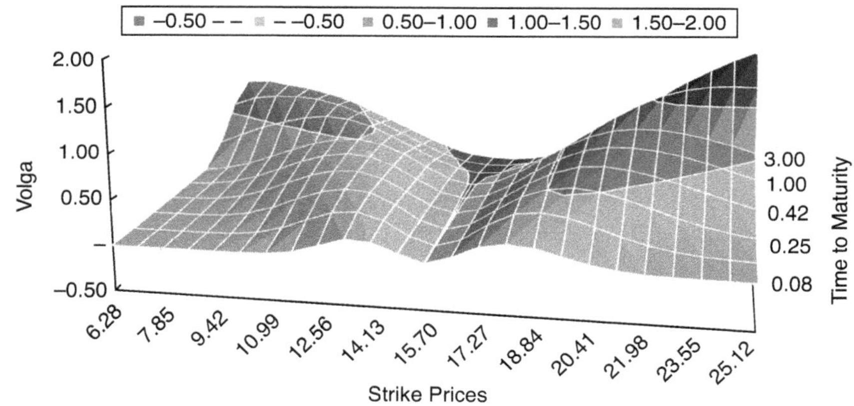

Figure 160 Volga surface plotted against time to expiry and strike prices
Source: FinanceTrainingCourse.com

7 Next steps, and questions

What do changes in volatility do to the distribution of P&L of a vanilla call or put options? What is the key driver of that change? How do surface plots help you answer that question?

With respect to volatility and P&L, the first component is the profit booked on account of the difference between the volatility at which the position is hedged or squared in the market and the implied volatility at which the option

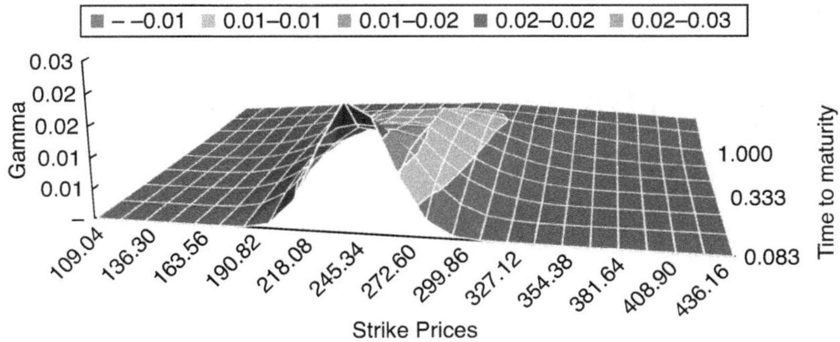

Figure 161 Gamma surface plotted against time to expiry and strike prices
Source: FinanceTrainingCourse.com

was sold. If you could square yourself with an offsetting option purchased at a lower volatility, the difference would be your immediate trading gain.

The second driver is the difference between the implied volatility at which the option position was sold and the actual realized volatility expressed over the life of the option. Should that really make a difference to your answer? Would that depend on your rebalancing frequency and the cost of each rebalance?

Each surface that we have examined here in this chapter can be mapped to a P&L surface. Once we have that P&L surface, we can stress it, flatten it, simulate it, project it or level it. But in order to do that, we would need to extend the simple hedge P&L model.

Think about these questions as we move forward to our next chapter on hedging higher-order Greeks.

10
Hedging Higher-Order Greeks

In earlier chapters, we set the foundation for hedging in practice. We did this by calculating option price sensitivities (Greeks) and Delta hedging for European call and put options. Our next step is to take a closer look at the next two important Greeks – Gamma and Vega.[1]

We begin with Gamma and a simple question: Why would you want to hedge Gamma?

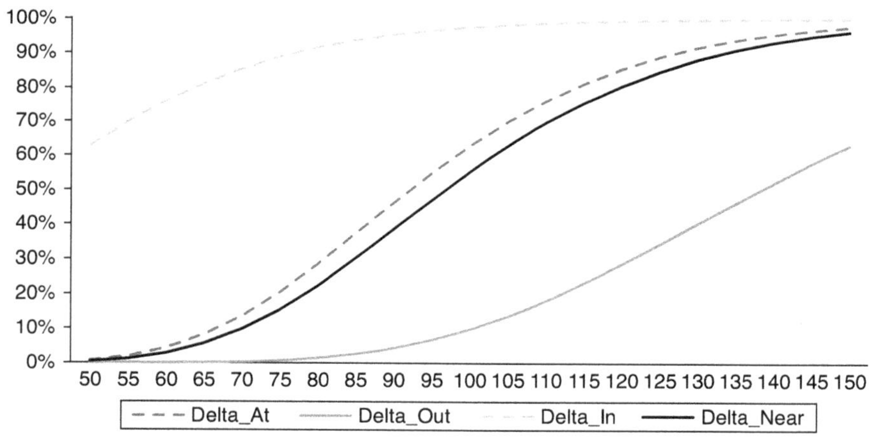

Figure 162 Delta and moneyness
Source: FinanceTrainingCourse.com

If you leave it unhedged you are exposed to the risk of large moves, especially when the option is at or near money. When you are deep out or deep in, Delta is flat and asymptotic, as shown above. But when are you not, a large move can result in a significant trading loss despite being Delta hedged. As long as prices move in small increments and do not jump dramatically, the Delta hedge will cover you. However, if the underlying jumps you will be exposed.

We saw this at work earlier with duration and convexity in the fixed income world. Delta is the first-order rate of change, and works well within a narrow band. Within and outside that band Gamma tracks not just the error but also the magnitude of your gain/loss in case of a large move (up/down); the magnitude of the error shifts dramatically as the option gets closer to the at/near money state. However, given the convex nature of the second derivative in this case, the impact of a large up move or a large down move is not symmetric.

The image below shows the impact of shifting Gamma curves across at, in, near and out of money options.

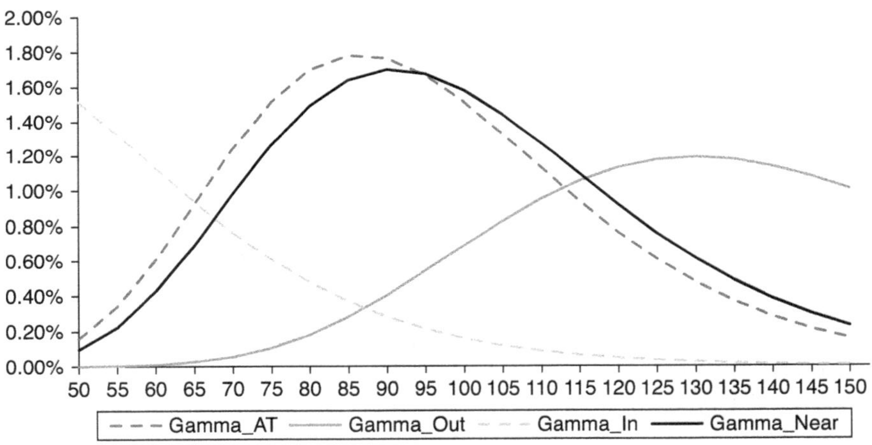

Figure 163 Gamma and moneyness
Source: FinanceTrainingCourse.com

We cannot hedge these Greeks (Gamma and Vega) by buying or selling the underlying. First the second derivative of a spot/forward/linear position is zero, so hedging Gamma through the underlying is out. The second complexity arises with Vega; we really don't know what shape or form realized volatility will take in the future. How can we effectively hedge it?

Then there is the issue of term structure of volatility. The implied volatility changes according to time to maturity (term structure) as well as moneyness (deep in, deep out, or at/near strike price), so taking a simple constant volatility view across all options irrespective of maturity or moneyness would be inaccurate.

The interesting thing for you to note is the shape of Gamma and Vega when viewed with respect to how much in or out of money the underlying option is. The second catch is that both Gamma and Vega use the same calculation function for calls and puts (Gamma for a call and a put has the same value; Vega for a call and a put has the same value). This creates interesting implications for

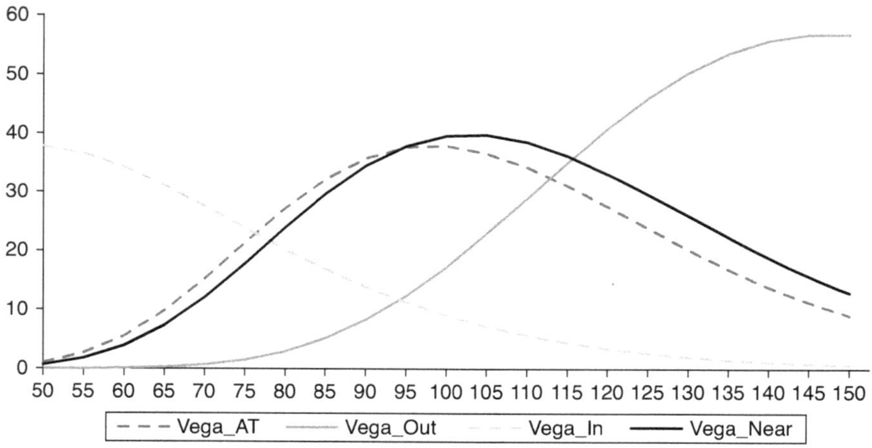

Figure 164 Vega and moneyness
Source: FinanceTrainingCourse.com

hedging a book of options with calls and puts; you may be perfectly hedged and squared with respect to your Gamma and Vega exposures, but the wrong universe of hedging choices can still wipe you out.

We hedge Gamma and Vega by buying other options (specifically cheaper out of money options) with similar maturities. As with Delta hedging, we do need to rebalance – but the rebalancing frequency is less frequent than with Delta hedging. Our final hedge is therefore a mix of exposure to the underlying (partial Delta hedge) and cheaper options with similar maturities.

The only question is that as there is a large universe of options out there, how do we manage multiple constraints including premium and sensitivities across Delta, Gamma and Vega? The answer is constraint optimization through Excel Solver.

1 Hedging Gamma and Vega – framework

Since a spot, forward or future position is linear in its payoff, it has no second-order derivative. Options on the other hand are non-linear (asymmetric payoffs). While we can get away with hedging Delta with a linear position because Delta is a linear approximation (a tangent used to estimate the rate of change) we cannot hedge the exposure of higher-order Greeks (such as Gamma) by buying a position in the underlying.

Vega brings new challenges. We do not directly observe volatility; furthermore, the impact of changes in volatility are not linear and cannot be modelled or hedged using linear instruments. They vary according to moneyness and the time to maturity of the option.

To hedge these non-linear changes represented by Gamma and Vega, we have to try a non-linear recipe; we have to buy similar (ideally cheaper) options.

We start with building a simple Excel spreadsheet that will allow us to hedge Gamma and Vega exposure for a single short position in a call option contract. Our Gamma and Vega hedge would be created by buying cheaper out of money options with maturities that are shorter than, or similar to, the original exposure.

For our first example, we will build a simplistic spreadsheet with a focus on learning to work within the hedging domain using Solver in Excel. We will hedge a single position with a portfolio of cheaper options, but our optimization metrics and our Solver constraints would be simplistic.

Our second example would hedge a portfolio of short option positions using the same available universe of cheaper options as in the first example. But we will add new optimization metrics and solution constraints to bring the model closer to practice. Please note that both examples are contrived to illustrate specific modelling points; actual hedging practice will vary from desk to desk and from one market to the next.

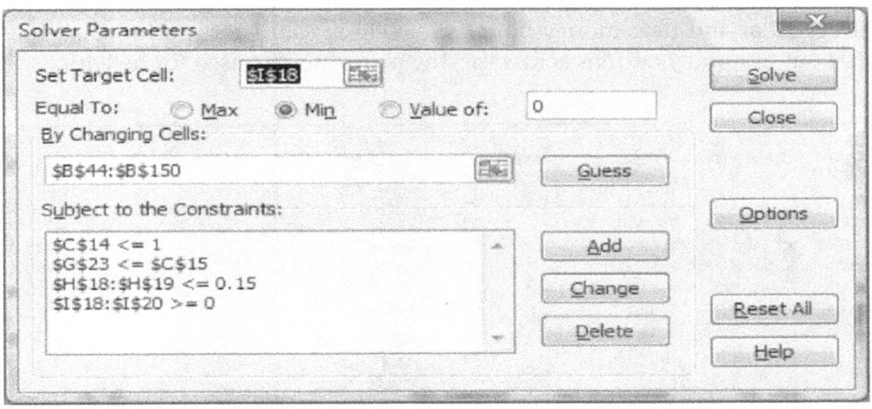

Figure 165 Using Solver to create a hedging portfolio for Gamma and Vega exposures

i Hedging higher-order Greeks for a single short position

Here is our step-by-step guide for building our Solver spreadsheet for hedging higher-order Greeks.

a Options universe dataset

For the date on which the hedge will be put in place, we need the entire universe of available options with implied volatility data. For ease of use, we sort the options universe by expiry and this becomes our raw dataset. We will now refer to this as the universe.

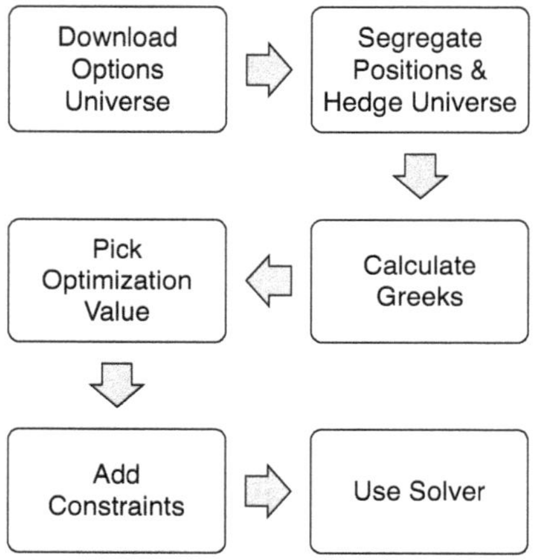

Figure 166 Steps required for hedging higher-order Greeks

We segregate the universe between the options we are going to sell, and the options we will use to hedge our short positions within the spreadsheet. We select 13 at and near money options for selling (our short positions), while 104 out of money options across varying maturities are used for hedging.

symbol	exchange	date	period	strike	out-of-the-money %	call/put	iv
NVDA	NASDAQ	05/14/14	30	18.1	0	C	0.27
NVDA	NASDAQ	05/14/14	30	19.005	5	C	0.2734
NVDA	NASDAQ	05/14/14	30	19.91	10	C	0.2987
NVDA	NASDAQ	05/14/14	30	20.815	15	C	0.301
NVDA	NASDAQ	05/14/14	30	21.72	20	C	0.301
NVDA	NASDAQ	05/14/14	30	22.625	25	C	0.301
NVDA	NASDAQ	05/14/14	30	23.53	30	C	0.301
NVDA	NASDAQ	05/14/14	30	24.435	35	C	0.301
NVDA	NASDAQ	05/14/14	30	25.34	40	C	0.301
NVDA	NASDAQ	05/14/14	30	26.245	45	C	0.301

Figure 167 The default options universe

Our next step is to calculate Greeks for the entire universe. Once we have this data, we can determine the appropriate optimization value and the associated constraints for our Solver model.

Date	Expiry (years)	Strike Price	Implied Vol.	d1	d2	N(d1)	N(d2)	Price	Delta	N'(d1)	Gamma	Vega	Rho	Theta
05/14/14	3	18.100	0.289	0.280	-0.220	0.610	0.413	3.684	0.610	0.384	0.042	0.416	0.221	-0.633
05/14/14	3	19.005	0.286	0.180	-0.316	0.571	0.376	3.301	0.571	0.392	0.044	0.430	0.211	-0.640
05/14/14	2	18.100	0.289	0.229	-0.180	0.590	0.429	3.005	0.590	0.389	0.053	0.344	0.154	-0.771
05/14/14	3	19.910	0.284	0.082	-0.409	0.533	0.341	2.949	0.533	0.398	0.045	0.439	0.201	-0.641
05/14/14	3	20.815	0.282	-0.012	-0.500	0.495	0.309	2.636	0.495	0.399	0.045	0.444	0.190	-0.638

Figure 168 Calculating Delta

b Hedging Gamma and Vega – building the Solver model

Our first attempt is to build a simple illustrative scenario with a single option contract.

We have sold (written) a single position in a call option on NVIDIA (NVDA) on 14 May 2014. Our objective is to hedge Gamma and Vega exposure using a universe of cheaper options on the same date. Our model will essentially look for an optimal combination of cheaper options that completely or partially offset our Gamma and Vega exposure. Since we have sold (that is, written) options, we are short Gamma and Vega. Our offsetting position requires a trade that will be positive Gamma and Vega. The positive Gamma and Vega trade becomes possible when we buy options or pay the premium.

Here is the original option specification for the call option contract that has been written by our desk. Each contract that we write includes a bundle of 100 options. In our initial model and trial run, we will solve for a single option and then scale the results for 100 contracts. This addresses the fractional purchase issue for non-integer hedge ratios.

Option Contract Size	100	
Exposure to be hedged	100 X	
Option Specification	1	1
Time to Expiry	1	
Strike Price	18.1	X 100
Option price	2.096	2.10
Delta	0.56	0.56
Gamma	0.076	0.08
Vega	0.250	0.25
Rho	0.081	0.08
Theta	− 1.069	− 1.07

Figure 169 Hedging Greeks – our short position

Of the above specification, the two things of immediate interest to us are the option premium (US$2.1) and the expiry (1 year). Our hedge portfolio cannot cost more than US$2.1, and while we can play with the expiry of our hedge portfolio, we would ideally like to match it as closely as possible with our short exposure.

c Gamma and Vega exposures – positive or negative?

Should we leave some residual Gamma and Vega exposure, or should our hedging portfolio neutralize the exposure in its entirety? From the fixed income and ALM world comes an interesting parallel; in the ALM world to preserve surplus or immunize capital from interest rate changes we match the weighted average of the first-order sensitivity (modified duration), but we require that second-order sensitivity (convexity) of assets (our long positions) should be greater than the convexity of liabilities (our short positions).

Similarly, while in the options world we may match Delta completely, we would aim to create a hedging portfolio with excess Gamma and Vega exposure compared to our original short position. If that is not possible, we will let the positions run with the Gamma and Vega mismatch, but use exposure limits to track our sensitivity to these two factors. Our hedge is going to be an imperfect semi-hedge, which would leave some room for benefiting from unanticipated changes in market volatility as well as large unexpected jumps in the price of the underlying.

d Structuring the problem

The first question that comes up for discussion is: Within the settings of Excel Solver, what objective function will we use to create our semi-perfect hedge? The objective function is the cell Solver will optimize. Since it is a single cell and we have two targets (Gamma and Vega exposure) we would need to be creative to structure a variable that will lead to exposure minimization under both the heads. An alternative approach would be to begin with a Gamma hedge objective, then hedge Vega on an incremental question. This raises a related question: Which exposure is more important to hedge first? The second-order price risk, or the first-order volatility risk?

The second question revolves around the constraints we need to define in order to achieve an acceptable solution. We address two of these questions below.

e Model design

Our first step is to put aside the universe of options available for hedging. For our first round, we limit the universe to call options. On 14 May 2014, there are 104 call options available across the combination of maturities and strikes. The universe excludes 13 longer-maturity options that we have selected for short positions.

We add a new column at the beginning of the universe titled Allocation, which we will use in our Solver model to allocate hedge portfolio weight to a given option contract.

Option Universe - Available for Hedging - Universe

Allocation	Date	Expiry	Expiry (Years)	Strike	Money-ness	C or P	Impl. Vol.
1%	05/14/14	720	2.00	28.96	60	C	0.2778
1%	05/14/14	30	0.08	19.005	5	C	0.2734
1%	05/14/14	1080	3.00	23.53	30	C	0.2785
1%	05/14/14	1080	3.00	24.435	35	C	0.2781
1%	05/14/14	1080	3.00	27.15	50	C	0.2778
1%	05/14/14	720	2.00	20.815	15	C	0.2817
1%	05/14/14	720	2.00	21.72	20	C	0.2799
1%	05/14/14	1080	3.00	28.055	55	C	0.2778
1%	05/14/14	720	2.00	25.34	40	C	0.2778
1%	05/14/14	720	2.00	26.245	45	C	0.2778
0%	05/14/14	30	0.08	18.100	0	C	0.27
0%	05/14/14	720	2.00	27.15	50	C	0.2778
0%	05/14/14	720	2.00	28.055	55	C	0.2778
0%	05/14/14	60	0.17	18.100	0	C	0.2666
0%	05/14/14	120	0.33	23.53	30	C	0.286
0%	05/14/14	30	0.08	19.910	10	C	0.2987

Figure 170 Option hedging universe – the selection of options available to hedge Gamma and Vega

We now add values for Greeks aga[illegible]nst each option in the hedge universe.

d_1	d_2	$N(d_1)$	$N(d_2)$	Price	Delta	$N'(d_1)$	Gamma	Vega	Rho	Theta
−0.97	−1.37	0.16	0.09	0.5[illegible]6	0.16	0.25	0.035	0.229	0.05	−0.46
−0.57	−0.65	0.28	0.26	0.2[illegible]2	0.28	0.34	0.237	0.065	0.00	−2.93
−0.27	−0.75	0.39	0.23	1.8[illegible]7	0.39	0.38	0.044	0.433	0.16	−0.60
−0.35	−0.83	0.36	0.20	1.6[illegible]2	0.36	0.38	0.043	0.423	0.15	−0.59
−0.57	−1.05	0.28	0.15	1.2[illegible]6	0.28	0.34	0.039	0.382	0.12	−0.53
−0.13	−0.52	0.45	0.30	1.9[illegible]0	0.45	0.40	0.055	0.360	0.12	−0.76
−0.24	−0.63	0.41	0.26	1.6[illegible]0	0.41	0.39	0.054	0.355	0.11	−0.74
−0.64	−1.12	0.26	0.13	1.1[illegible]2	0.26	0.33	0.037	0.367	0.11	−0.51
−0.63	−1.03	0.26	0.15	0.9[illegible]2	0.26	0.33	0.046	0.301	0.08	−0.61
−0.72	−1.12	0.23	0.13	0.8[illegible]5	0.23	0.31	0.043	0.283	0.07	−0.58
0.04	−0.03	0.52	0.49	0.5[illegible]6	0.52	0.40	0.282	0.077	0.01	−3.42
−0.81	−1.20	0.21	0.11	0.7[illegible]4	0.21	0.29	0.040	0.265	0.06	−0.54
−0.89	−1.29	0.19	0.10	0.6[illegible]9	0.19	0.27	0.038	0.247	0.06	−0.50
0.06	−0.05	0.52	0.48	0.7[illegible]3	0.52	0.40	0.202	0.110	0.01	−2.40
−1.50	−1.66	0.07	0.05	0.0[illegible]3	0.07	0.13	0.044	0.048	0.00	−0.59
−1.06	−1.14	0.15	0.13	0.1[illegible]2	0.15	0.23	0.146	0.040	0.00	−2.15

Figure 171 Adding Greeks to the optic[illegible]ns universe

Option Greeks are then used to calculate our hedge portfolio Greeks. For each of the Greeks in the table below, the formula is a sum product of the hedge portfolio allocation weight and the Greeks in question; the first vector in the formula below is the portfolio allocation weight, and the second is the Greek in question across the universe. The multiplier is the scaling factor that we will use later to scale results from 1 option contract to 100 contracts.

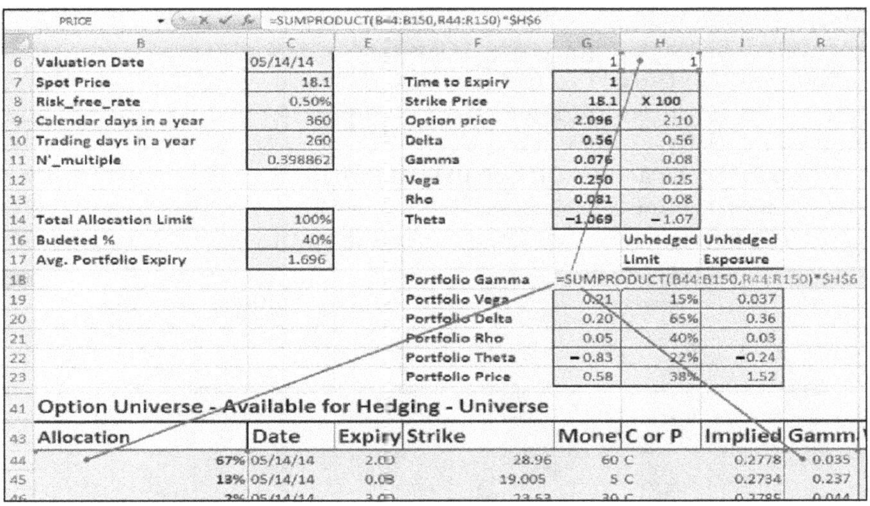

Figure 172 Calculating hedge portfoli[illegible] metrics

Applying this formula for each of the Greeks gives us the following table of hedge portfolio Greeks. We will use elements of this table in our model.

		Unhedged Limit	Unhedged Exposure
Portfolio Gamma	0.01	84%	0.064
Portfolio Vega	0.04	82%	0.205
Portfolio Delta	0.05	91%	0.51
Portfolio Rho	0.01	85%	0.07
Portfolio Theta	−0.16	85%	−0.91
Portfolio Price	0.17	9%	1.93

Figure 173 Hedging portfolio metrics

We have most of the components we need to setup the Solver model.

For our objective function, we create a new cell titled Gamma-Vega-Unhedged, which is the sum of Gamma Vega unhedged exposure from the table above. Our first iteration Solver model will aim to minimize this number. To ensure that we do not run into negative territory, we will assume a non-negative model.

Portfolio Expiry	**0.299**	1	0.70
Gamma-Vega-Unhedged	**0.269**		

Figure 174 Solver objective function

In terms of constraints, the first constraint we want to set up will ensure that our average hedge portfolio expiry is less than the short position maturity. A second constraint would be to ensure that the hedge portfolio Gamma and Vega values are at least the same as, but ideally greater than, the Gamma and Vega estimates for our short position.

To use the Solver add-in, click on the Data tab in Excel and chose the Solver add-in (available in the professional edition of Microsoft Office/Excel). If you have the professional edition and you do not see the Solver add-in, use the Excel Settings to enable it.

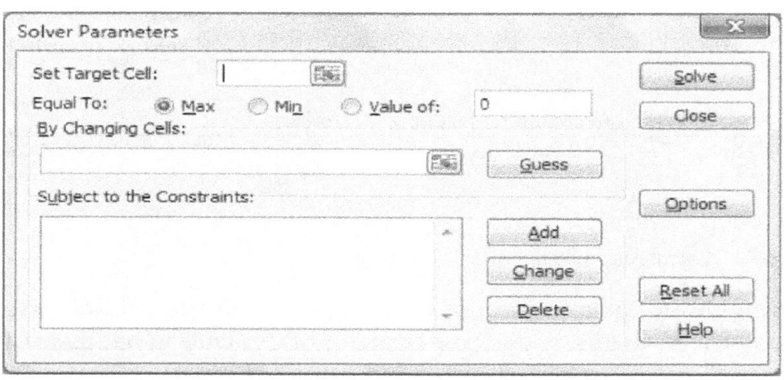

Figure 175 Solver screen at step zero

You now have the required blank slate.

Step 1 is to configure Solver's options to ensure non-negative values. In addition to the non-negative values, we also want to use a quadratic model for estimates and the conjugate method for searching optimal solutions.

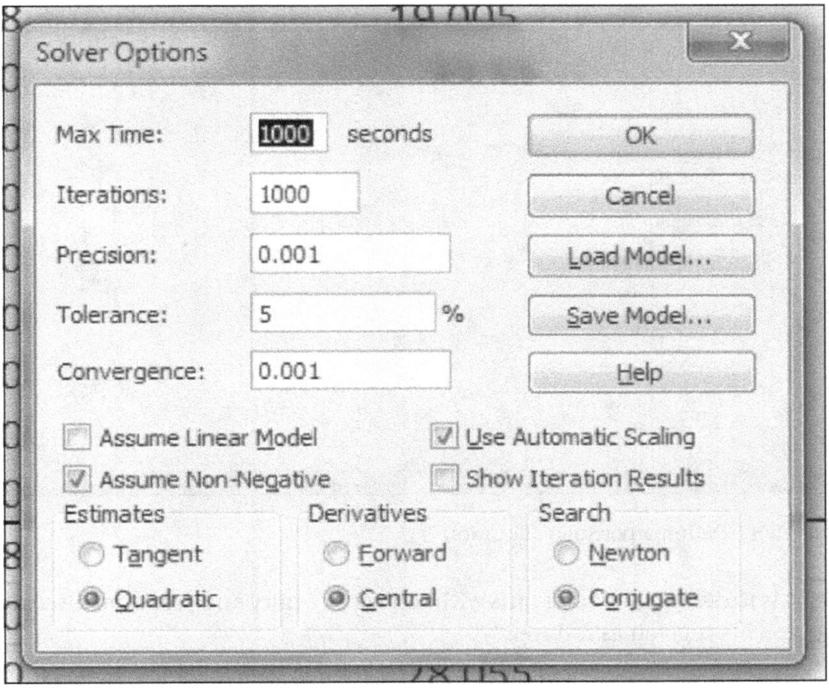

Figure 176 Setting Solver option parameters

Step 2 is to set the target cell to the objective function cell, the Gamma-Vega-Unhedged cell, and select the option to minimize it.

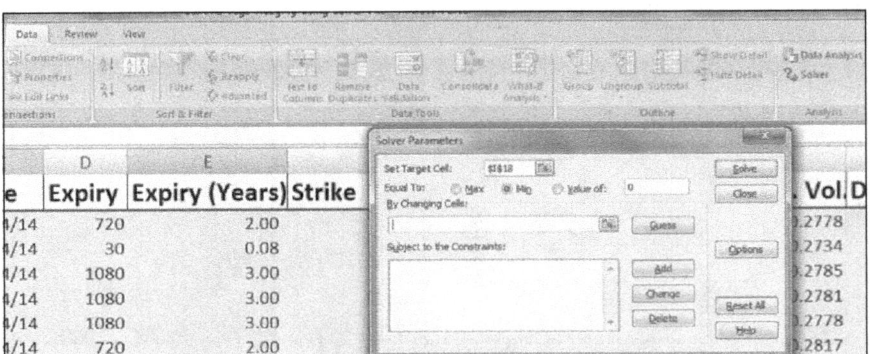

Figure 177 Solver screen at step 2

Step 3 is to identify the cells that Solver will change; this is the range of cells for the portfolio allocation weight given in the Allocation column of the Excel spreadsheet.

Once you are done with Steps 2 and 3, the Solver model will look like this:

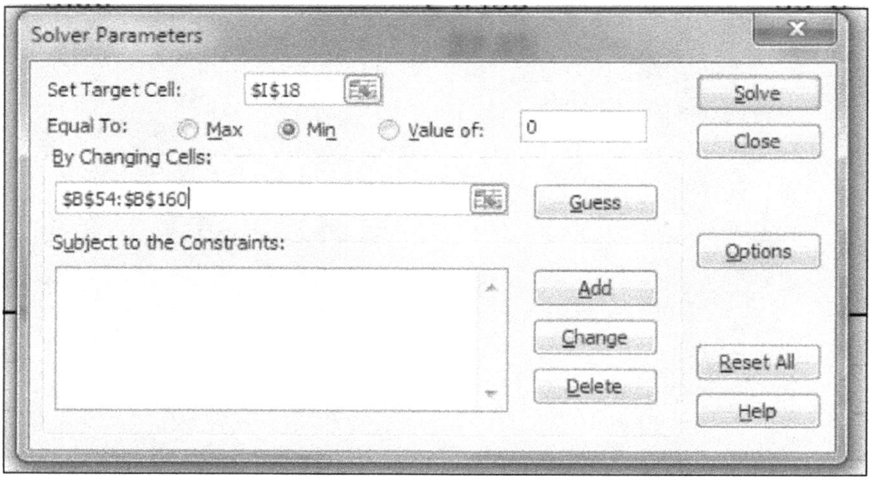

Figure 178 Defining portfolio allocation

Step 4 is to define the constraints with respect to expiry and premium discussed above. This is given as follows:

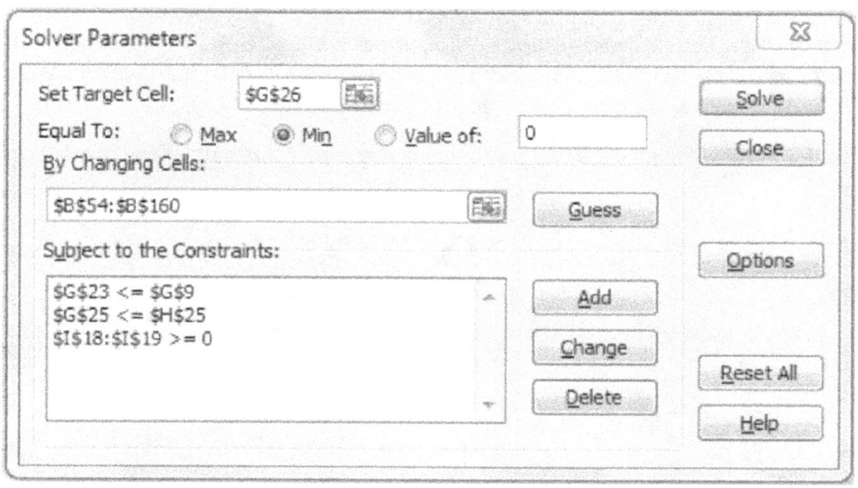

Figure 179 Adding constraints

Here is how the objective function and two of the constraints link up with the relevant cells.

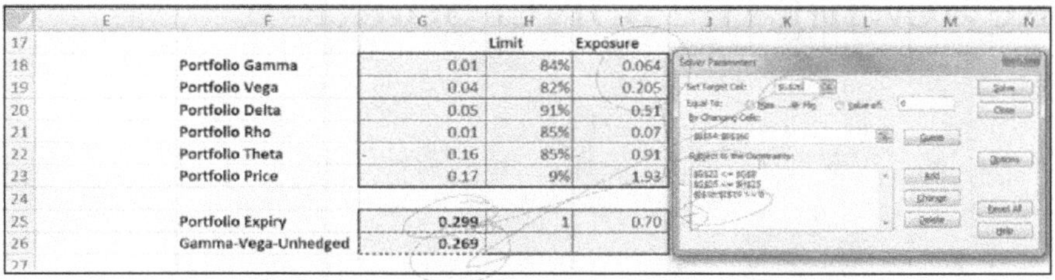

Figure 180 Bringing it together

Note that there are a number of additional constraints on the number of option contracts that the hedge portfolio can include, as well as the proportion of the original premium available for hedging that we have not defined. What we would like to do is to try and run this model with these bare minimal conditions to see what kind of a solution Solver throws up, then refine and fine-tune the model by adding additional constraints.

If you want to give it a shot, go ahead: first save your work, then press Solve to run Solver on your newly built Gamma and Vega hedging optimizer model. What does your solution look like? What is the recommended allocation and cost? We review the results and the tweaks in our next chapter.

11

Reviewing the Solver Solution

When we press the solve button on the Solver add in, what does our initial solution looks like?

		Unhedged Limit	Unhedged Exposure
Portfolio Gamma	0.076	0%	0.000
Portfolio Vega	0.203	19%	0.047
Portfolio Delta	0.269	52%	0.29
Portfolio Rho	0.038	53%	0.04
Portfolio Theta	– 0.988	8%	– 0.08
Portfolio Price	0.670	47%	1.43
Portfolio Expiry	**1.000**	1	0.00
Gamma-Vega-Unhedged	**0.047**		

Figure 181 The higher order Greeks hedging solution – first pass

We can see that the Gamma Vega unhedged objective function has been minimized to 0.047%. Within that minimization, Gamma has been completely neutralized while there is some residual Vega exposure left. While we did not focus on the minor Greeks (Delta, Rho, Theta), their exposures have also been reduced.

How does it compare to the original short position? Let's take a quick look.

Option price	**2.096**	2.10
Delta	**0.56**	0.56
Gamma	**0.076**	0.08
Vega	**0.250**	0.25
Rho	**0.081**	0.08
Theta	**– 1.069**	– 1.07

Figure 182 Comparing the two sets of Greeks: the hedge versus the short position

What instruments were picked and recommended by the Solver solution? The solution picked two major positions and five minor. The majors were out of money options with expiries within a year. The minors were all deep out of money options with longer-dated expiries.

Allocation	Date	Expiry	Expiry (Years)	Strike	Money-ness	C
71%	05/14/14	360	1.00	23.53	30	C
24%	05/14/14	150	0.42	19.91	10	C
2%	05/14/14	720	2.00	20.815	15	C
2%	05/14/14	720	2.00	21.72	20	C
1%	05/14/14	1080	3.00	23.53	30	C
1%	05/14/14	1080	3.00	24.435	35	C
1%	05/14/14	720	2.00	25.34	40	C
0%	05/14/14	720	2.00	26.245	45	C
0%	05/14/14	720	2.00	27.15	50	C
0%	05/14/14	90	0.25	24.435	35	C

Figure 183 Hedge portfolio – first pass

Why? Let's take a look at their Greeks to understand the logic behind these recommendations. The model is essentially calculating the cheapest Gamma to premium ratio while focusing on the constraints it has been asked to optimize. The Vega solution is possibly more intricate, so it focuses on minimizing what it can solve.

N(d1)	N(d2)	Price	Delta	N'(d1)	Gamma	Vega	Rho	Theta
0.21	0.14	**0.541**	0.21	0.29	0.058	0.191	0.03	−0.76
0.33	0.27	**0.645**	0.33	0.36	0.112	0.153	0.02	−1.44
0.45	0.30	**1.960**	0.45	0.40	0.055	0.360	0.12	−0.76
0.41	0.26	**1.690**	0.41	0.39	0.054	0.355	0.11	−0.74
0.39	0.23	**1.887**	0.39	0.38	0.044	0.433	0.16	−0.60
0.36	0.20	**1.692**	0.36	0.38	0.043	0.423	0.15	−0.59
0.26	0.15	**0.942**	0.26	0.33	0.046	0.301	0.08	−0.61
0.23	0.13	**0.815**	0.23	0.31	0.043	0.283	0.07	−0.58
0.21	0.11	**0.704**	0.21	0.29	0.040	0.265	0.06	−0.54
0.02	0.02	**0.019**	0.02	0.05	0.020	0.016	0.00	−0.27

Figure 184 Hedge portfolio Greeks – first pass

Is a better solution possible? Let's add some new conditions to refine our model.

1. Hedge portfolio Gamma and Vega should be greater than short position.
2. To ensure that this happens, we force the model to purchase multiple options. This is a condition that did not exist before. Now the model can

purchase multiple option positions rather than limiting us to just 100% allocation. The purchase restriction is given in cell C14.

Here is what the revised Solver model looks like:

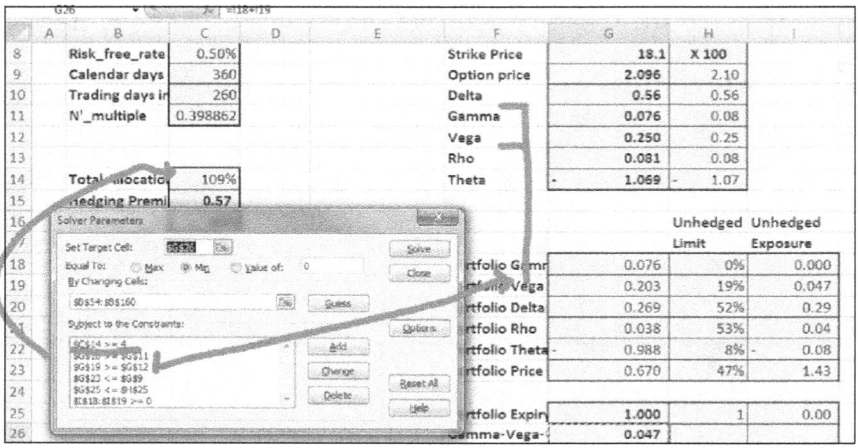

Figure 185 Tweaking the Solver hedging model

How do these new conditions change the solution?

		Unhedged Limit	Unhedged Exposure
Portfolio Gamma	0.076	0%	-0.000
Portfolio Vega	0.075	70%	0.174
Portfolio Delta	0.113	80%	0.45
Portfolio Rho	0.009	89%	0.07
Portfolio Theta	- 1.031	4%	- 0.04
Portfolio Price	0.202	11%	1.89
Portfolio Expiry	**1.000**	1	- 0.00
Gamma-Vega-Unhedged	**0.174**		

Figure 186 Hedging higher-order Greeks – second pass

What does the universe of recommended solutions look like now? Solver fails to find a perfect solution – but at the point it gives up, we have a partial solution that we can review.

Option Universe - Available for Hedging - Universe

Allocation	Date	Expiry	Expiry (Years)	Strike	Money-ness	C
317%	05/14/14	90	0.25	24.435	35	C
14%	05/14/14	30	0.08	22.625	25	C
11%	05/14/14	60	0.17	24.435	35	C
8%	05/14/14	360	1.00	19.005	5	C
7%	05/14/14	60	0.17	23.530	30	C
7%	05/14/14	90	0.25	26.245	45	C
6%	05/14/14	30	0.08	21.720	20	C
6%	05/14/14	30	0.08	23.530	30	C
5%	05/14/14	60	0.17	25.340	40	C
5%	05/14/14	120	0.33	27.15	50	C
4%	05/14/14	90	0.25	27.15	50	C
2%	05/14/14	120	0.33	28.055	55	C
1%	05/14/14	90	0.25	25.34	40	C
1%	05/14/14	120	0.33	28.96	60	C
1%	05/14/14	90	0.25	28.055	55	C
1%	05/14/14	60	0.17	26.245	45	C
1%	05/14/14	30	0.08	24.435	35	C

Figure 187 Hedging solution – forcing a deep out of money solution

The recommendations for the original solutions have changed dramatically; we now have ten major positions, and seven minor. Unlike our earlier solution, in this instance they are all under one year maturity and they all are deep out of money options.

What if rather than focusing on Gamma and Vega we only focus our attention on Vega? What would that do to our recommended hedges?

Here is the revised Solver model; note that the objective function now focuses only on minimizing the Vega difference between the hedge portfolio and the original short position. We have also jacked up the allocation by force to 900%.

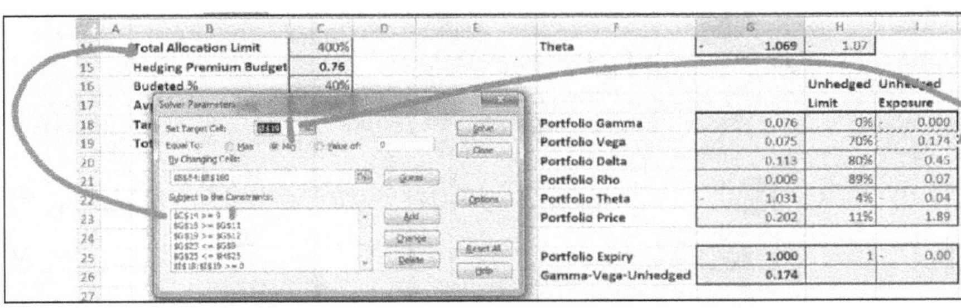

Figure 188 Hedging higher-order Greeks – third and fourth passes

What does the solution look like now?

Solver fails to find a solution, so we go ahead and change two of the conditions above from our Solver model;we drop the constraints that force multiple positions and we remove an additional Vega limit condition that may confuse Solver. Under the revised set of conditions, Solver immediately finds a solution:

		Unhedged Limit	Unhedged Exposure
Portfolio Gamma	0.077	-1%	−0.000
Portfolio Vega	0.234	6%	0.015
Portfolio Delta	0.333	41%	0.23
Portfolio Rho	0.048	41%	0.03
Portfolio Theta	– 1.006	6%	– 0.06
Portfolio Price	0.917	78%	1.18
Portfolio Expiry	**1.000**	1	−0.00
Gamma-Vega-Unhedged	**0.015**		

Figure 189 Minimizing Gamma and Vega exposure

Despite the fact that Gamma is no longer part of the objective function, we still have a solution that now minimizes both Gamma and Vega unhedged exposures. The cost of the hedging portfolio has, however, gone up. This is one instance of a step-by-step Solver solution for a complex problem that may not reach an optimal solution using a single-step approach.

What instruments are recommended and used by Solver? Positions are down to two with shorter maturities. You can now see why the multiple-position force was added as a condition; it pushes Solver to focus on deep out of money options, and it allows us to keep the hedging cost to a minimum.

Option Universe - Available for Hedging - Universe

Allocation	Date	Expiry	Expiry (Years)	Strike	Money-ness	C
94%	05/14/14	360	1.00	21.72	20	C
8%	05/14/14	180	0.50	19.005	5	C
0%	05/14/14	180	0.50	19.91	10	C
0%	05/14/14	360	1.00	19.005	5	C
0%	05/14/14	180	0.50	20.815	15	C

Figure 190 Hedging higher-order Greeks – final solution

1 Hedging Gamma and Vega for a book of options

We are now ready to move to a more sophisticated version of our hedging problem. Rather than limiting ourselves to a single short position, we are going to go ahead and sell multiple options.

Here is an inventory of our short positions. We have sold 13 (for luck) at and near money options across maturities ranging from 30 days to three years. We now need to determine an acceptable approach allowing us to hedge higher-order Greeks for this portfolio of short positions.

Option Universe - Sold Positions

	Date	Expiry	Expiry-years	Strike Price	Money-ness	C
1	05/14/14	30	0.08	18.100	0	C
2	05/14/14	60	0.17	18.100	0	C
3	**05/14/14**	90	0.25	18.1	0	C
4	05/14/14	120	0.33	18.1	0	C
5	05/14/14	150	0.42	18.1	0	C
6	05/14/14	180	0.50	18.1	0	C
7	**05/14/14**	**360**	**1**	**18.1**	**0**	**C**
8	05/14/14	720	2	18.1	0	C
9	05/14/14	720	2	19.005	5	C
10	05/14/14	**720**	**2**	**19.91**	**10**	**C**
11	05/14/14	1080	3	18.1	0	C
12	05/14/14	1080	3	19.005	5	C
13	05/14/14	1080	3	19.91	10	C

Figure 191 Portfolio of short positions

To hedge Greeks in our new model, we have the same universe of 104 call options that we used earlier for hedging a single option position.

In our initial model, we used a single Gamma and Vega bucket, because we only had a single short position with a single expiry. Given the fact that we have a range of maturities in our short portfolio and the fact that volatility varies across maturity buckets, we would need to revise our approach by tracking Vega and Gamma exposures across maturity buckets. Our hedging strategy would also aim at ensuring that we track excess unhedged exposure by bucket as well as the Greek in question.

In Asset Liability Management, we are comfortable and familiar with the concept of tracking interest rate risk exposure by maturity buckets. We will use the same process here. The only difference is that rather than tracking interest rate sensitivity we would be tracking sensitivity to changes in implied volatility (Vega) and the second-order rate of change of the underlying spot price (Gamma).

In an ideal world, our methodology would allow us to match Gamma and Vega exposures by maturity bucket across our original short position and our optimal hedge portfolio. Once our optimization process is complete, we would be able to generate the table that would document the perfect match across buckets.

	Short Position		Hedge Portfolio	
Maturity	Bucket	Bucket	Bucket	Bucket
Bucket	Vega	Gamma	Vega	Gamma
30	0.077	0.282	0.077	0.282
60	0.110	0.202	0.110	0.202
90	0.131	0.160	0.131	0.160
120	0.149	0.136	0.149	0.136
150	0.165	0.121	0.165	0.121
180	0.179	0.109	0.179	0.109
360	0.250	0.076	0.250	0.076
720	1.059	0.162	1.059	0.162
1080	1.286	0.131	1.286	0.131
	3.406	1.380		

Figure 192 Bucketing Gamma and Vega of short positions by maturity

From an optimization point of view, though, given the complexity of this problem and Solver's inherent limitations, we still want to create a reasonable objective function that Excel can use to search for the optimal solution. So we use the grid created above to calculate absolute as well as relative differences by bucket and create an objective function[1] using either of the sums of the two difference figures (absolute or relative) shown below.

Maturity	Difference	Difference	Relative Difference	
Bucket	Vega	Gamma	Vega	Gamma
30	-	-	-	-
60	-	-	-	-
90	-	-	-	-
120	-	-	-	-
150	-0.00	-0.00	-0.00	-0.00
180	-	-	-	-
360	-	-	-	-
720	-	-	-	-
1080	-	-	-	-
	-0.00	-0.00	-0.00	-0.00
	-0.00		-0.00	

Figure 193 Relative and absolute differences between Gammas and Vegas for short position and hedge portfolio

This obviously complicates our optimization criteria and the constraints we would need to add to help Solver reach an acceptable solution. Compared to our original criteria for hedging a single short position, the revised optimization criteria have many more potential elements.

Optimization Criteria	
Premium Available	23.62
Cummulative Bucket Gap	−0.00
Relative Bucket Gap	−0.00
Hedge Portfolio Price	14.64
Cummulative Vega Gap	−0.00
Cummulatie Gamma Gap	−0.00
Total Short Positions	13
Total Hedge Allocation	1768%
Hedge Position Allowed	20
Original Premium	26.24
Left over Premium	44.2%
Delta % left over	40%
Leftover Delta Margin	4.2%
Leftover Delta Premium	1.09
Avg. Hedge Portfolio Maturity	1.062
Avg. Short Position Maturity	1.37
Total Allocation Limit	1768%

Figure 194 Elements of revised hedging model for a book of options

As we saw earlier with our simple model for a single short position, hedging Gamma and Vega still leaves some exposure when it comes to Delta, Rho and Theta. The left-over Delta exposure can be hedged using the Delta hedging approach we covered earlier. Rho and Theta are minor Greeks that are managed through a limit and control process.

Specification Short Position	Short Position	Net Position
Gamma	1.38	-0.00
Vega	3.41	-0.00
Delta	7.10	2.84
Rho	1.29	0.35
Theta	-18.03	0.33
Premium	26.24	11.60

Figure 195 Original and hedged exposures for Greeks of the short position

Our Solver model has also changed. The objective function has been modified and now solves for minimizing the cumulative bucket gap. The constraints and conditions have been changed to accommodate multiple maturity buckets.

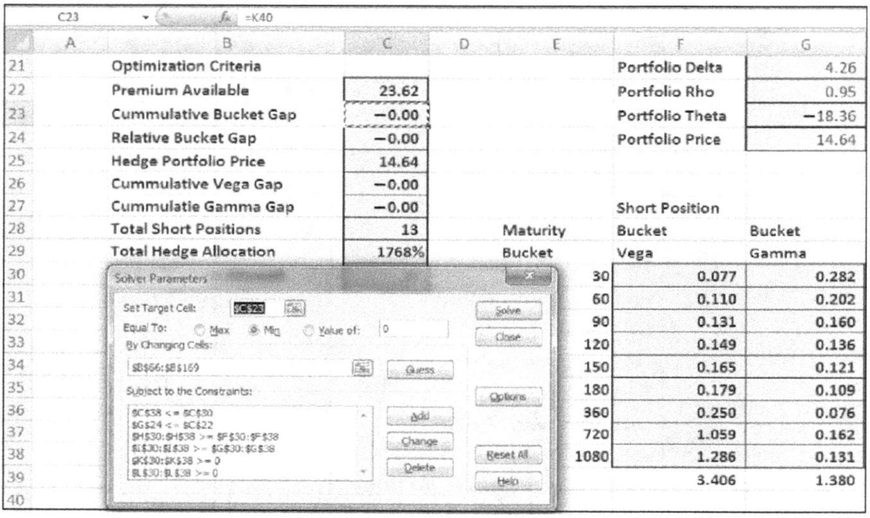

Figure 196 Initial Solver function setup for hedging a book of options

In our next section we discuss creating the Solver model and running variations between possible solutions and constraints.

2 Hedging portfolio Vega and Gamma using Solver

For our portfolio model, we need an objective function that allows us to minimize the cumulative Greek gap across maturity buckets with respect to Vega and Gamma. The gap is measured between the short positions and the proposed hedge portfolio.

We will try two alternatives. In the first instance, we calculate the cumulative gap and use that as the objective function. In the second instance, we keep the constraints around the gap by maturity, but switch to a different objective function to see if Solver can still find the correct solution.

But before we proceed, a word about cumulative bucket gap and the constraints used in the Solver model.

Our first objective function is a value that summarizes the differences across 18 different cells in four separate steps. Let's review these steps.

The objective function as shown above is defined in cell **C23** (tagged as **Step 1** in the image that follows). **C23** is a summary cell linked to cell **K40** (tagged

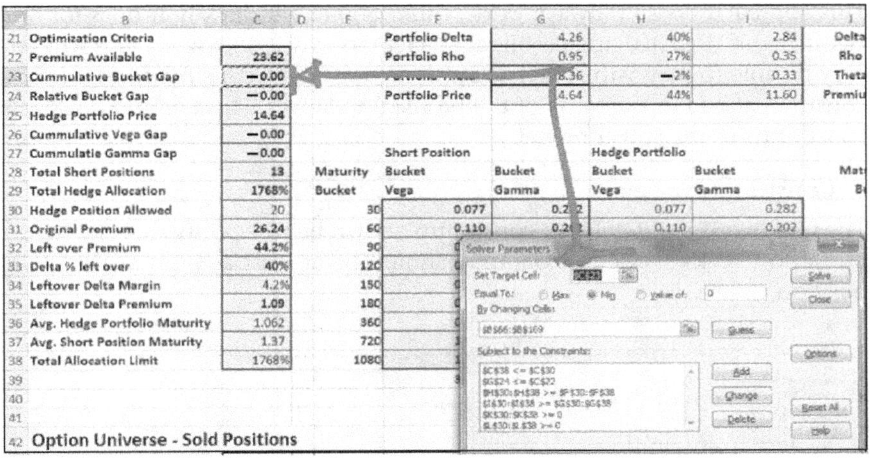

Figure 197 The Solver objective function

as **Step 2**). **K40** is the sum of **K39** and **L39**, which in turn sum up the Greek gap differences by maturity bucket in the K and L columns immediately above (tagged as **Step 3**). The differences are calculated by comparing the portfolio Greeks for the original short position and the hedge portfolio in columns **F, G, H and I** (tagged as **Step 4**).

Even though the objective function appears to be one cell, its value is driven by differences that exist across four columns summarized in two additional columns summarized further in two cells finally linked to a single cell. In the image below, (1) is the cumulative bucket gap which is calculated by the cells tagged in (2), based on the two columns marked by (3), which in turn are calculated through the four columns marked by (4).

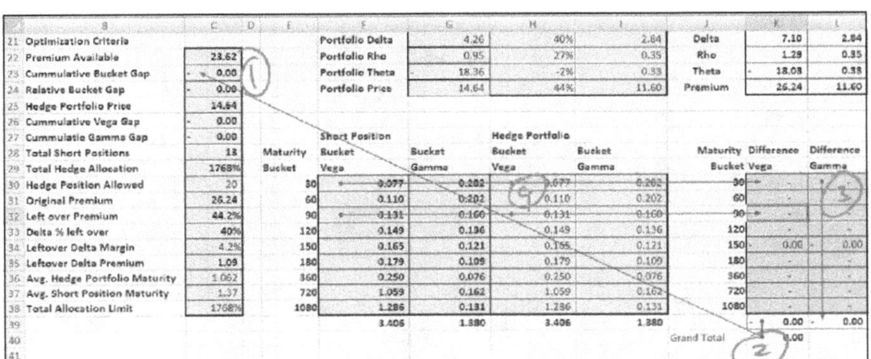

Figure 198 Understanding the objective function components

This approach doesn't always work within Solver, but luckily it does for our Gamma and Vega hedging problem. The reason why it does work, and why we may be able to play with other definitions of the objective function, are the constraints used in the setup of the problem in Solver. There are four column constraints in the Solver model.

i Constraints review

The first two **H** and **I** column constraints shown below specify that the hedge portfolio Greeks (Vega and Gamma) should be at least as high as the short position Greeks.

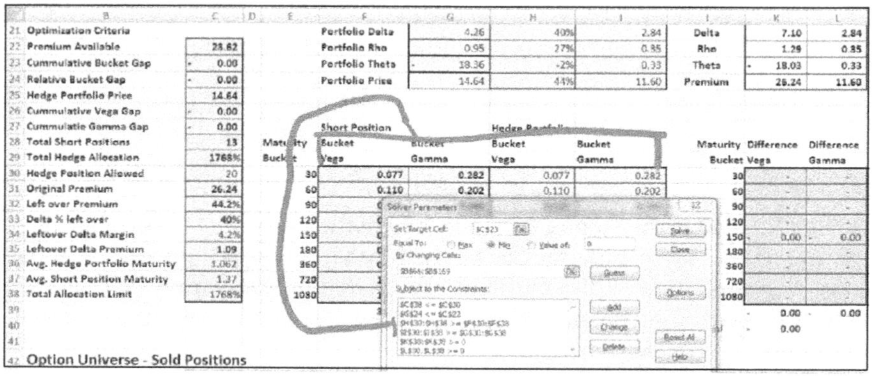

Figure 199 The first two constraints

The next two (columns **K** and **L**) require that Greek differences in each maturity bucket amount to zero. There is some element of redundancy here, but once we have found a solution we can play with the constraints to see which one is required and which is redundant.

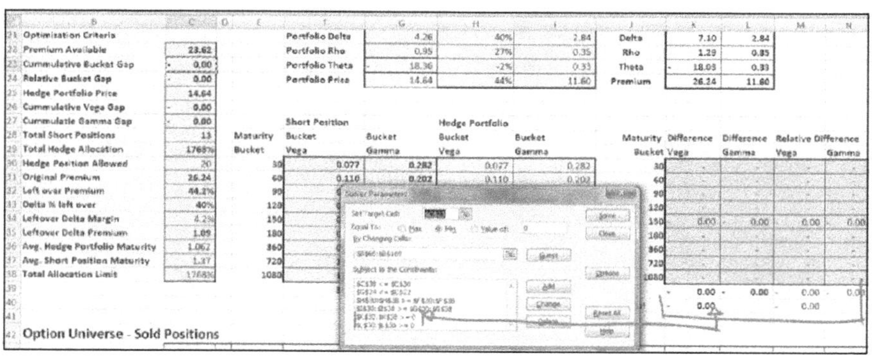

Figure 200 The last two constraints

The first two single-cell constraints ensure that we do not spend more than we have (the premium available) and force hedge portfolio allocation across multiple positions.

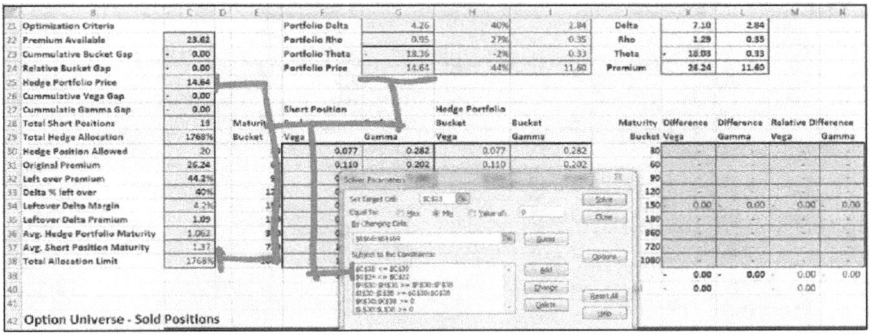

Figure 201 Premiums and allocations

ii Solver solution – first pass

Our first solution does a reasonable job of hedging Gamma and Vega exposure, but appears to be a bit pricey (at US$14.64) compared to the solutions we saw in our simpler model.

Specification Short Position	Short Position	Net Position
Gamma	1.38	-0.00
Vega	3.41	-0.00
Delta	7.10	2.84
Rho	1.29	0.35
Theta	-18.03	0.33
Premium	26.24	11.60

Figure 202 Solver solution – first pass

Greeks by maturity buckets also perfectly offset each other between the short position and the hedge portfolio:

	Short Position		Hedge Portfolio	
Maturity	Bucket	Bucket	Bucket	Bucket
Bucket	Vega	Gamma	Vega	Gamma
30	0.077	0.282	0.077	0.282
60	0.110	0.202	0.110	0.202
90	0.131	0.160	0.131	0.160
120	0.149	0.136	0.149	0.136
150	0.165	0.121	0.165	0.121
180	0.179	0.109	0.179	0.109
360	0.250	0.076	0.250	0.076
720	1.059	0.162	1.059	0.162
1080	1.286	0.131	1.286	0.131
	3.406	1.380	3.406	1.380

Figure 203 The two portfolios side by side

The differences grid also sums up to zero.

Maturity	Difference	Difference	Relative Difference	
Bucket	Vega	Gamma	Vega	Gamma
30	-	-	-	-
60	-	-	-	-
90	-	-	-	-
120	-	-	-	-
150	-0.00	-0.00	-0.00	-0.00
180	-	-	-	-
360	-	-	-	-
720	-	-	-	-
1080	-	-	-	-
	-0.00	-0.00	-0.00	-0.00

Figure 204 Absolute and relative differences

However, when we review the portfolio allocation we run into issues. The first is the number of options used to hedge the short portfolio. There are 29 individual positions to hedge our 13 short positions across 9 maturity buckets. So we would like to see if we can reduce the number of positions, as well as the cost of our hedge portfolio, by playing around with the objective function and the constraints.

Allocation	Date	Expiry	Expiry in	Strike	Money-nes	C	Implied Vol.
376%	05/14/14	30	0.08	20.815	15	C	0.3010
307%	05/14/14	720	2.00	22.625	25	C	0.2790
134%	05/14/14	1080	3	21.72	20	C	0.2799
118%	05/14/14	360	1.00	22.625	25	C	0.2774
112%	05/14/14	60	0.17	19.910	10	C	0.2688
112%	05/14/14	120	0.33	19.91	10	C	0.2746
102%	05/14/14	90	0.25	19.005	5	C	0.2707
99%	05/14/14	180	0.50	19.005	5	C	0.2801
99%	05/14/14	1080	3	22.625	25	C	0.2790
47%	05/14/14	60	0.17	21.720	20	C	0.2819
28%	05/14/14	150	0.42	19.005	5	C	0.2785
26%	05/14/14	150	0.42	19.91	10	C	0.2765
26%	05/14/14	60	0.17	22.625	25	C	0.2819
24%	05/14/14	1080	3.00	27.15	50	C	0.2778
23%	05/14/14	1080	3.00	28.055	55	C	0.2778
22%	05/14/14	150	0.42	20.815	15	C	0.2763
22%	05/14/14	1080	3.00	28.96	60	C	0.2778
18%	05/14/14	150	0.42	21.72	20	C	0.2773
15%	05/14/14	150	0.42	22.625	25	C	0.2801
13%	05/14/14	60	0.17	23.530	30	C	0.2819
11%	05/14/14	150	0.42	23.53	30	C	0.2837
9%	05/14/14	150	0.42	24.435	35	C	0.2861
6%	05/14/14	150	0.42	25.34	40	C	0.2875
6%	05/14/14	60	0.17	24.435	35	C	0.2819
5%	05/14/14	150	0.42	26.245	45	C	0.2893
3%	05/14/14	150	0.42	27.15	50	C	0.2893
2%	05/14/14	60	0.17	25.340	40	C	0.2819
1%	05/14/14	150	0.42	28.96	60	C	0.2882
1%	05/14/14	60	0.17	26.245	45	C	0.2819

Figure 205 The hedge solution allocation – first pass

3 Minimizing hedge portfolio cost

To minimize hedge portfolio cost we will change the objective function. Previously, we minimized cumulative bucket gap. In this iteration, we will minimize the cell representing hedge portfolio cost. We will also remove the additional constraint around total portfolio allocation, to give Solver the freedom to move around our hedge universe and pick as many positions as it needs to come up with a more cost-effective solution. Here is what the revised Solver model looks like.

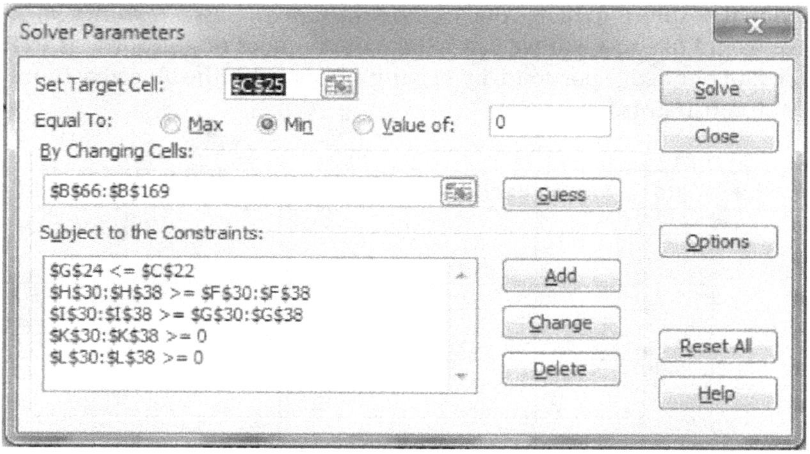

Figure 206 Solver model – minimize cost

Note that we are short of one constraint as compared to the first pass, and the objective function has changed. We press Solve and it finds a solution.

The maturity bucket grid is a match:

	Short Position		Hedge Portfolio	
Maturity Bucket	Bucket Vega	Bucket Gamma	Bucket Vega	Bucket Gamma
30	**0.077**	**0.282**	0.077	0.282
60	**0.110**	**0.202**	0.110	0.202
90	**0.131**	**0.160**	0.131	0.160
120	**0.149**	**0.136**	0.149	0.136
150	**0.165**	**0.121**	0.165	0.121
180	**0.179**	**0.109**	0.179	0.109
360	**0.250**	**0.076**	0.250	0.076
720	**1.059**	**0.162**	1.059	0.162
1080	**1.286**	**0.131**	1.286	0.131
	3.406	**1.380**	**3.406**	**1.380**

Figure 207 Minimize cost – maturity bucket grid

The differences grid adds up to zero.

Maturity Bucket	Difference Vega	Difference Gamma	Relative Difference Vega	Gamma
30	0.00	0.00	0.00	0.00
60	-0.00	-0.00	-0.00	-0.00
90	0.00	0.00	0.00	0.00
120	0.00	0.00	0.00	0.00
150	-0.00	-0.00	-0.00	-0.00
180	-0.00	-0.00	-0.00	-0.00
360	-0.00	-0.00	-0.00	-0.00
720	-0.00	-0.00	-0.00	-0.00
1080	-0.00	-0.00	-0.00	-0.00
	-0.00	0.00	0.00	0.00

Figure 208 Relative differences grid – second pass

The hedge portfolio cost has also declined, from our earlier US$14.64 to US$9.62.

Specification Short Position	Short Position	Net Position
Gamma	1.38	0.00
Vega	3.41	-0.00
Delta	7.10	4.02
Rho	1.29	0.53
Theta	-18.03	0.62
Premium	26.24	16.62

Figure 209 Solver solution – optimized for lowest hedge cost
Source: FinanceTrainingCourse.com

Specification Short Position	Short Position	Net Position
Gamma	1.38	- 0.00
Vega	3.41	- 0.00
Delta	7.10	2.84
Rho	1.29	0.35
Theta	- 18.03	0.33
Premium	26.24	11.60

Figure 210 Solver solution – optimized for minimum cumulative gap
Source: FinanceTrainingCourse.com

When we put the two solutions side by side, we see that while Gamma and Vega remain perfectly hedged, the Delta, Rho and Theta unhedged exposures have risen. However, the premium saving of US$5 adequately compensates us for this change.

Our next question deals with redundant constraints.

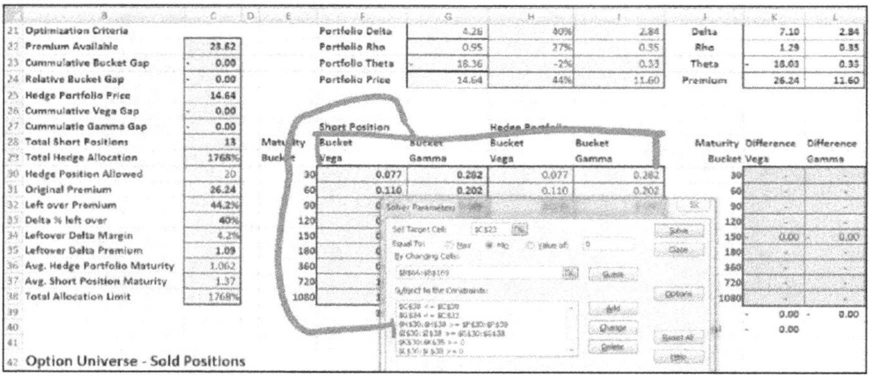

Figure 211 Solver model – redundant constraints
Source: FinanceTrainingCourse.com

Do we really need all the four column constraints pertaining to maturity buckets, in particular the differences for each Greek by maturity bucket? Could we get by with two, rather than four, of these constraints? We go ahead and drop both sets (Vega and Gamma) of individual maturity bucket grid constraints, on the basis that the cumulative difference by maturity bucket constraints should be sufficient to reach a solution.

But the answer is unfortunately no; Solver cannot find an optimal solution without these constraints, so they are not redundant.

To address this, rather than using the cumulative difference that adds both Gamma and Vega buckets together, we use the cumulative difference for the Gamma bucket only. When we solve, we reach a solution quite close to our second pass; there is a marginal difference in premium over our previous solution. So we do not need the Vega bucket constraint to solve for the optimal solution.

Specification Short Position	Short Position	Net Position
Gamma	1.38	−0.00
Vega	3.41	0.00
Delta	7.10	4.08
Rho	1.29	0.54
Theta	−18.03	0.63
Premium	26.24	16.85

Figure 212 Solver solution – with Vega maturity bucket constraint removed
Source: FinanceTrainingCourse.com

However, a bigger issue now is the number of positions required to hedge the portfolio. While our new and improved solution is certainly cheaper than our first pass, there are now 86 positions required to hedge our 13 short call positions.

We add a new constraint that restricts the number of positions first to 30 and then to 50. However, in both instances a feasible solution is not found.

However, when we increase the limit to 55, a feasible solution is identified, and it comes with the added bonus of lower cost.

Specification Short Position	Short Position	Net Position
Gamma	1.38	0.00
Vega	3.41	0.00
Delta	7.10	4.38
Rho	1.29	0.60
Theta	– 18.03	0.83
Premium	26.24	18.30

Figure 213 Solver solution – allocation constraint adjusted

Specification Short Position	Short Position	Net Position
Gamma	1.38	−0.00
Vega	3.41	0.00
Delta	7.10	4.08
Rho	1.29	0.54
Theta	−18.03	0.63
Premium	26.24	16.85

Figure 214 Solver solution – Vega constraint removed

Source: FinanceTrainingCourse.com

In the last iteration, the number of positions are down to 52 and the premium is down to US$7.94 from the earlier US$9.62.

4 Optimizing Delta

Let's now look at the solution from a slightly different point of view. While our Gamma and Vega exposures stay perfectly hedged, the hedge premium cost and leftover Delta exposure go up and down in an inverse manner; the premium cost comes down, while Delta goes up. Or if Delta goes down, the premium cost goes up. Rather than minimize premium we would like to see if we could find an optimal solution that would also balance the leftover Delta amount side by side with our Gamma and Vega hedging solution.

So we create a new objective function that focuses on Delta, and run Solver again.

Specification Short Position	Short Position	Net Position
Gamma	1.38	-0.00
Vega	3.41	-0.00
Delta	7.10	3.29
Rho	1.29	0.54
Theta	-18.03	0.12
Premium	26.24	15.54

Figure 215 Solver solution – optimizing Delta hedge
Source: FinanceTrainingCourse.com

Interestingly enough in this solution it is not just Delta that comes down, but also the number of positions required to hedge our exposure drop from 52 all the way down to 26, with about 11 major positions and 15 minor exposures. However, the premium jumps up from US$7 and change to US$10 and change. Playing with the model allows you to push Delta all the way down to US$1.9 at a cost of US$19.

Specification Short Position	Short Position	Net Position
Gamma	1.38	0.00
Vega	3.41	0.00
Delta	7.10	1.90
Rho	1.29	0.19
Theta	-18.03	0.30
Premium	26.24	7.07

Figure 216 Optimizing Delta – second pass
Source: FinanceTrainingCourse.com

Here is what the revised portfolio allocation looks like for Delta at 3.9, premium at US$10.4:

Allocation	Date	Expiry	Expiry in	Strike	Money-nes	C
463%	05/14/14	720	2.00	28.96	60	C
366%	05/14/14	1080	3.00	28.96	60	C
190%	05/14/14	30	0.08	19.910	10	C
112%	05/14/14	360	1.00	25.34	40	C
106%	05/14/14	60	0.17	19.005	5	C
102%	05/14/14	90	0.25	19.005	5	C
101%	05/14/14	120	0.33	19.005	5	C
100%	05/14/14	150	0.42	19.005	5	C
99%	05/14/14	180	0.50	19.005	5	C
62%	05/14/14	360	1.00	28.055	55	C
13%	05/14/14	360	1.00	27.15	50	C
8%	05/14/14	60	0.17	25.340	40	C
7%	05/14/14	90	0.25	28.055	55	C
6%	05/14/14	90	0.25	27.15	50	C
6%	05/14/14	360	1.00	26.245	45	C
6%	05/14/14	120	0.33	28.96	60	C
5%	05/14/14	30	0.08	22.625	25	C

Figure 217 Revised allocation

Source: FinanceTrainingCourse.com

Compare this to the optimal solution at US$7.94 with 53 positions:

Allocation	Date	Expiry	Expiry in	Strike	Money-nes	C
366%	05/14/14	1080	3.00	28.96	60	C
315%	05/14/14	720	2.00	28.96	60	C
163%	05/14/14	30	0.08	20.815	15	C
143%	05/14/14	360	1.00	28.96	60	C
138%	05/14/14	720	2.00	28.055	55	C
129%	05/14/14	60	0.17	21.720	20	C
123%	05/14/14	90	0.25	22.625	25	C
120%	05/14/14	360	1.00	28.055	55	C
108%	05/14/14	120	0.33	23.53	30	C
106%	05/14/14	150	0.42	24.435	35	C
105%	05/14/14	150	0.42	25.34	40	C
103%	05/14/14	90	0.25	23.53	30	C
103%	05/14/14	120	0.33	24.435	35	C
101%	05/14/14	180	0.50	25.34	40	C
98%	05/14/14	180	0.50	26.245	45	C
95%	05/14/14	60	0.17	22.625	25	C
90%	05/14/14	150	0.42	26.245	45	C
90%	05/14/14	180	0.50	27.15	50	C
86%	05/14/14	120	0.33	25.34	40	C
84%	05/14/14	30	0.08	21.720	20	C
82%	05/14/14	60	0.17	20.815	15	C
77%	05/14/14	180	0.50	28.055	55	C
75%	05/14/14	90	0.25	24.435	35	C
73%	05/14/14	150	0.42	27.15	50	C
64%	05/14/14	120	0.33	26.245	45	C
62%	05/14/14	180	0.50	28.96	60	C
56%	05/14/14	90	0.25	21.72	20	C

Figure 218 Optimal allocation – final pass

Source: FinanceTrainingCourse.com

The two solutions should point out an obvious lesson; shorter dated options are more sensitive to changes in the price of the underlying (Gamma at work) and less sensitive to changes in implied volatility (Vega at work). Longer-dated options are more sensitive to changes in implied volatility.

To find the optimal solution, you need to find the right balance between the two, which, within our limited setting, Solver does reasonably well. Any leftover Delta exposure can then be hedged using the Delta hedging models we discussed earlier.

5 Next steps, and question

1. How would the Solver model change when you opt to work with modified Vega as well as with Vanna and Volga?
2. What happens when you replace the Delta neutral constraint with a Delta Gamma neutral constraint? What kind of an impact does it have on the recommended solution?

Part V
Applications

12
Rebalancing, Implied Vol and Rho

Now that we have a Delta hedging model for calls and puts, let's try and use it to answer the following questions:

a. What is the impact of rebalancing frequency on hedging profitability?
b. What is the impact of a rise in volatility on profitability? How does implied volatility help in interpreting this change?
c. What is the impact of a change in risk-free rate on profitability?

These are all questions that should occur naturally to you as you spend more time with the Delta hedging model. They are also essential to building a deeper understanding of the concept of implied volatility, Rho and Theta. The first two are covered here, the third in Chapter 13.

1 Assumptions and securities

Let's take a look at these questions one by one. We will begin work with a call option on a non-dividend paying stock assuming the following valuation parameters:

ASSUMPTIONS	
Spot	US$162.30
Strike	US$200.00
Model Volatility	20%
Time	1
Risk_Free	1%
Steps	12
Delta_T	0.083

Figure 219 P&L review assumptions
Source: FinanceTrainingCourse.com

The theoretical value of the call option is US$3.01 based on the above assumptions. The resulting Cash Accounting P&L for a single run of the dynamic Delta hedging model is this:

P	Q	R
Cash Accounting P&L		
Cash Inflow		
Premium Received	3.010	
Strike Price Received	200.000	
Gross Inflow		203.010
Cash out at Maturity		
Interest Paid	0.65	
Principal repaid	200.11	
Gross Outflow		200.76
Net Cash Inflow		2.25

Figure 220 P&L review – base case
Source: FinanceTrainingCourse.com

2 Rebalancing frequency and efficiency of the hedge: implications for profitability?

Theoretically speaking, in the Black–Scholes world, the cost of the hedge should be close to the theoretical value of the option. In our cash accounting P&L we have included the theoretical premium received, which is used in determining the initial amount to be borrowed. If we take the premium out of consideration in the P&L, the P&L figure should be centred around zero.

To see if increasing the frequency would lead to better results, we increase the number of time steps used from 12 to 365. The graph below plots the Net P&L to Theoretical Value across 100 simulated runs; a value close to 100% means that it is a close match to the premium, whereas a value farther away for 100% indicates a poor match.

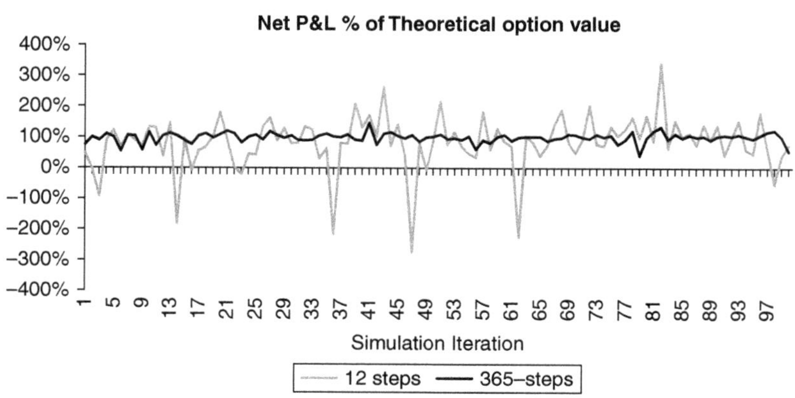

Figure 221 P&L simulation – rebalancing frequency
Source: FinanceTrainingCourse.com

We can clearly see that there is greater variation when rebalancing is carried out on a monthly basis than on a daily basis.

The graph below gives a similar picture. In this case, however, the premium is not considered in the net P&L calculation. A value of 0% indicates that the net P&L – that is, the cost of the hedge – exactly matches the theoretical value of the call option.

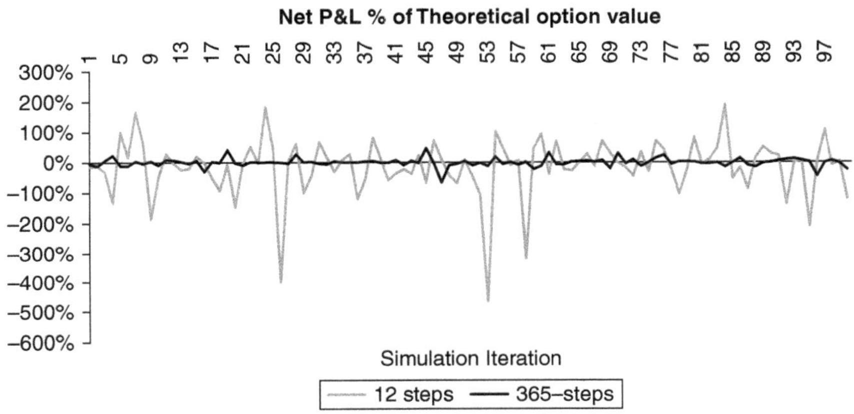

Figure 222 P&L simulation – hedge effectiveness
Source: FinanceTrainingCourse.com

An alternative way to look at the same dataset is to plot a histogram for daily as well as monthly hedging. The next two figures present the results when we plot a histogram for P&L results from 100 iterations from our 12-step as well as our 365-step model.

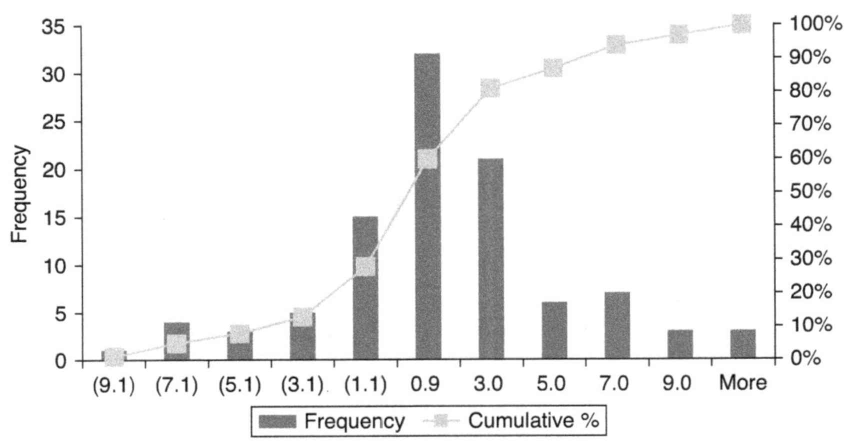

Figure 223 Cash P&L – 12 steps – low-volatility world
Source: FinanceTrainingCourse.com

We see the same trend again.

P&L distribution for the 12-step model, as expected, is significantly more dispersed than the 365-step model. From a probability point of view, only 47% of the distribution is centred around zero for the 12-step model, whereas that number rises to 67% for the 365-step model.

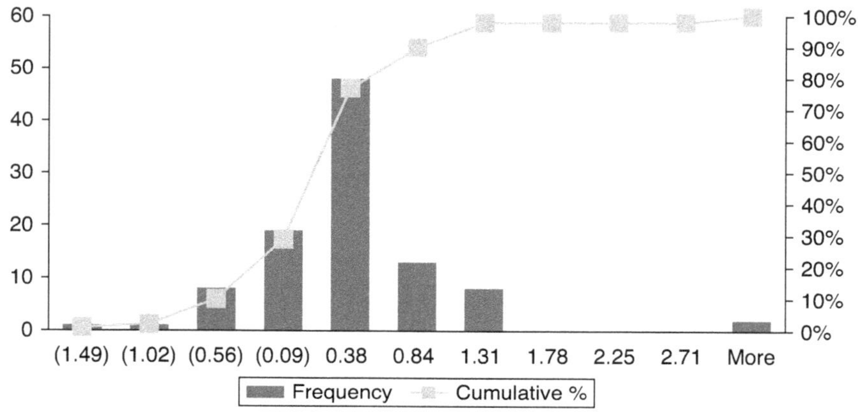

Figure 224 Cash P&L – 365 steps – low-volatility world
Source: FinanceTrainingCourse.com

But that is the risk manager's point of view. What about a trader's?

From a trading point of view, there are two lessons here. First, it would appear that the large variation in P&L linked to jumps in the underlying price is the unhedged Gamma at work (Is that true? Think about it.) By daily rebalancing, we update prices and Delta on a daily basis. In the monthly model, our Delta model is supposedly correct for the entire month, which we know is not true; the error creeps in and is responsible for the divergence in the results we see.

Second, would you prefer to limit the cost of hedging the option to the amount you have charged your customer, or less? If you are in the business of earning a living from writing options, the premium you charge on the options you sell should always be higher than the cost to you of effectively hedging the option.

Now back to the Gamma question: Is the large variation in the P&L due to the unhedged Gamma? Gamma is your second-order error term. Conceptually it is similar to convexity, and linked to changes in not just the underlying price but also volatility.

$$Gamma = \frac{\partial Delta}{\partial S} = \frac{N'(d_1)}{S\sigma\sqrt{T-t}}$$

Is your true P&L (the premium received less the actual cost of hedging) the summation of the hedge error? How would you go about answering this question?

i The Gamma correction

Here is one approach that we can use to answer the above question. How big is the impact of Gamma correction? And if we made it, how would that change the distribution of P&L that we have seen so far?

To make the Gamma correction, we need to adjust our estimate of Delta and plug in a revised (and hopefully improved) Delta in our simulation model.

We modify our original 365-day model by making a simple adjustment. Rather than using Delta in estimating the units of the underlying security that we need to purchase to hedge our exposure, we will use Delta plus the Gamma correction adjustment. This revised value will now include the second-order error term we missed out when we used our linear unadjusted Delta estimates.

Rather than using the Black–Scholes formal definition of Gamma, we will numerically estimate it using the modified Gamma methodology covered earlier, by observing the actual change in Delta in our simulation and using that as an input to our Gamma approximation.

Once we have made the adjustment, we run our hedge P&L simulation again. The results of 100 iterations are summarized below in the form of our standard P&L histogram. For comparison, we reproduce the original (unadjusted Delta P&L). Since visual comparison can be uncertain, we also reproduce the actual distribution results from the two simulations.

With Gamma Correction				Unadjusted Delta Without Gamma Correction		
Bin	Frequency	Cumulative %		Bin	Frequency	Cumulative %
(1.06)	1	1.00%		(1.49)	1	1.00%
(0.82)	2	3.00%		(1.02)	1	2.00%
(0.57)	5	8.00%		(0.56)	8	10.00%
(0.33)	3	11.00%		(0.09)	19	29.00%
(0.09)	19	30.00%		0.38	48	77.00%
0.15	40	70.00%		0.84	13	90.00%
0.39	20	90.00%		1.31	8	98.00%
0.63	6	96.00%		1.78	0	98.00%
0.88	1	97.00%		2.25	0	98.00%
1.12	0	97.00%		2.71	0	98.00%
More	3	100.00%		More	2	100.00%
	100				100	

Figure 225 Comparison – distribution of P&L with and without Gamma correction
Source: FinanceTrainingCourse.com

We can see that the results in the revised simulation with Gamma correction are more tightly centred around zero, and the dispersion we had seen in the original 365-step simulation has also been reduced by making the Gamma adjustment.

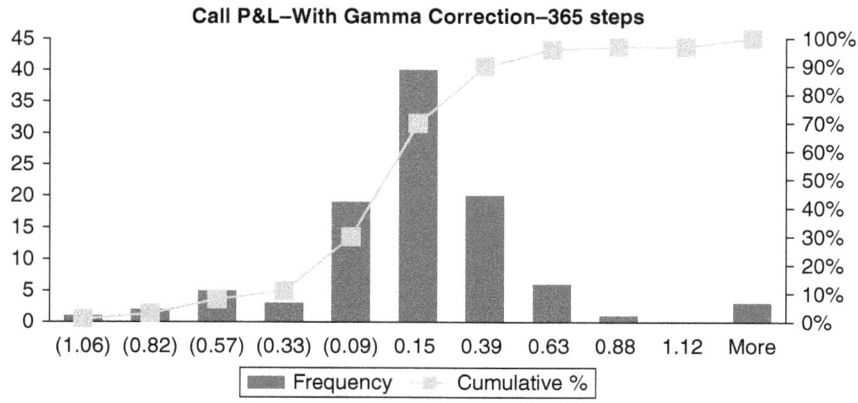

Figure 226 Call P&L with Gamma correction
Source: FinanceTrainingCourse.com

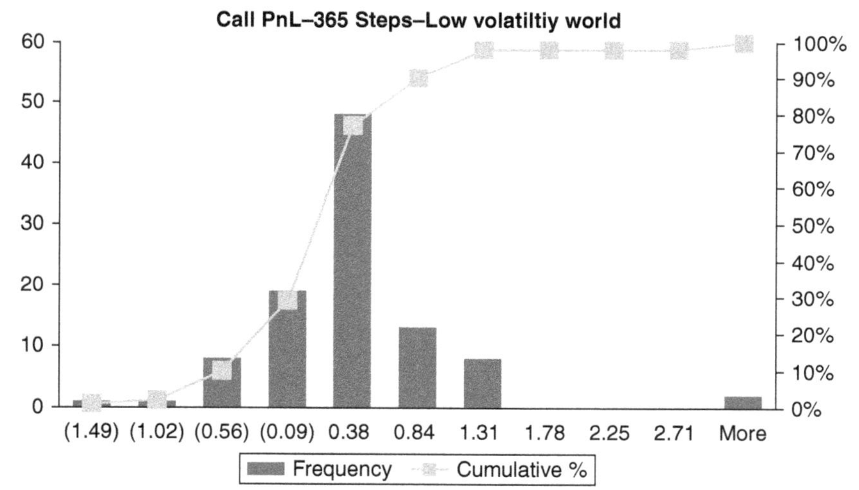

Figure 227 Call P&L without Gamma correction
Source: FinanceTrainingCourse.com

3 Volatility and profitability: the question of implied volatility

With volatility, there are multiple questions. How does profitability change when the general environment moves from low volatility to high volatility?

How does profitability change when you have already written an option and volatility moves for or against you?

Let's start with the first question. Using the 12-step model, we calculate the impact on Net P&L. In our base case, we have assumed a volatility of 20%. Now let's assume that the volatility increases to 30%. What is the impact on hedge efficiency for options written in two different environments?

Implied Volatility	**20%**
Simulated P&L Summary	**Results**
Simulated P&L - 100 runs average	**3.02**
Simulated Trading Gain/(Loss) - 100 runs average	**(2.15)**
Average Interest Paid	**0.25**
Average Principal Repaid on Maturity	**27.74**

Figure 228 Low-volatility world
Source: FinanceTrainingCourse.com

Premium Received	**8.128**
Implied Volatility	**30%**
Simulated P&L Summary	**Results**
Simulated P&L - 100 runs average	**8.51**
Simulated Trading Gain/(Loss) - 100 runs average	**(5.93)**
Average Interest Paid	**0.38**
Average Principal Repaid on Maturity	**45.24**

Figure 229 High-volatility world
Source: FinanceTrainingCourse.com

Premiums are clearly higher, and so is profitability in absolute terms. But is that true in the relative world? Let's take a quick look by plotting the Net P&L to Theoretical Value across 100 simulated runs. In relative terms (as a percentage of premiums) there is not much difference. Why is that? Was it a result you had expected?

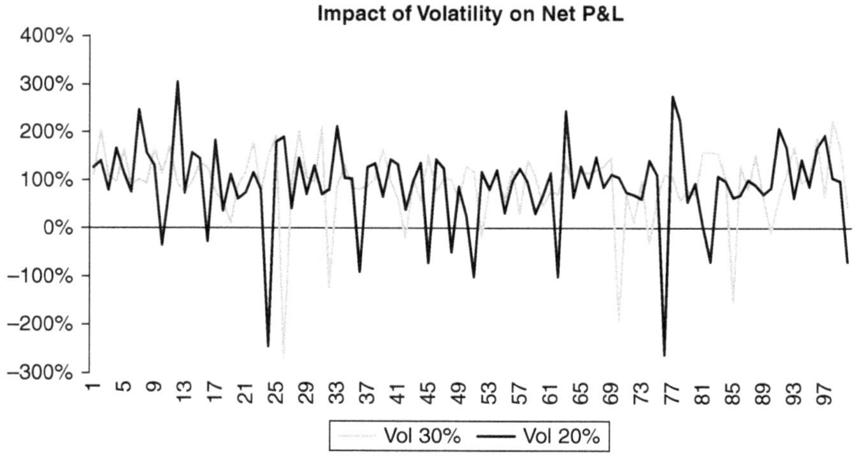

Figure 230 Volatility impact
Source: FinanceTrainingCourse.com

To answer these questions, you have to revisit implied volatility.

i Implied volatility and P&L – four scenarios to set things right

We go back to a simple world where implied volatility can take four possible values: 10%, 20%, 30% and 40%. As a trading desk, we can write and sell options at each of these implied volatility levels.

Premium Received	0.072
Implied Volatility	10%
Simulated P&L Summary	Results
Simulated P&L - 100 runs average	0.07
Simulated Trading Gain/(Loss) - 100 runs average	(0.00)
Average Interest Paid	0.02
Average Principal Repaid on Maturity	3.10

Figure 231 Implied volatility scenario 1
Source: FinanceTrainingCourse.com

Premium Received	3.022
Implied Volatility	20%
Simulated P&L Summary	**Results**
Simulated P&L - 100 runs average	3.58
Simulated Trading Gain/(Loss) - 100 runs average	(2.00)
Average Interest Paid	0.30
Average Principal Repaid on Maturity	36.55

Figure 232 Implied volatility scenario 2
Source: FinanceTrainingCourse.com

Premium Received	9.732
Implied Volatility	30%
Simulated P&L Summary	**Results**
Simulated P&L - 100 runs average	10.67
Simulated Trading Gain/(Loss) - 100 runs average	(6.96)
Average Interest Paid	0.54
Average Principal Repaid on Maturity	42.16

Figure 233 Implied volatility scenario 3
Source: FinanceTrainingCourse.com

Premium Received	18.172
Implied Volatility	40%
Simulated P&L Summary	**Results**
Simulated P&L - 100 runs average	16.43
Simulated Trading Gain/(Loss) - 100 runs average	(14.70)
Average Interest Paid	0.62
Average Principal Repaid on Maturity	66.59

Figure 234 Implied volatility scenaric 4
Source: FinanceTrainingCourse.com

As a trading desk, your best case is a combination where you write an option at 40% implied volatility and book a premium of 16.43. The next day or week, when the volatility falls to 10%, you square yourself in the market at a cost of 7 cents and book a profit of 16.36.

Your worst case is writing an option at 10% and seeing implied volatility levels rise to 40% with premium income limited to 7 cents, and hedging costs rising all the way up to US$16.

But the tabular scenarios presented above do not do justice to the case. To truly appreciate the depth of our payoff (in the first case) or your misery (in the second) it is just as important to plot the P&L distribution for the four implied volatility scenarios. We do that next.

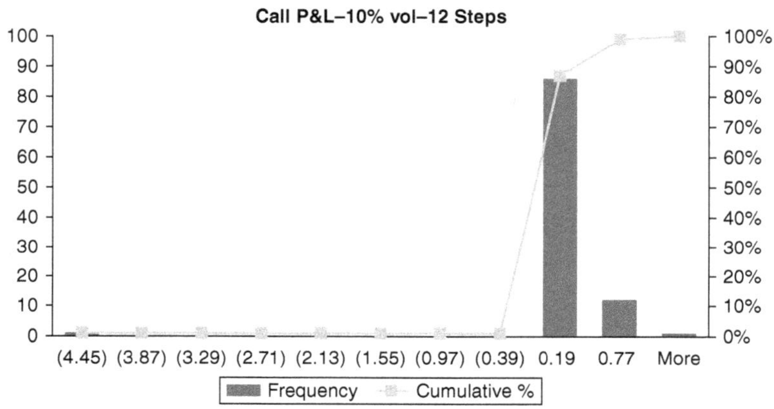

Figure 235 The distribution of P&L for 10% volatility
Source: FinanceTrainingCourse.com

The P&L distribution shows that while the average cost of hedging (premium) may be 7 cents, for the 10% volatility case it can cross 77 cents in extreme scenarios.

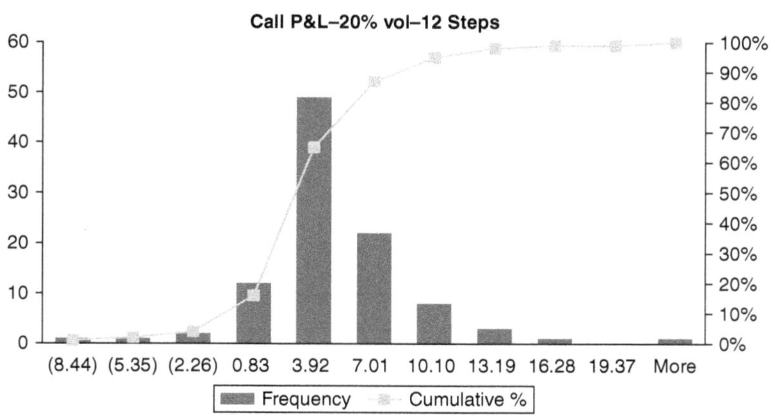

Figure 236 The distribution of P&L for 20% volatility
Source: FinanceTrainingCourse.com

The extreme for 20% volatility is $19 and change; for 30% volatility it is $26; and for the 40% volatility case, north of $26.

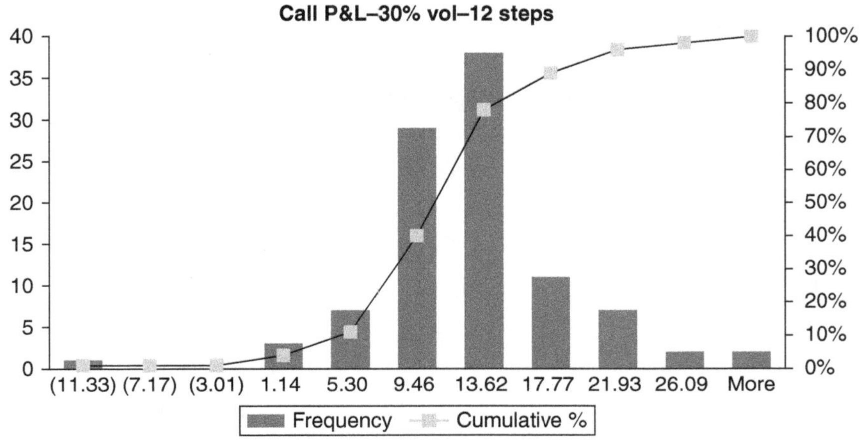

Figure 237 The distribution of P&L for 30% volatility
Source: FinanceTrainingCourse.com

But these are absolute numbers and they do not give a true sense of how extreme these numbers can be unless we plot the relative distribution – the P&L relative to the premium received.

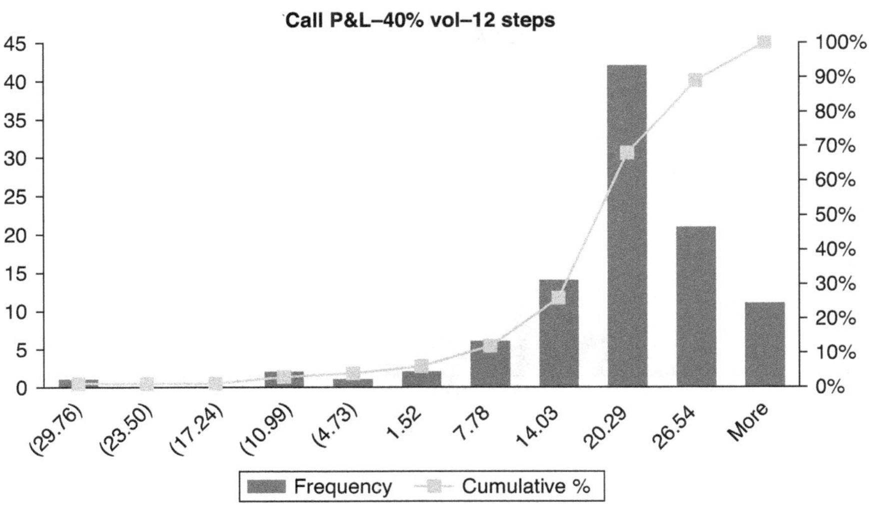

Figure 238 The distribution of P&L for 40% volatility
Source: FinanceTrainingCourse.com

To calculate the relative P&L we divide the absolute P&L figure by the premium and then use Excel to draw a histogram for the series. The results for the four scenarios are presented below.

ii Relative P&L comparison

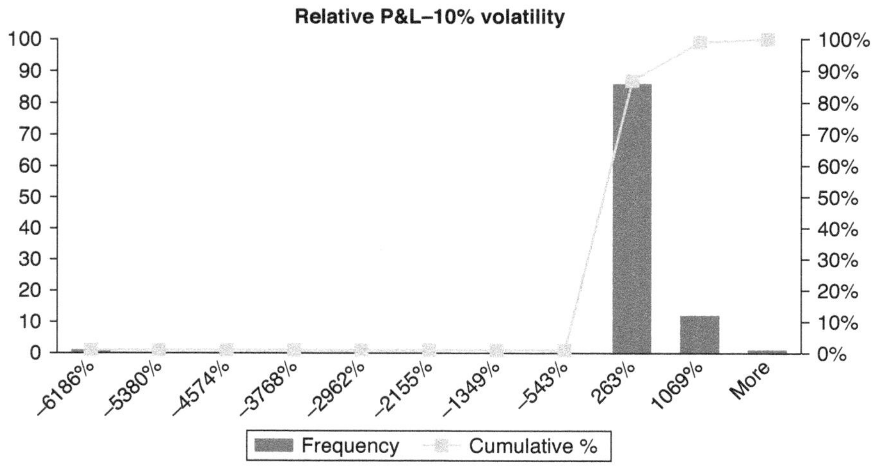

Figure 239 P&L relative to premium at 10%
Source: FinanceTrainingCourse.com

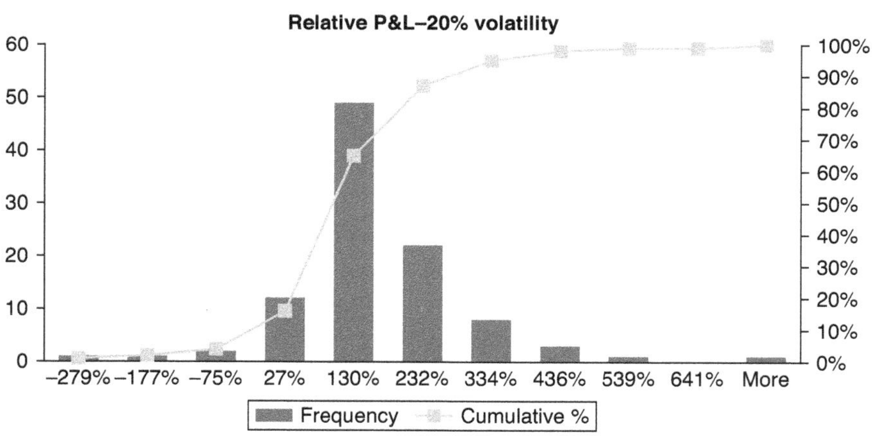

Figure 240 P&L relative to premium at 20%
Source: FinanceTrainingCourse.com

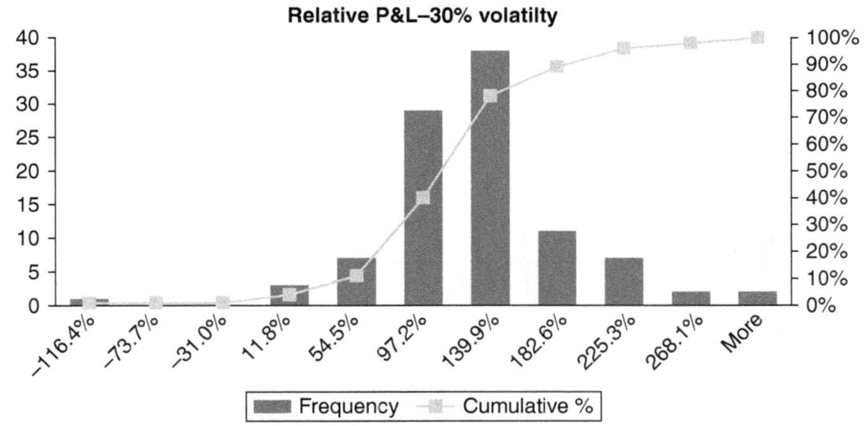

Figure 241 P&L relative to premium at 30%
Source: FinanceTrainingCourse.com

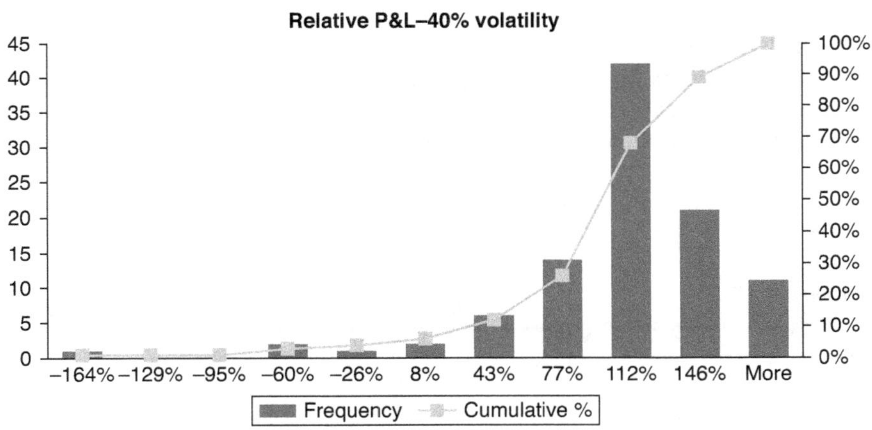

Figure 242 P&L relative to premium at 40%
Source: FinanceTrainingCourse.com

No, it's not your imagination. There is a definite trend here; something is happening to the relative P&L distribution. As we raise volatility, the P&L distribution is stabilizing. A large part of that stability has to do with the fact that premiums are rising, and with that increase the magnitude of extreme swings in relative P&L is reducing.

We use two more plots (the last two, we promise) to make the point clear. The first plot shows the relative volatility for the 20%, 30% and 40% scenarios. The second plot includes the 10% scenario.

We won't comment on the trend. You be the judge.

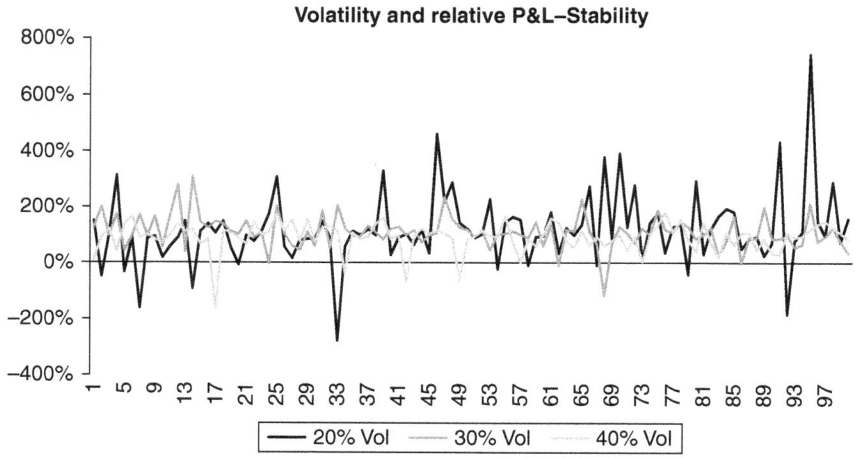

Figure 243 Relative P&L plot for 20%, 30%, 40% scenarios
Source: FinanceTrainingCourse.com

A quick question or two before we end this chapter. In your opinion, what do these two charts imply for supply and demand curves for option writers? How do you compare the curves when implied volatility levels are low versus instances when implied volatilities levels are at a historical high?

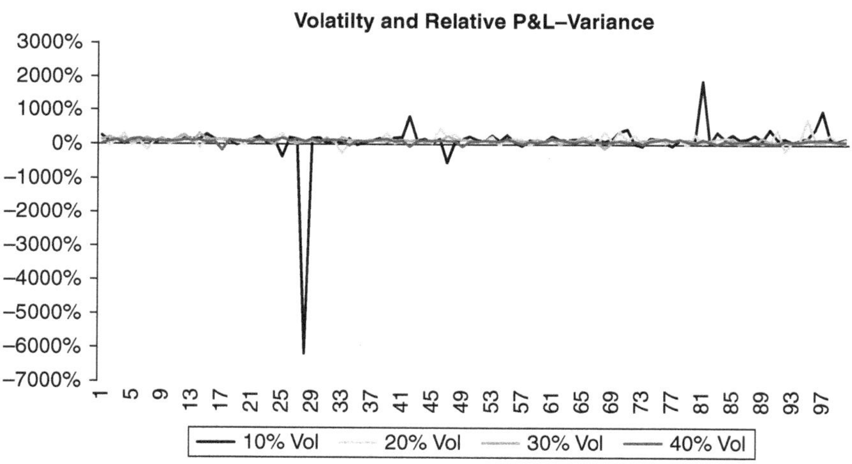

Figure 244 Relative P&L plot for 10%, 20%, 30%, 40% implied volatility scenarios
Source: FinanceTrainingCourse.com

iii More vexing questions

For your P&L simulation or actual hedging implementation, which Delta should you use? One calculated using the implied volatility? Or one calculated using your expectation of future realized volatility? How frequently should you update that Delta estimate? Would you favour a crude Delta hedge over a Delta Gamma hedge, or an even more sophisticated Delta Vega hedge? There is some fascinating research on the topic by Riaz and Wilmott (list of papers here).[1]

4 Dissecting Rho

One of the first relationships to stand out in our plot of Greeks is the similarity in the curves for Rho and Delta. What drives that relationship?

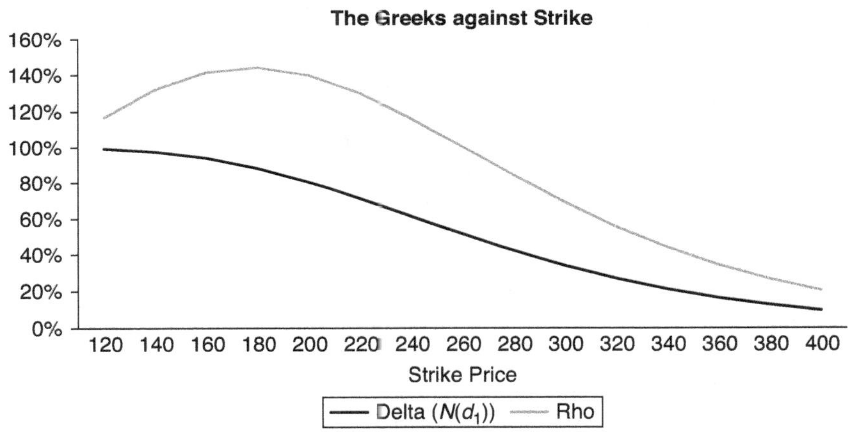

Figure 245 Delta and Rho
Source: FinanceTrainingCourse.com

To investigate, we look at the equations for Delta and Rho, and find the common denominator in both equations – the probabilities $N(d_1)$ and $N(d_2)$.

Delta and Rho are given by their respective equations, $Delta_{call} = N(d_1)$ and $Rho_{call} = K(T-t)e^{-r(T-t)}N(d_2)$. The first uses a conditional probability of exercise $N(d_1)$; the second an unconditional probability, $N(d_2)$.

A plot of the probabilities shows how closely the two track each other. Since Rho is a function of $N(d_2)$ and Delta a function of $N(d_1)$, the Greeks' curves are close to each other.

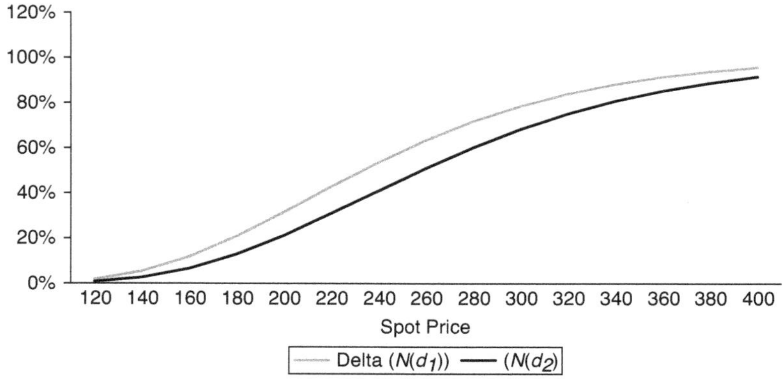

Figure 246 $N(d_1)$ and $N(d_2)$ against spot
Source: FinanceTrainingCourse.com

The variation that exists between the two Greeks is accounted by the multipliers used in Rho. $Rho_{call} = K(T-t)e^{-r(T-t)}N(d_2)$. K, the strike, $(T-t)$ the time differential, and the present value factor. All three tie in with our interpretation of Rho. We will see later, in that when it comes to interest rates and option pricing there are two components where a change in interest rates has an impact. The bigger of these two is financing cost. Since we purchase the underlying in and around the strike price, our total borrowing is unlikely to exceed K. Multiply that by the remaining time to maturity, the present value factor for the period and the unconditional probability of exercise, and you have the rate of change in option price on account of changes in interest rates.

It is also instructive to plot Rho, $N(d_1)$ and $N(d_2)$ against changing spot and changing strikes to see how Rho transitions from deep out of money to at money and from at money to deep in the money options. The next two graphs show that transition.

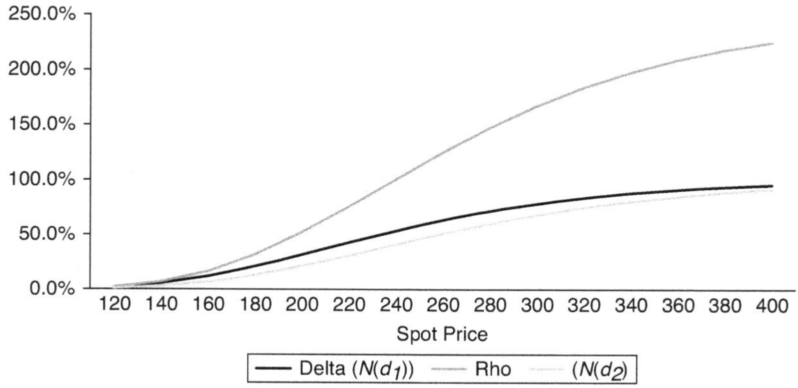

Figure 247 Rho, $N(d_1)$, $N(d_2)$ against changing spot
Source: FinanceTrainingCourse.com

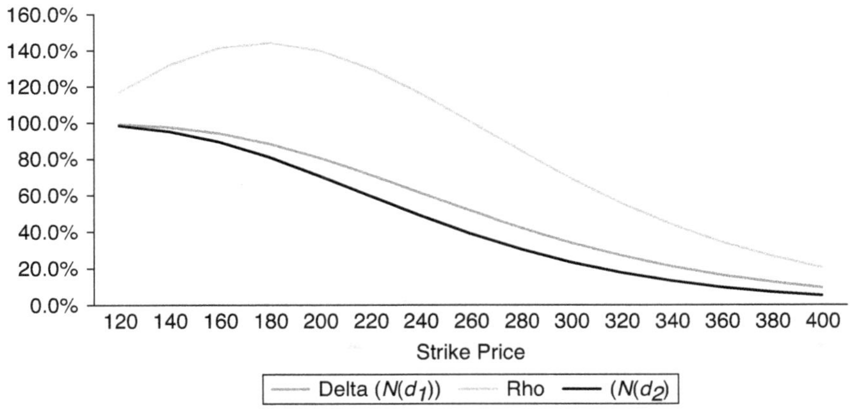

Figure 248 Rho, $N(d_1)$, $N(d_2)$ against changing strikes
Source: FinanceTrainingCourse.com

5 Risk-free rates and profitability: the question of Rho

We present the results of three P&L simulation runs in the tables below. The first assumes a risk-free interest rate of 1%, the second uses 2%, and the third uses a risk-free interest rate estimate of 5%.

The first is easy; rates go up, premiums go up, and a European call option becomes more expensive. Why is that?

Premium Received	**3.010**
Risk Free Rate	**1%**
Simulated P&L Summary	**Results**
Simulated P&L - 100 runs average	**3.37**
Simulated Trading Gain/(Loss) - 100 runs average	**(1.83)**
Average Interest Paid	**0.30**
Average Principal Repaid on Maturity	**37.34**

Figure 249 P&L at 1% interest rates
Source: FinanceTrainingCourse.com

The reason is the Average Interest Paid column. The premium goes up by 28 cents, of which 21 cents is the increased cost of financing the borrowed position. Where do the other 7 cents come from? (Need a hint? – Other than the borrowing component, what else benefits from or uses r, the risk-free rate?)

Premium Received	3.291
Risk Free Rate	2%
Simulated P&L Summary	**Results**
Simulated P&L - 100 runs average	2.87
Simulated Trading Gain/(Loss) - 100 runs average	(2.69)
Average Interest Paid	0.51
Average Principal Repaid on Maturity	19.91

Figure 250 P&L at 2% interest rates
Source: FinanceTrainingCourse.com

The second one is more difficult. In this instance as rates increase from the original 1% to 5%, the cost of borrowing balloons from the original US$0.30 to US$1.95, but the impact in option premium is only US$1.244. How does this work? (Hint: think about what other driver/factor in the Black–Scholes analysis uses *r*.)

Premium Received	4.254
Risk Free Rate	5%
Simulated P&L Summary	**Results**
Simulated P&L - 100 runs average	4.05
Simulated Trading Gain/(Loss) - 100 runs average	(2.00)
Average Interest Paid	1.95
Average Principal Repaid on Maturity	46.25

Figure 251 P&L at 5% interest rates
Source: FinanceTrainingCourse.com

In addition to borrowing the difference between premium received and Delta hedge, the other usage of the risk-free rate, *r*, is to estimate the future value of the underlying asset in the BSM (Black–Scholes model's) risk-neutral world. This implies that there are other components of Rho in addition to the borrowing cost.

An alternative way of looking at the same question is to push volatility down to a very low level in the dynamic hedging model. You cannot use zero as an input for volatility, since it will break the model; but any low number such as 0.001% will do. Our revised low-volatility model assumptions are as follows.

ASSUMPTIONS	
Spot	US$200.00
Strike	US$200.00
Model Volatility	0%
Time	1
Risk_Free	1%
Steps	12
Delta_T	0.083

Figure 252 Low-volatility analysis
Source: FinanceTrainingCourse.com

We now evaluate a call option struck at US$200, with the underlying spot price also at US$200.

The option has one year to expiry and the risk-free interest rate is 1% per annum. With volatility at a level where it makes very little contribution to changes in the value of the underlying, the only operator on the stock price is the risk-free interest rate. Remember in the risk-neutral Black–Scholes world, all assets grow at the risk-free rate, and all investors are content to earn the risk-free rate.

The daily accrual on spot at time zero (US$200) on a continuously compounded basis is 0.167. You can see that the value of the underlying changes by a month's worth of interest at every time step:

However, even more interesting is the premium and profitability calculation in the close to zero volatility world using our standard dynamic hedging model. It is the sum of interest paid on the borrowed amount required to deliver the underlying at the strike price of US$200.

Change in Underlying	New Spot Price
	200.00
0.1667	200.17
0.1667	200.33
0.1673	200.50
0.1672	200.67
0.1674	200.84
0.1680	201.00
0.1685	201.17
0.1673	201.34
0.1678	201.51
0.1685	201.68
0.1677	201.84
0.1676	202.01

Figure 253 Change in underlying asset value
Source: FinanceTrainingCourse.com

Premium Received	**1.990**
Implied Volatility	**0.001%**
Simulated P&L Summary	**Results**
Simulated P&L - 100 runs average	**1.99**
Simulated Trading Gain/(Loss) - 100 runs average	-
Average Interest Paid	**1.99**
Average Principal Repaid on Maturity	**198.01**

Figure 254 Premium and profitability calculations in the low-volatility world
Source: FinanceTrainingCourse.com

What does the breakdown of interest paid looks like? No surprises here. A little less than 0.167, since the principal amount is US$198 rather than US$200.

Cash Out flow on Maturity	
Interest Paid	Principal Amount Borrowed
0.165	198.01
0.165	–
0.165	–
0.165	–
0.166	–
0.166	–
0.166	–
0.166	–
0.166	–
0.166	–
0.166	–
0.167	–
0.000	–
1.990	**198.01**

Figure 255 Interest under extreme low-volatility assumptions

The low-volatility world is a great learning device, since it clearly shows the interaction of the risk-free rate with the growth in the value of the asset, as well as the financing cost of the amount borrowed to hedge the underlying asset.

When the underlying asset is dependent on two or more rates (the dividend rate for a dividend paying stock, or a currency exchange rate dependent on interest rates on the two currencies), the model becomes even more intricate.

13
Understanding Theta

1 Theta against Gamma and Rho

Theta tracks the change in option value for a change in time to expiry, assuming that all other drivers of option value remain the same.

Theta's calculation includes reference to the underlying Spot price, volatility, the two probabilities – $N(d_1)$ and $N(d_2)$ – and the difference between the risk-free rate and the dividend yield on the underlying share (interest rate differential on currencies).

Of all the Greeks we calculate, the formula for Theta is the most intricate, because the underlying relationships linking Theta to option value are so complex. Think about it for a second.

$$c(S,t) = SN(d_1)e^{-q(T-t)} - Xe^{-r(T-t)}N(d_2)$$

Where

c is the value of a European call option

$N(x)$ is the cumulative probability distribution function (pdf) for a standardized normal distribution

S_0 is the price of the underlying asset at time zero

K is the strike or exercise price

r is the continuously compounded risk-free rate

σ is the volatility of the asset price

T is the time to maturity of the option

q is the yield rate on the underlying asset. (Alternatively, if the asset provides cash income instead of a yield, q will be set to zero in the formula and the present value of the cash income during the life of the option will be subtracted from S_0.)

And,

$$d_1 = \frac{\ln(S_0/K) + (r - q + \sigma^2/2)T}{\sigma\sqrt{T}}$$

$$d_2 = \frac{\ln(S_0/K) + (r - q + \sigma^2/2)T}{\sigma\sqrt{T}} = d_1 - \sigma\sqrt{T}$$

Where do you see time (T or Delta_T) in the above equation? Not just in the two components on the right-hand side, but also within $N(d_1)$ and $N(d_2)$.

Now calculate the rate of change of the above function with respect to time. The two probabilities plus the amount borrowed, the interest paid and earned and volatility – Theta ends up including sensitivities across the equation, because in the Black–Scholes model, time touches everything.

It is instructive to plot Theta against Gamma and Rho to see how the three Greeks differ from each other.

When you compare the figure above with one below, what should stand out immediately is the inverse relationship between Gamma and Theta. For the same at the money option, a large Gamma value corresponds to a negative Theta value. As Gamma declines, Theta tends to move in the opposite direction.

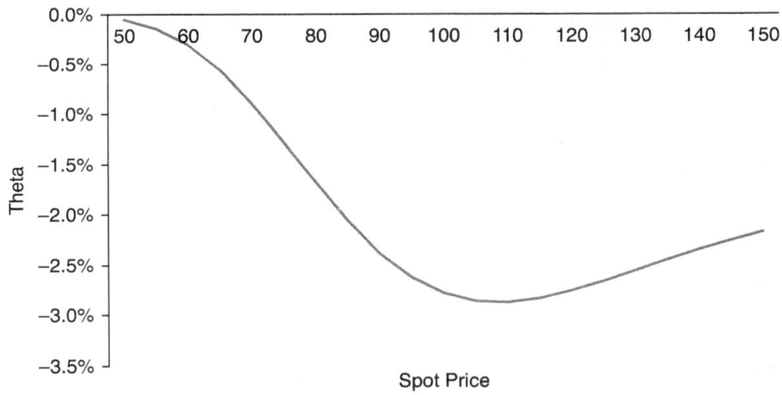

Figure 256 Theta against rising spot for an at the money call option
Source: FinanceTrainingCourse.com

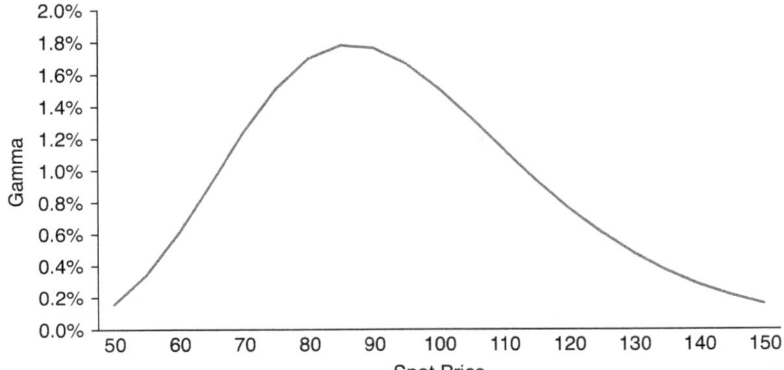

Figure 257 Gamma against rising spot for an at the money call
Source: FinanceTrainingCourse.com

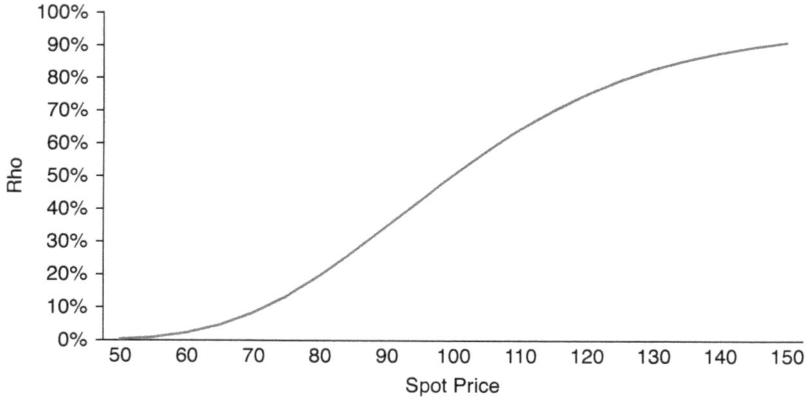

Figure 258 Rho against rising spot for an at the money call option
Source: FinanceTrainingCourse.com

The relationship with Rho is less obvious, but becomes clearer when you compare the formulas for the two Greeks (take a look at the last term used in the Theta calculation).

i Theta for a call option

$$Theta_{call} = \frac{\partial C}{\partial (T-t)}$$

$$Theta_{call} = \frac{-SN'(d_1)\sigma\, e^{-q(T-t)}}{2\sqrt{T-t}} + qSN(d_1)e^{-q(T-t)} - rKN(d_2)e^{-r(T-t)}$$

Assuming zero dividends reduces the above formula to:

$$Theta_{call} = \frac{\partial C}{\partial (T-t)} = \frac{-SN'(d_1)\sigma}{2\sqrt{T-t}} - rKN(d_2)e^{-r(T-t)}$$

ii Theta for a put option

$$Theta_{put} = \frac{\partial C}{\partial (T-t)} = \frac{-SN'(d_1)\sigma e^{-q(T-t)}}{2\sqrt{T-t}} - qSN(-d_1)e^{-q(T-t)} + rKN(-d_2)e^{-r(T-t)}$$

simplifies to the following for zero dividends:

$$Theta_{put} = \frac{\partial C}{\partial (T-t)} = \frac{-SN'(d_1)\sigma}{2\sqrt{T-t}} + rKN(-d_2)e^{-r(T-t)}$$

iii Rho for a call option

$$Rho_{call} = K(T-t)e^{-r(T-t)}N(d_2)$$

where
S = Stock spot price
σ = Implied volatility
r = Risk-free rate
T = Time to maturity in years
t = Current time
q = Dividend rate

$$d_1 = \frac{Ln\left(\frac{S}{K}\right) + \left(r + \frac{\sigma^2}{2}\right)(T-t)}{\sigma\sqrt{T-t}}$$

$$d_2 = d_1 - \sigma\sqrt{T-t}$$

iv Rho for a put option

$$Rho_{put} = -K(T-t)e^{-r(T-t)}N(-d_2)$$

2 Theta plots for at the money call and put options

It is also useful to plot the Theta of a call and put against each other for at the money options struck at the same strike price.

You can see that while Theta shapes for calls and puts are similar, the values are pegged to different scales; take another look at the Theta formula above and the reason should become clear.

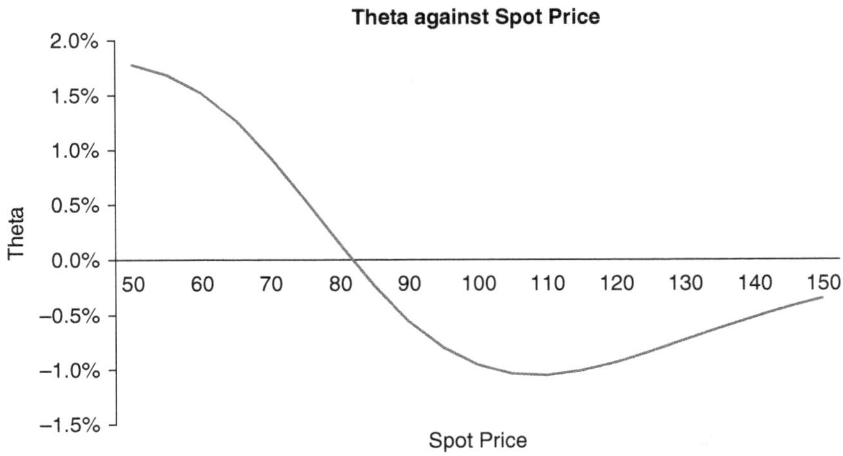

Figure 259 Theta plot for an at the money put option
Source: FinanceTrainingCourse.com

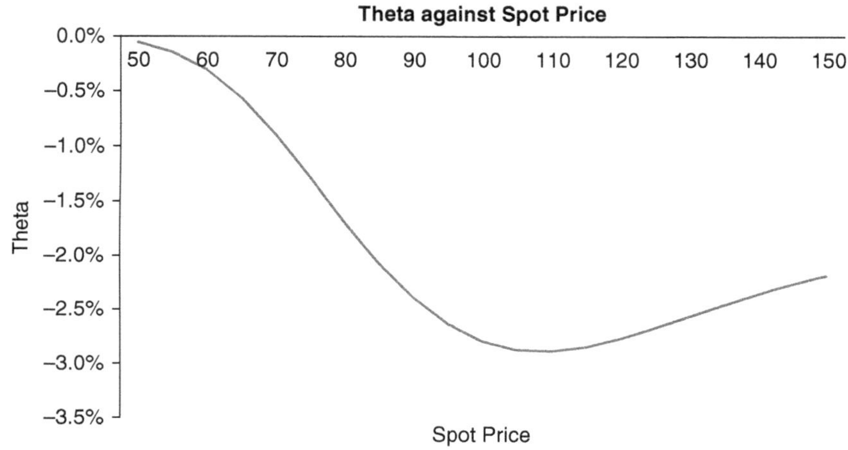

Figure 260 Theta plot for an at the money call option
Source: FinanceTrainingCourse.com

The same relationship holds true (similar curves, different scale) when we plot Theta for a call and a put against changing volatility and changing time to expiry, as shown in the next four snapshots.

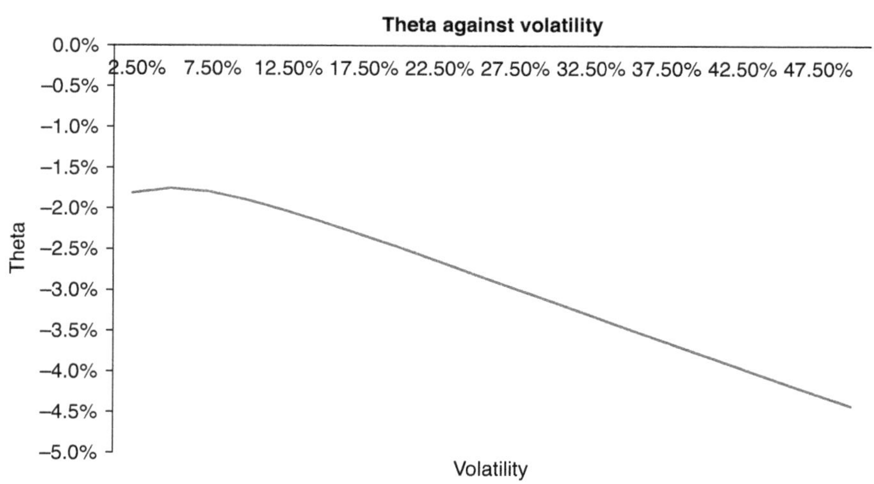

Figure 261 Theta against changing volatility for at the money call
Source: FinanceTrainingCourse.com

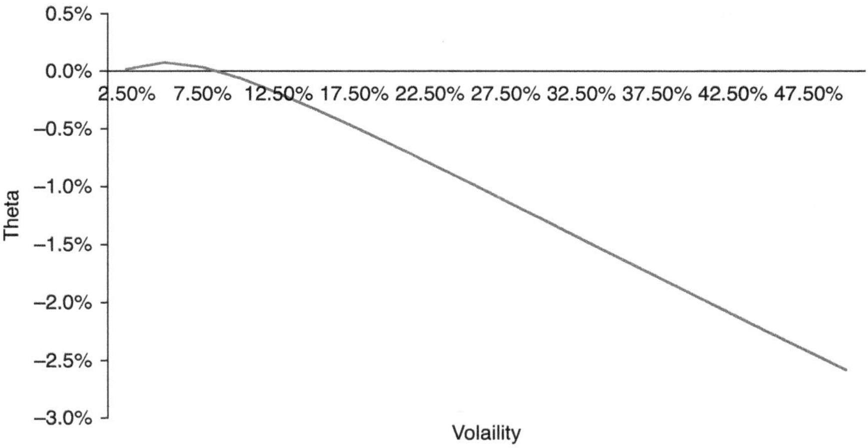

Figure 262 Theta against changing volatility for at the money put
Source: FinanceTrainingCourse.com

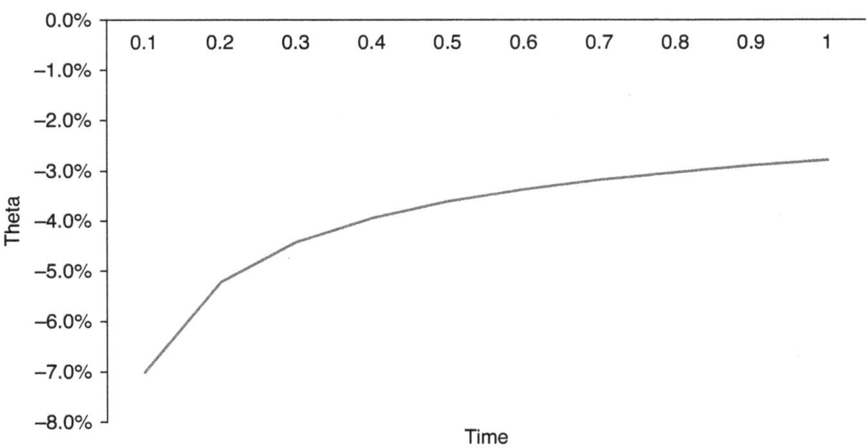

Figure 263 Theta against changing time for at the money call
Source: FinanceTrainingCourse.com

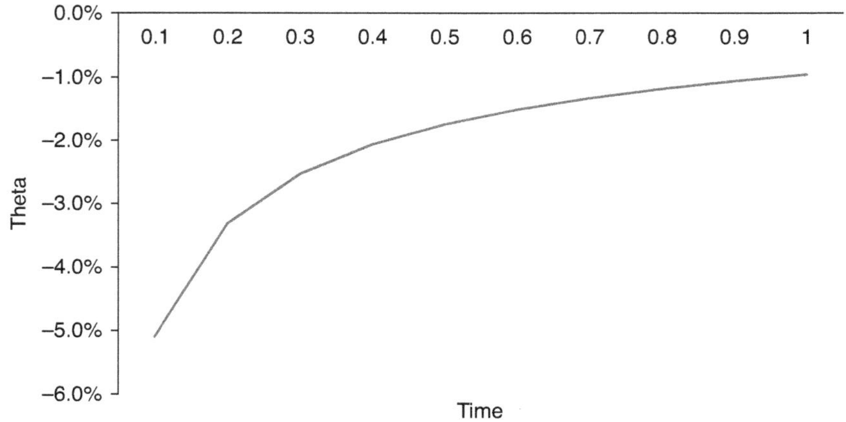

Figure 264 Theta against changing time for at the money put
Source: FinanceTrainingCourse.com

However, the same does not hold when you plot Theta against changing interest rates for the two options. It reflects the relationship between rising cost of financing and the price of calls and puts.

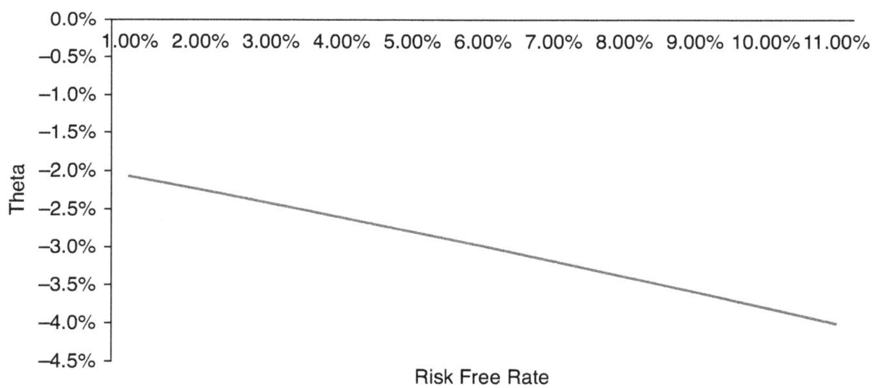

Figure 265 Theta against changing interest rates for at the money call
Source: FinanceTrainingCourse.com

For call options, as interest rates rise Theta becomes increasingly negative. For put options the opposite is true.

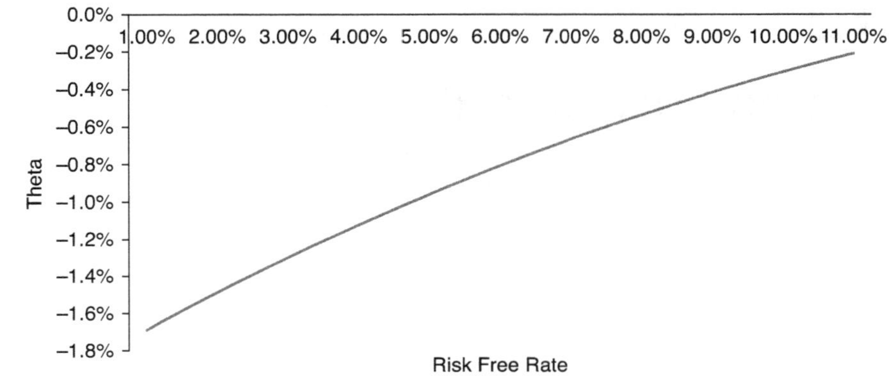

Figure 266 Theta against changing rates for at the money put
Source: FinanceTrainingCourse.com

14

Option Prices and Time to Expiry

Douglas, Guo and Su in their October 2007 paper[1] (A Closer Look at Black–Scholes option Thetas) introduce the concept of **Time Premium**, the difference between an option at time 1 and another similar option very close to expiry. We calculate time premium and compare it to Theta. We use the framework presented in the research paper to look at Theta for European call options from a slightly different perspective.

Consider the following at the money European call option on a non-dividend-paying stock:

Spot	100
Strike	100
RiskFree Rate	5%
Annualized Vol	25%
Daily Vol	1.6%
Time to Maturity	1
Notional	1

Figure 267 Theta experiment – setting the stage

Call option Theta is calculated as follows:

$$Theta_{call} = \frac{-SN'(d_1)\sigma\, e^{-q(T-t)}}{2\sqrt{T-t}} + qSN(d_1)e^{-q(T-t)} - rKN(d_2)e^{-r(T-t)}$$

1 Theta relative to underlying asset value *S*

The following graph shows the value of the option at varying times to maturity. Each line represents the value over time for a different underlying asset value *S*.

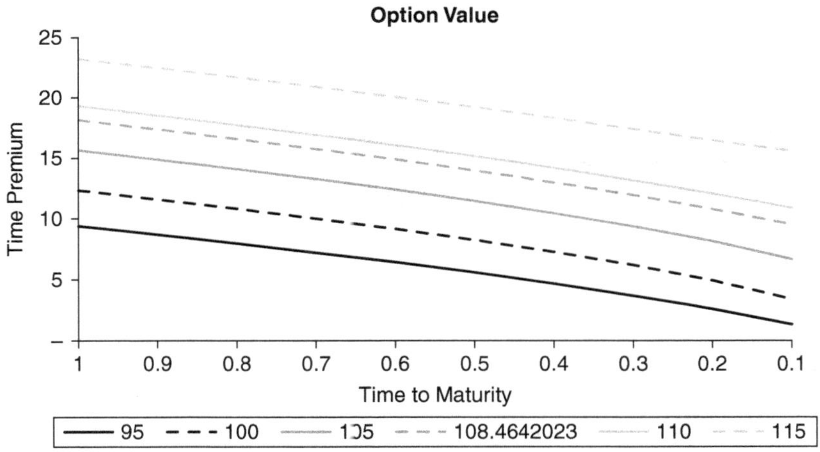

Figure 268 Theta – plot against different spots
Source: FinanceTrainingCourse.com

In general, as the option approaches maturity the value of the option declines.

The option's time premium is greatest when $S = X$, as shown in the following graph. Keeping all other parameters/assumptions constant, the time premium represents the change in the value of the option as the option approaches expiration. It is calculated as the difference between the value of the option at inception and its value at expiry:

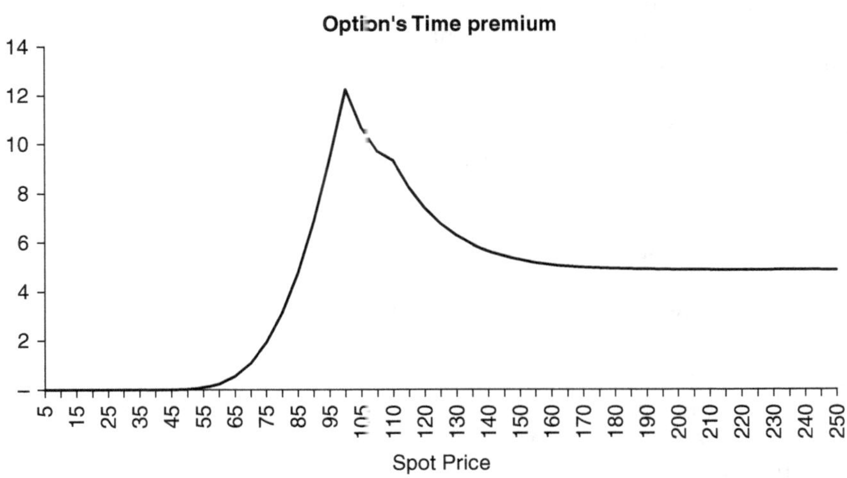

Figure 269 Theta – maximum time premium
Source: FinanceTrainingCourse.com

The rate at which this time premium dissipates for different values of *S* is given in the following graph, which plots option Thetas on the *Y* axis against the underlying asset value on the *X* axis:

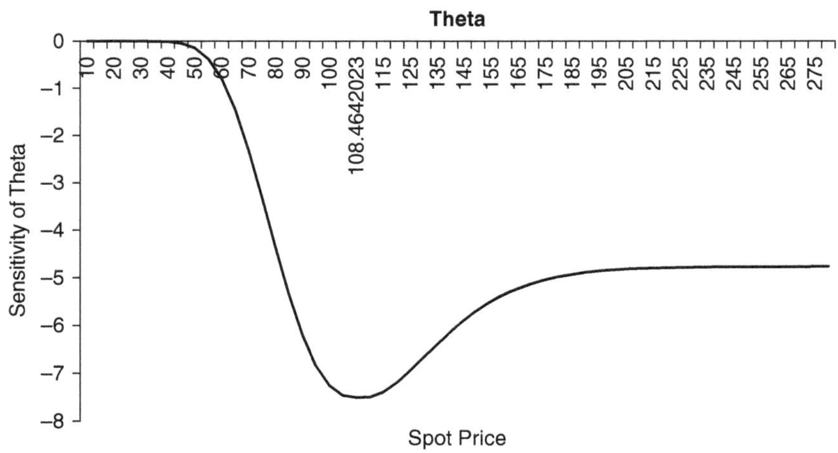

Figure 270 Theta – plot against spot reloaded
Source: FinanceTrainingCourse.com

The graph shows the sensitivity of Theta for the option to various spot prices. It indicates the rate at which the value of the option's time premium declines over time. For a call option the Theta is always negative, which means that the value of the option's time premium will always dissipate as the option approaches maturity. For deep out of the money options, there is no dissipation in the time premium. As the underlying asset value approaches the strike price, the rate of dissipation increases. When the option is in the money the rate of decay falls, and then levels out for deep in the money options.

As S approaches positive infinity, that is, the option is deep, deep in the money, Theta approaches the value:

Risk free rate * Strike * exp(–Risk free rate * Time to expiry)

For the given option, this value is –4.75615.

As S approaches 0, meaning the option is deep out of the money, Theta approaches the value of zero.

The maximum rate of dissipation is reached around the point where the option is at the money, more specifically when the spot price is slightly greater than the strike price, i.e. when:

$$S = \text{Strike} * \exp(\text{Risk-free rate} \times \text{time to maturity} + (\text{Vol}^2) \times \text{time to maturity}/2)$$

In this instance, the maximum value of Theta is reached when S = 108.464, as seen in the graph above and more clearly in the table below:

Spot	Theta
95	– 6.83533
100	– 7.25050
105	– 7.45810
108.4642	– 7.49615
110	–7.48933
115	–7.38496

Figure 271 Theta values for out and near money options

2 Theta and option time premium relative to volatility

The option's time premium is an increasing function of volatility. As volatility increases, the value of the option increases:

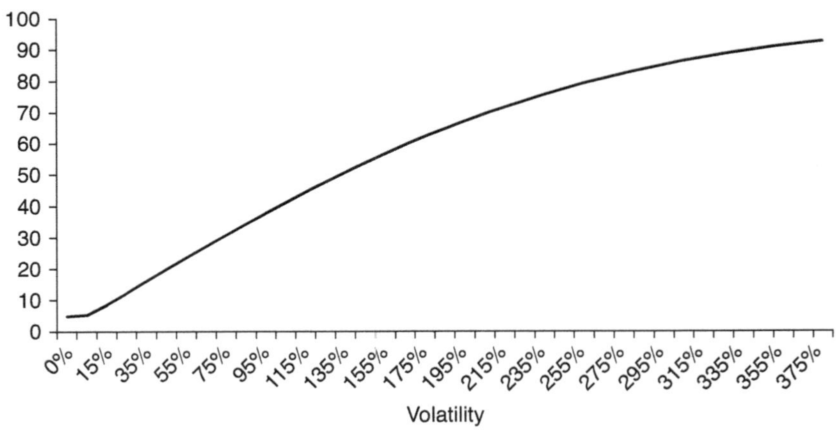

Figure 272 Option time premium against volatility
Source: FinanceTrainingCourse.com

While the option value declines over time regardless of the level of volatility:

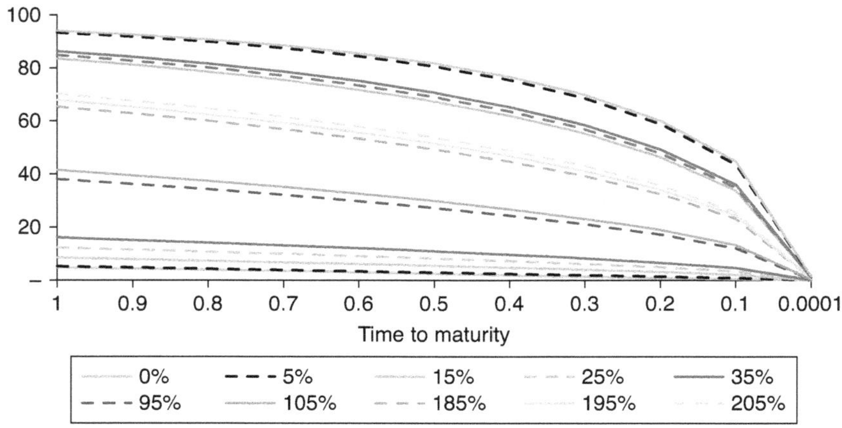

Figure 273 Option value against time to expiry
Source: FinanceTrainingCourse.com

The rate at which the time premium declines over time depends on the level of asset volatility. It is not a monotonic (i.e. only increasing or only decreasing) function in volatility.

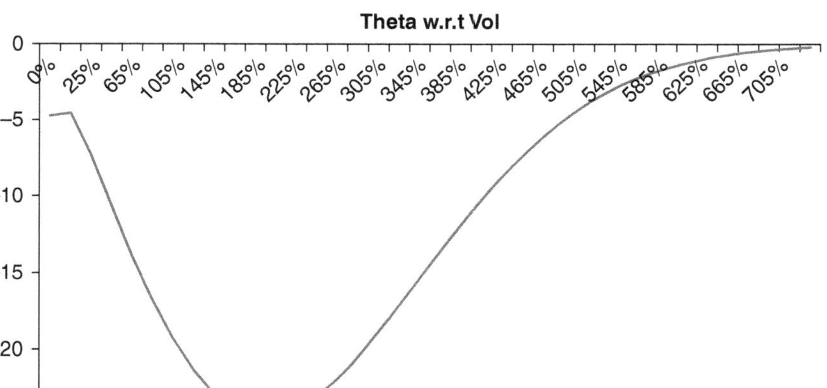

Figure 274 Theta against rising volatility
Source: FinanceTrainingCourse.com

3 Theta relative to time to maturity

As already seen above, the option value declines as the option approaches maturity; however, depending on the moneyness of the option, the Theta may be an increasing or a decreasing function of time:

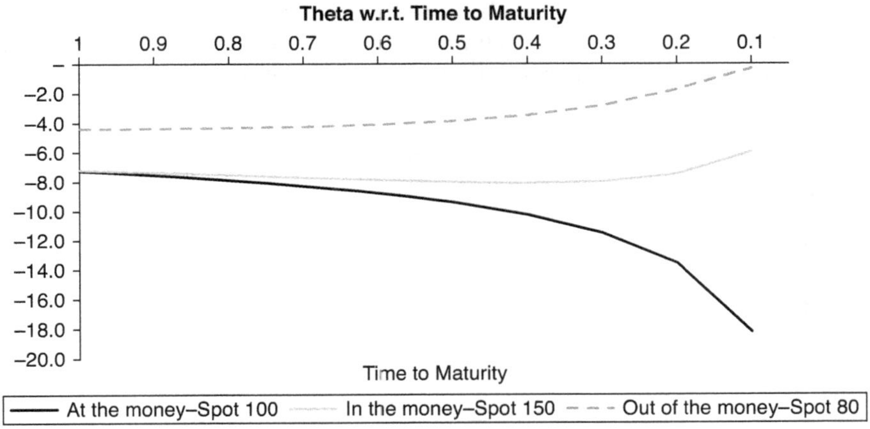

Figure 275 Theta against time to maturity and moneyness
Source: FinanceTrainingCourse.com

For in and out of the money options, the rate at which the option's time premium declines remains fairly constant over the life of the option, then decreases as the option approaches expiry. For at the money options, the rate of decay is much higher, increasing as the option approaches maturity.

4 Theta and option time premium relative to risk-free rate

The option's time premium increases as the risk-free rate increases.

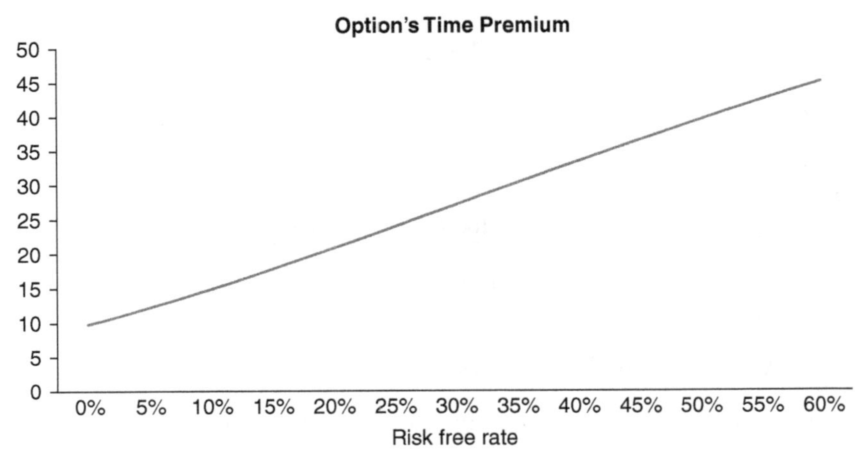

Figure 276 Time premium against risk-free rates
Source: FinanceTrainingCourse.com

At first glance, the option Theta also appears to be a monotonically decreasing function of the risk-free rate, declining as the risk-free rate increases, that is, as the risk-free rate increases, the rate of decay of the options time premium increases.

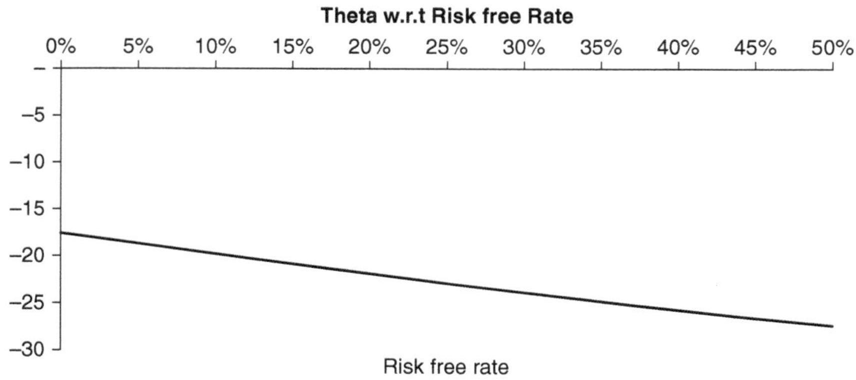

Figure 277 Theta against risk-free rates
Source: FinanceTrainingCourse.com

However, at extreme values of volatility, the rate of dissipation tends to reduce when the risk-free rate increases.

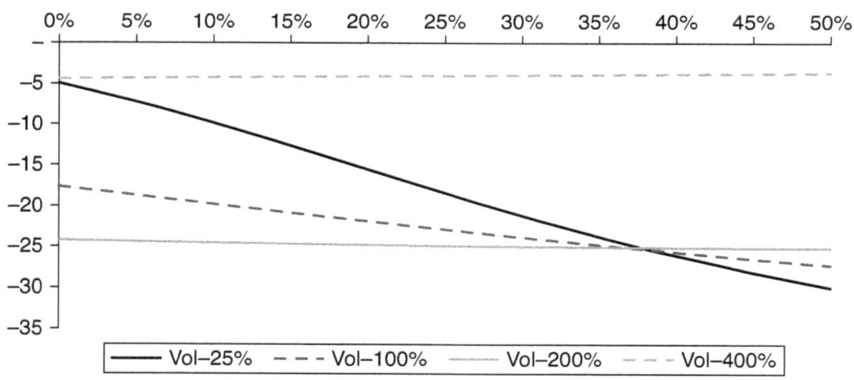

Figure 278 Theta against risk-free rates and bands of high volatility
Source: FinanceTrainingCourse.com

Appendix 1 Implied Volatility

Implied volatility is a tool for calibrating option pricing models based on market prices and using market expectations of future volatility rather than historical (empirical) volatility.

The process for finding implied volatility is the reverse of pricing an option; take the market price of an option, then derive the implied volatility from that price. In other words, now that we know the output, arrive at input volatility using this market price; hence the name implied volatility.

For our discussion, we will consider in the money, out of money and at the money options.

a Calculating implied volatility using Excel

We start with out of money call options with one year to expiry. Assume we have the following inputs:

Parameter	Explanation	Inputs
S_0	stock price at time zero	140
K	strike or exercise price	200
r	continuously compounded risk free rate	7%
q	continuous dividend yield rate on the underlying stock	2%
σ	annualized volatility of the stock price	
T	time to maturity of the option (in years)	1

Figure 279 Implied volatility using Excel – inputs
Source: FinanceTrainingCourse.com

Note that r, q and T will remain the same for all the cases. We are interested in just changing the stock price at time zero S_0 and the strike price K, and then using the market price of the option to arrive at the implied volatility, which is the unknown in the Black–Scholes call option price equation.

The volatility box is shaded black because we are still in the dark as to its value.

Let's assume that the market price of call option is US$18. Using Excel's Goal Seek function, we determine the volatility that will generate a Black–Scholes call option price of US$18.

The following image shows the Goal Seek setup.

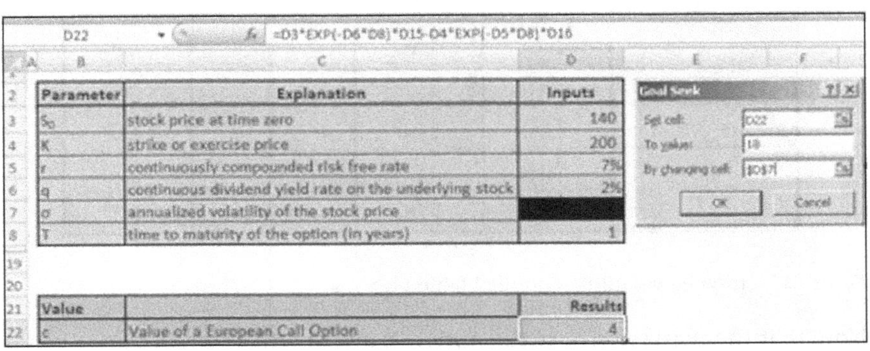

Figure 280 Using Goal Seek to calculate implied volatility
Source: FinanceTrainingCourse.com

In Excel, go to the Data tab, then to What-if Analysis and select Goal Seek. Currently for a dummy volatility of 30.52%, the Black–Scholes call option value has been calculated as US$4. However, we now want to set this value (cell **D22**) equal to US$18 and see what the resultant volatility would be. Hence we do this by changing volatilities (cell **D7**). On pressing OK, the Goal Seek functionality solves for the defined parameters using an iterative process and arrives at the solution below.

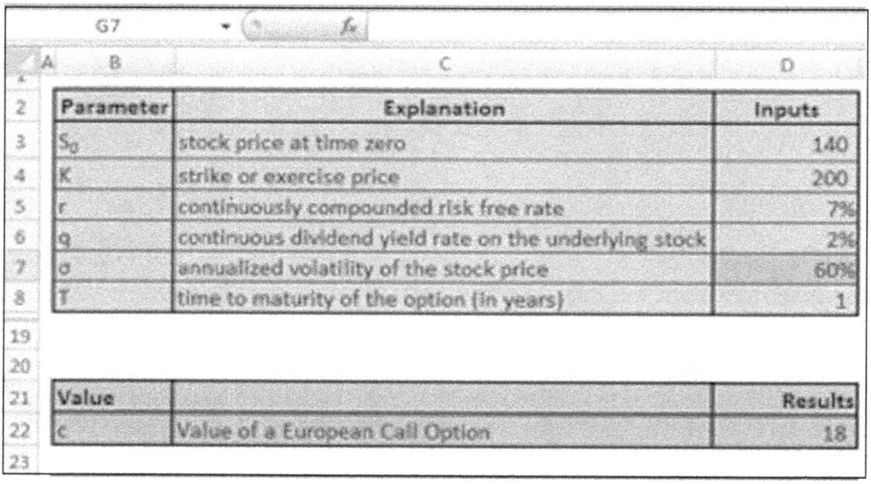

Parameter	Explanation	Inputs
S_0	stock price at time zero	140
K	strike or exercise price	200
r	continuously compounded risk free rate	7%
q	continuous dividend yield rate on the underlying stock	2%
σ	annualized volatility of the stock price	60%
T	time to maturity of the option (in years)	1

Value		Results
c	Value of a European Call Option	18

Figure 281 Implied volatility using Excel – result of the Goal Seek

The Goal Seek result is an implied volatility of 60%.

Using the same Goal Seek function and the approach specified above, we attempt to fill the following table.

	S_0	k	implied vol	price
in the money	140	110		50
	140	120		35
at the money	140	140		20
out of money	140	180		15
	140	200	60%	18

Figure 282 Implied volatility – unfilled table

Note that the market price of the option is already filled in. The price is not calculated but obtained from the market. Using the Goal Seek function four times in turn, with each revised combination of spot, strike and call option price, the table is populated as shown here.

	S_0	k	implied vol	price
in the money	140	110	63%	50
	140	120	40%	35
at the money	140	140	31%	20
out of money	140	180	46%	15
	140	200	60%	18

Figure 283 Implied volatilities – filled table

Appendix 2 Formula and Plot Reference

- For convenience, this reference guide has been broken down into three sections:Greeks Formula Reference
- Greeks Plot – a visual review of option Greeks across dimensions and moneyness
- Greeks Plot – Vega and Rho edition

While there are many ways of dissecting Greeks, a framework is always useful. Here are some basic ground rules.

1. Remember the first-order Greeks and separate them from second-order sensitivities. **Delta, Theta and Rho** are firs-order (linear) Greeks, which means that they will be different for call options and put options. Gamma and Vega are second-order (non-linear) Greeks, which means that they use the same values for calls and puts.
2. Remember that in most cases Greeks behave differently depending on the moneyness of the option. Greeks will behave and look differently between deep out, at, near and deep in the money options.
3. Think how the Greeks will change or move as you change the following parameters:
   - Spot
   - Strike Price
   - Time to Maturity or Expiry
   - Volatility of the Underlying
   - Interest Rates.

Rather than remembering the formula, try to remember behaviour, shape and shifts. For example, see the following three panels that show the shift in the shape of the five Greeks across spot prices and moneyness. Starting off with a deep out of money call option we plot the same curves for an at or near money call option as well as a deep in money option. Can you see the shift and the transition?

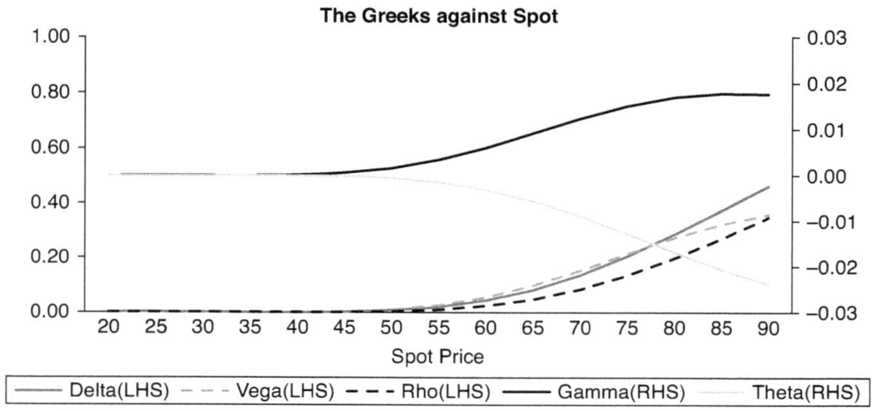

Figure 284 Delta, Gamma, Vega, Theta and Rho for a deep out of money call option
Source: FinanceTrainingCourse.com

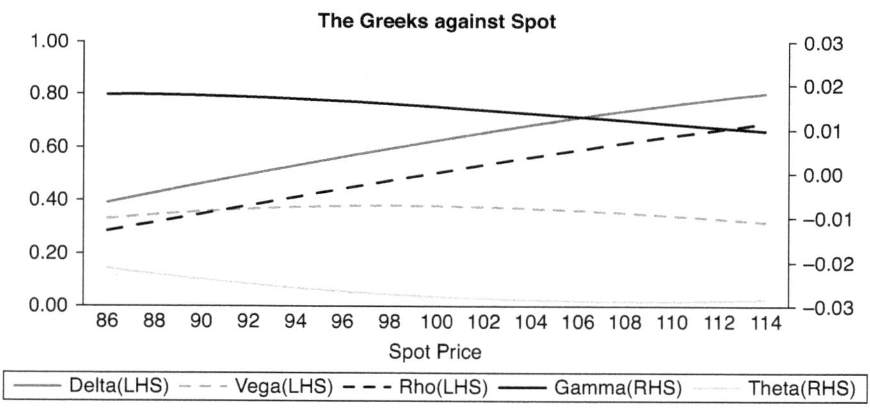

Figure 285 Delta, Gamma, Vega, Theta and Rho for at and near money call option
Source: FinanceTrainingCourse.com

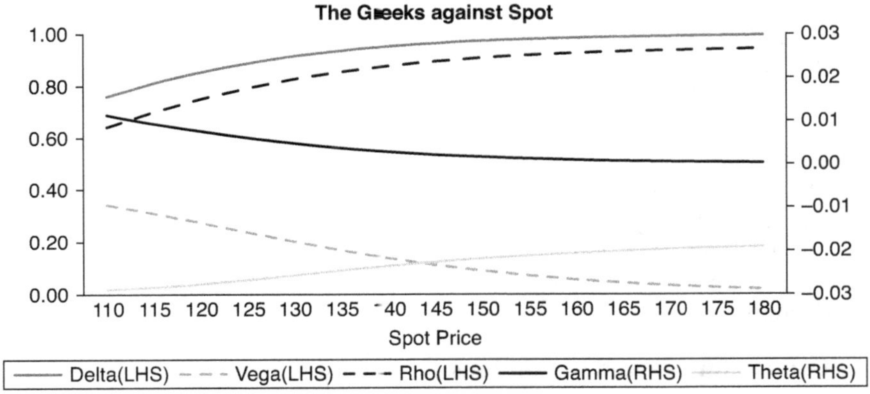

Figure 286 Delta, Gamma, Vega, Theta and Rho for a deep in money call option
Source: FinanceTrainingCourse.com

They are snapshots of the same curve, sliced into three different frames.

i Greeks formula summarized reference – continuous edition

We present calculation equations and definition references for Greeks presented in this book.

a Delta for a call option

$$Delta_{call} = \frac{\partial C}{\partial S} = N(d_1)$$

$$d_1 = \frac{\ln\left(\frac{S}{K}\right) + \left(r + \frac{\sigma^2}{2}\right)(T-t)}{\sigma\sqrt{T-t}}$$

where
S = Stock spot price
σ = Implied volatility
r = Risk-free rate
T = Time to maturity in years
t = Current time

b Delta for a put option

$$Delta_{put} = \frac{\partial P}{\partial S} = N(d_1) - 1$$

$$d_1 = \frac{\ln\left(\frac{S}{K}\right) + \left(r + \frac{\sigma^2}{2}\right)(T-t)}{\sigma\sqrt{T-t}}$$

where
S = Stock spot price
σ = Implied volatility
r = Risk-free rate
T = Time to maturity in years
t = Current time

c Gamma for call and put options

$$Gamma = \frac{\partial Delta}{\partial S} = \frac{N'(d_1)}{S\sigma\sqrt{T-t}}$$

$$N'(d_1) = \frac{1}{\sqrt{2\pi}} e^{-(d_1)^2/2}$$

$$d_1 = \frac{\ln\left(\frac{S}{K}\right) + \left(r + \frac{\sigma^2}{2}\right)(T-t)}{\sigma\sqrt{T-t}}$$

where
S = Stock spot price
σ = Implied volatility
r = Risk-free rate
T = Time to maturity in years
t = Current time

d Vega for call and put options

$$Vega = S\sqrt{T-t}N'(d_1)e^{-q(T-t)}$$

$$N'(d_1) = \frac{1}{\sqrt{2\pi}} e^{-(d_1)^2/2}$$

$$d_1 = \frac{\ln\left(\frac{S}{K}\right) + \left(r + \frac{\sigma^2}{2}\right)(T-t)}{\sigma\sqrt{T-t}}$$

where
S = Stock spot price
σ = Implied volatility
r = Risk-free rate
T = Time to maturity in years
t = Current time
q = Dividend rate

e Vanna for call and put options

$$vanna = e^{-qt}\sqrt{T-t}N'(d_1)\left(\frac{d_2}{\sigma}\right)$$

where
S = Stock spot price
σ = Implied volatility
r = Risk-free rate
T = Time to maturity in years
t = Current time
q = Dividend rate

$$N'(d_1) = \frac{1}{\sqrt{2\pi}}e^{-(d_1)^2/2}$$

$$d_1 = \frac{\ln\left(\frac{S}{K}\right)+\left(r+\frac{\sigma^2}{2}\right)(T-t)}{\sigma\sqrt{T-t}}$$

The assumption of zero dividends simplifies the above equation to:

$$vanna = \sqrt{T-t}N'(d_1)\left(\frac{d_2}{\sigma}\right)$$

f Volga for call and put options

$$volga = e^{-qt}\sqrt{T-t}N'(d_1)\left(\frac{d_1 d_2}{\sigma}\right)$$

where
S = Stock spot price
σ = Implied volatility
r = Risk-free rate

T = Time to maturity in years
t = Current time
q = Dividend rate

$$N'(d_1) = \frac{1}{\sqrt{2\pi}} e^{-(d_1)^2/2}$$

$$d_1 = \frac{\ln\left(\frac{S}{K}\right) + \left(r + \frac{\sigma^2}{2}\right)(T-t)}{\sigma\sqrt{T-t}}$$

$$d_2 = d_1 - \sigma\sqrt{T-t}$$

The assumption of zero dividends simplifies the above equation to:

$$volga = \sqrt{T-t}N'(d_1)\left(\frac{d_1 d_2}{\sigma}\right)$$

or

$$volga = Vega\left(\frac{d_1 d_2}{S\sigma}\right)$$

g Theta for a call option

$$Theta_{call} = \frac{\partial C}{\partial(T-t)}$$

$$Theta_{call} = \frac{-SN'(d_1)\sigma e^{-q(T-t)}}{2\sqrt{T-t}} + qSN(d_1)e^{-q(T-t)} - rKN(d_2)e^{-r(T-t)}$$

Assuming zero dividends reduces the above formula to:

$$Theta_{call} = \frac{\partial C}{\partial(T-t)} = \frac{-SN'(d_1)\sigma}{2\sqrt{T-t}} - rKN(d_2)e^{-r(T-t)}$$

h Theta for a put option

$$Theta_{put} = \frac{\partial C}{\partial(T-t)} = \frac{-SN'(d_1)\sigma e^{-q(T-t)}}{2\sqrt{T-t}} - qSN(-d_1)e^{-q(T-t)} + rKN(-d_2)e^{-r(T-t)}$$

Simplifies to the following for zero dividends:

$$Theta_{put} = \frac{\partial C}{\partial(T-t)} = \frac{-SN'(d_1)\sigma}{2\sqrt{T-t}} + rKN(-d_2)e^{-r(T-t)}$$

i Rho for a call option

$$Rho_{call} = K(T-t)e^{-r(T-t)}N(d_2)$$

$$d_1 = \frac{Ln\left(\frac{S}{K}\right) + \left(r + \frac{\sigma^2}{2}\right)(T-t)}{\sigma\sqrt{T-t}}$$

$$d_2 = d_1 - \sigma\sqrt{T-t}$$

where
S = Stock spot price
σ = Implied volatility
r = Risk-free rate
T = Time to maturity in years
t = Current time
q = Dividend rate

j Rho for a put option

$$Rho_{put} = -K(T-t)e^{-r(T-t)}N(-d_2)$$

ii Greeks formula reference – discrete edition

a Delta

$$\frac{OP_2 - OP_1}{S_2 - S_1}$$

where
OP_2 = New option price after the change in spot price
OP_1 = Old option price before the change in spot price
S_2 = New spot rate
S_1 = Old spot rate

b Theta

$$\frac{OP_2 - OP_1}{t_2 - t_1}$$

where
OP_2 = New option price after the change in period
OP_1 = Old option price before the change in period
$t_2 - t_1$ = Change in time (in years)

c Vega

$$\frac{(OP_2 - OP_1)}{(v_2 - v_1)} * 100$$

where
OP_2 = New option price after the change in volatility price
OP_1 = Old option price before the change in volatility price
$v_2 - v_1$ = Change in volatility

d Rho

$$\frac{(OP_2 - OP_1)}{(r_2 - r_1)} * 100$$

where
OP_2 = New option price after the change in risk-free rate
OP_1 = Old option price before the change in risk-free rate
$r_2 - r_1$ = Change in risk-free rate

e Gamma

(*Note*: The approximations work when we take only one of the Greeks as a discrete variable, therefore my previous approach was wrong.)

$$\frac{(OP_3 - 2OP_2 + OP_1)}{(S_2 - S_1)^2}$$

where
OP_3 = New option price after a unit increase in spot price
OP_2 = Old option price
OP_1 = New option price after a unit decrease in spot price
S_2 = New spot rate
S_1 = Old spot rate

iii Greeks suspects gallery

a Greeks against spot prices

Earlier we showed the shifts and transitions for deep out, at and deep in the money call options. Here is the short series for deep in, at and deep out of money put options.

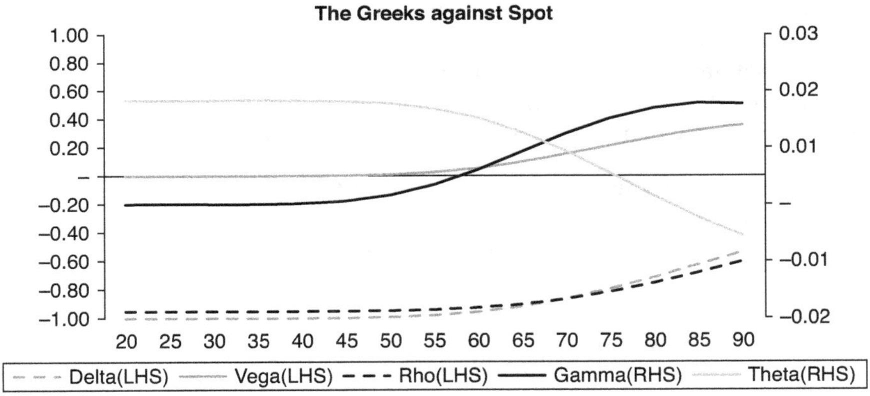

Figure 287 Deep in money put options – Greeks plot
Source: FinanceTrainingCourse.com

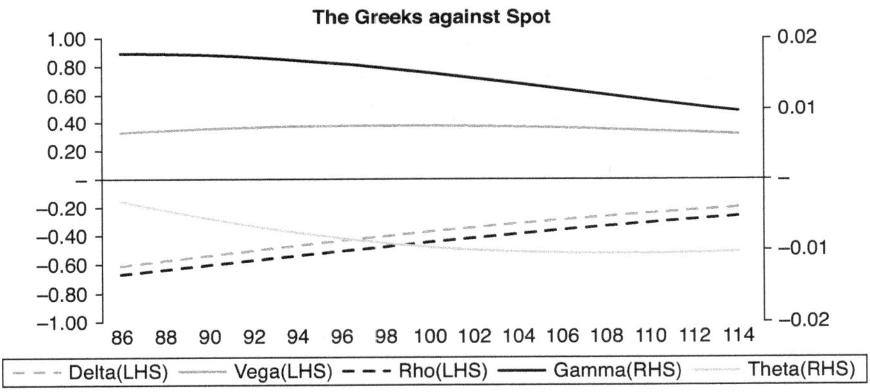

Figure 288 At the money put options – Greeks plot
Source: FinanceTrainingCourse.com

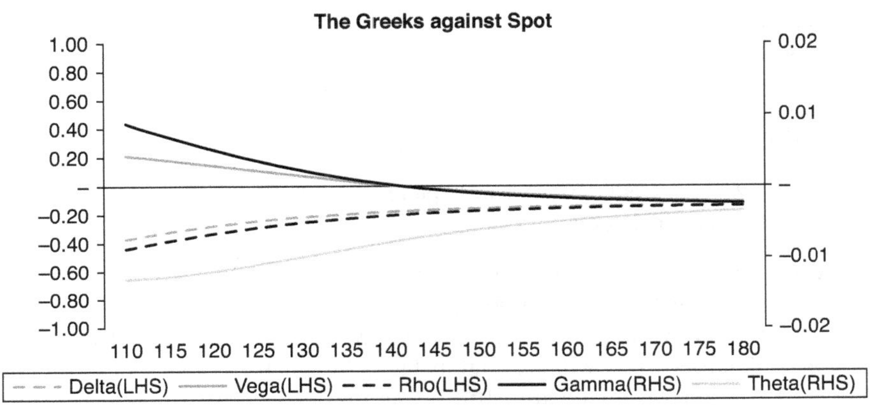

Figure 289 Deep out of money put option – Greeks plot
Source: FinanceTrainingCourse.com

The way to read the earlier graphical sets and the one above is to take one Greek at a time. So, starting with Delta you will see that while the shape is the same, the sign is different between the call and the put. While there are some similarities between the deep out of money call and the deep in money put, they disappear completely when we look at the deep out of money put contracts.

b Plotting Greeks against changing volatility

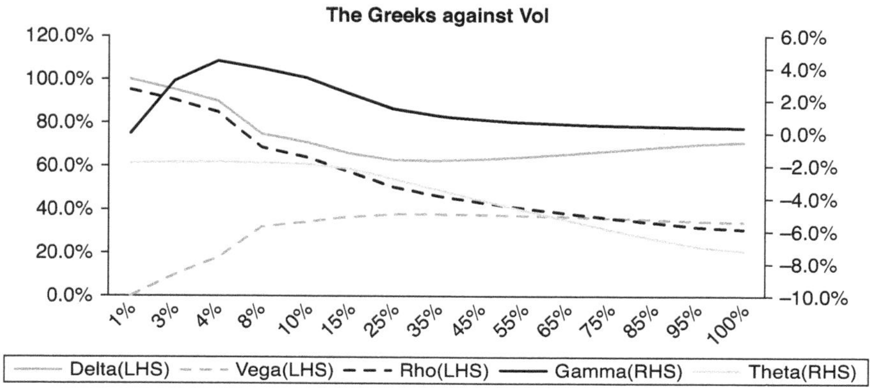

Figure 290 At money call option – Greeks plot against changing volatilities
Source: FinanceTrainingCourse.com

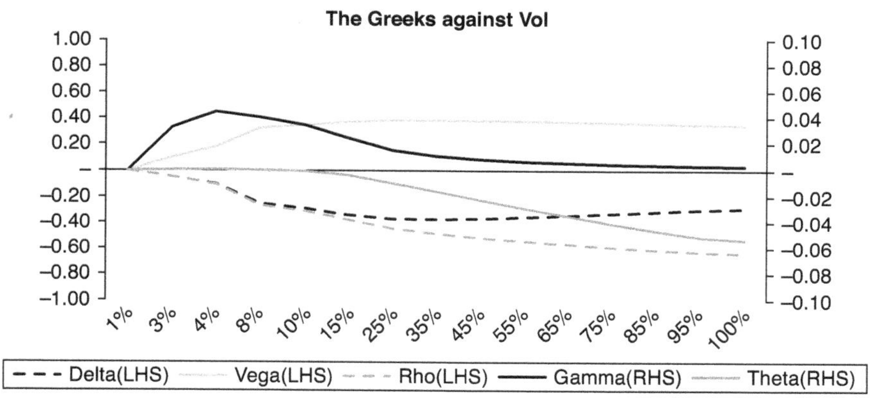

Figure 291 At money put option – Greeks plot against changing volatilities
Source: FinanceTrainingCourse.com

However, the difference really crops up between calls and puts when you switch the frame of reference from changing spot prices to changing volatilities. From this new point of view, calls and put are clearly different animals. Why is that? If you look closely, you will see that as far as Vega, Delta, Theta and Rho are concerned, the basic shape and shift are similar; they look different because the LHS axis has shifted. Delta and Theta vary across calls and puts.

c Greeks – an alternate dimension

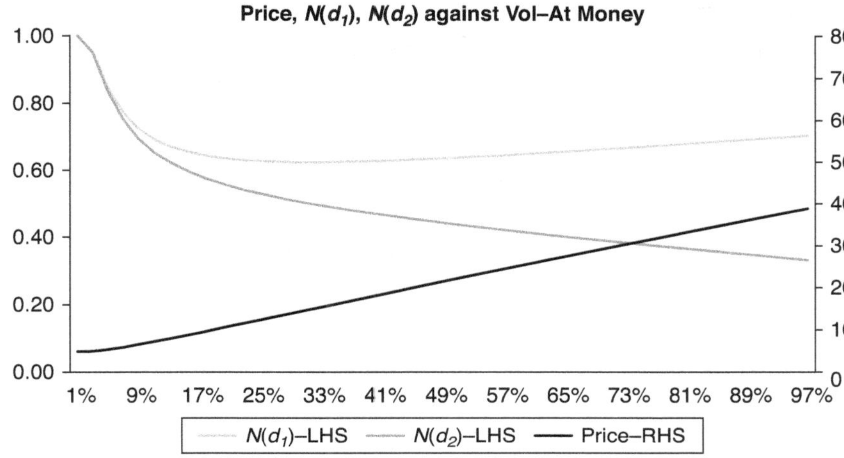

Figure 292 Plotting $N(d_1)$, $N(d_2)$ and price against volatility
Source: FinanceTrainingCourse.com

What do you think audiences expect when they see figures of the Greeks plotted against volatilities for at the money options? Do you see a contradiction? Take a look at Delta. Then think about how we calculate Delta for a European call option. We look at $N(d_1)$ as a conditional probability. Intuitively speaking, what should we expect $N(d_1)$ to do as volatility rises? Rise or fall? What is $N(d_1)$ doing in that figure?

Now take a look at figure immediately above. What are $N(d_1)$ and $N(d_2)$ doing as volatility rises? Is that intuitive or counterintuitive?

iv Greeks suspects gallery – Vega and Rho edition

a Vega plots for at the money European call (put) options

Vega, like Gamma, uses the same calculation function for European call and put options. The plot below will remain the same for a European call or put option.

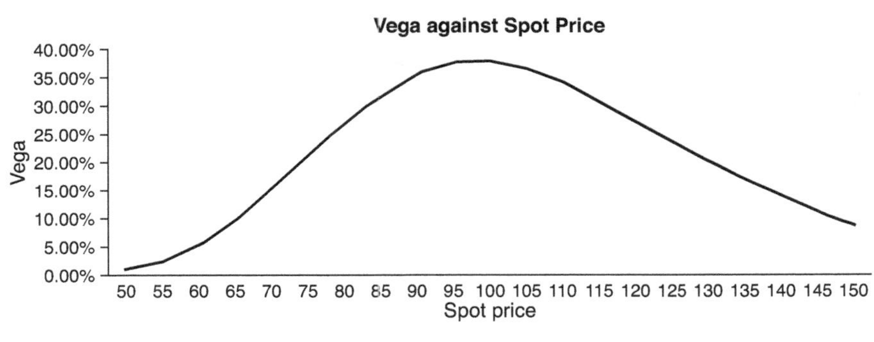

Figure 293 Vega plot against changing spot for at the money call options

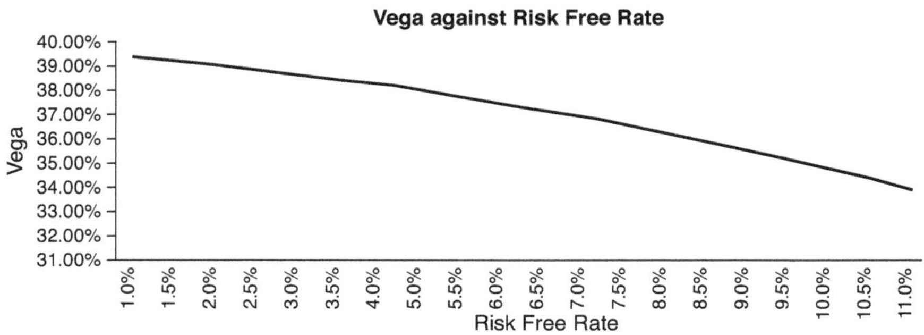

Figure 294 Vega plot against changing risk-free rate for at the money call options

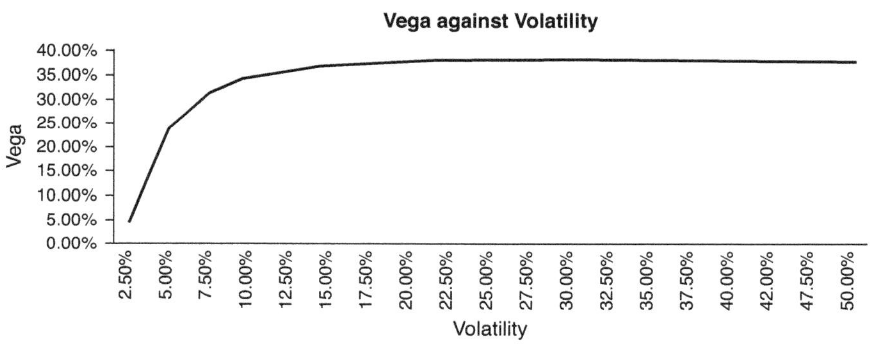

Figure 295 Vega plot against changing volatility for at the money call options

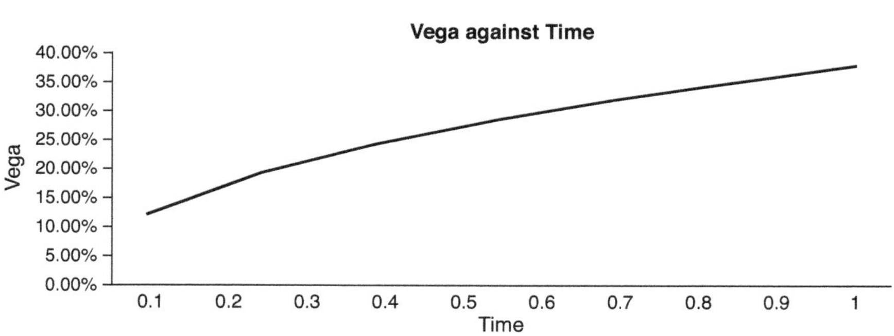

Figure 296 Vega plot against changing time for at the money call options

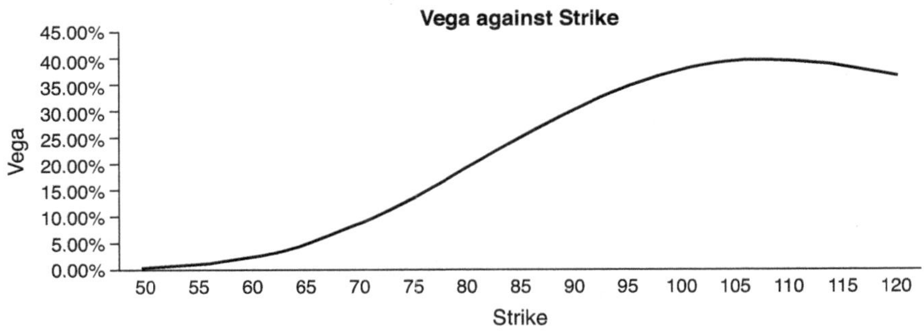

Figure 297 Vega plot against changing strike for at the money call options

b Rho plots for at the money call and put options

In the case of Rho, the overall shape of the curve remains the same, but in the case of European call and put options it is pegged to a different scale. The only exception to this is the plot of Rho against time, where the curves go in the opposite direction.

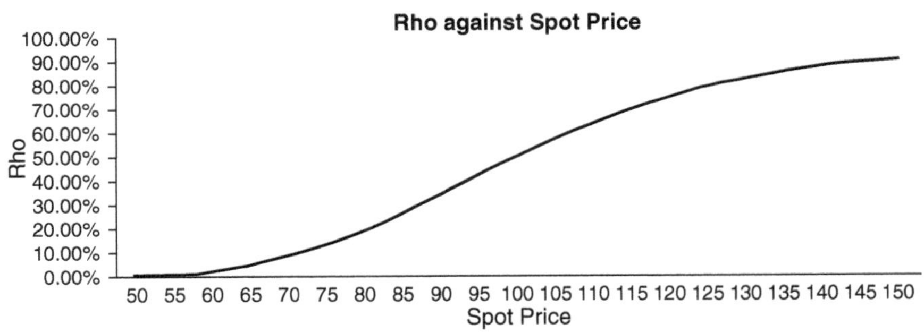

Figure 298 Rho plot against changing spot for at the money call options

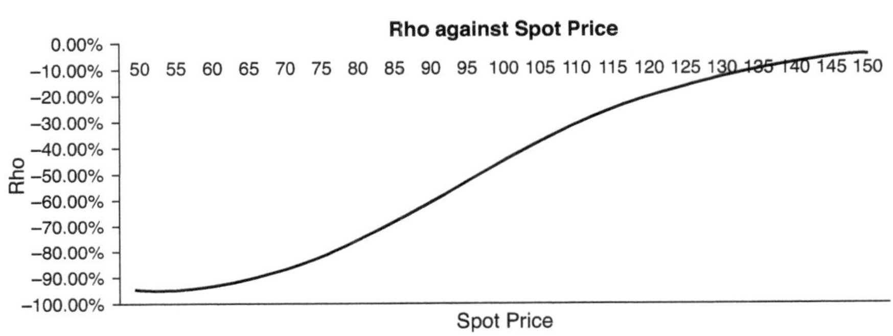

Figure 299 Rho plot against changing spot for at the money put options

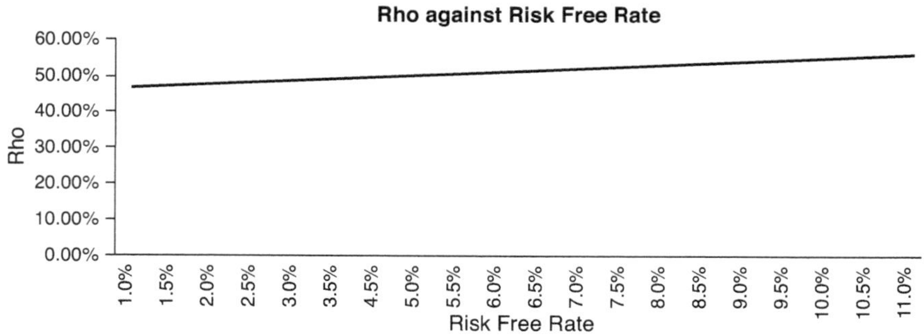

Figure 300 Rho plot against changing risk-free rates for at the money call options

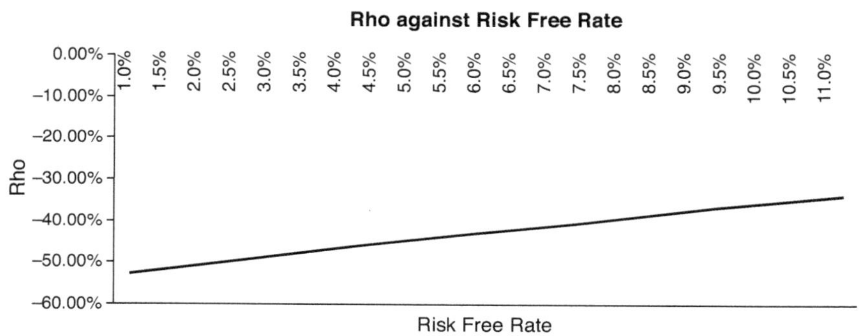

Figure 301 Rho plot against changing risk-free rates for at the money put options

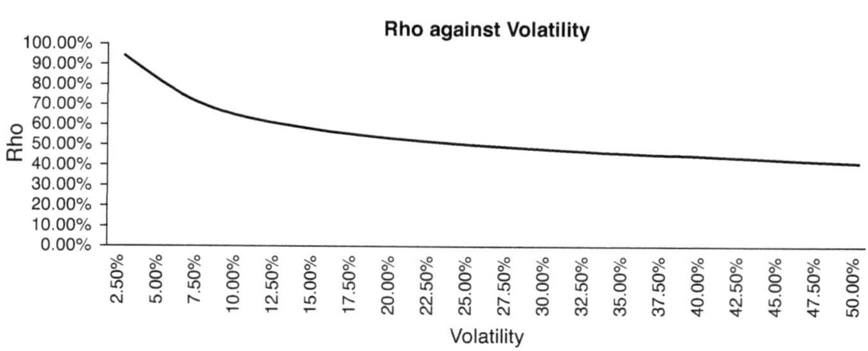

Figure 302 Rho plot against changing volatility for at the money call options

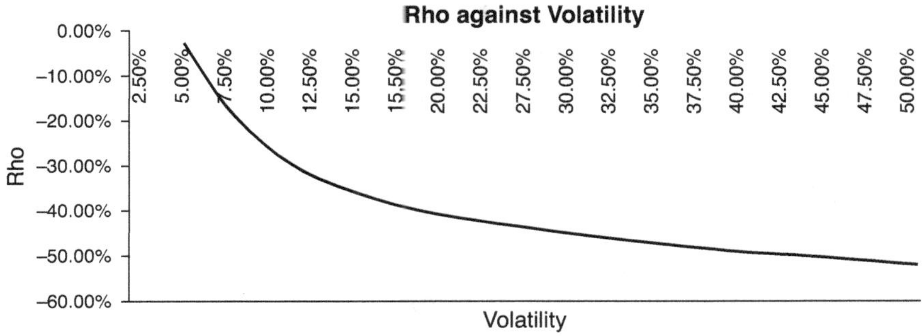

Figure 303 Rho plot against changing volatility for at the money put options

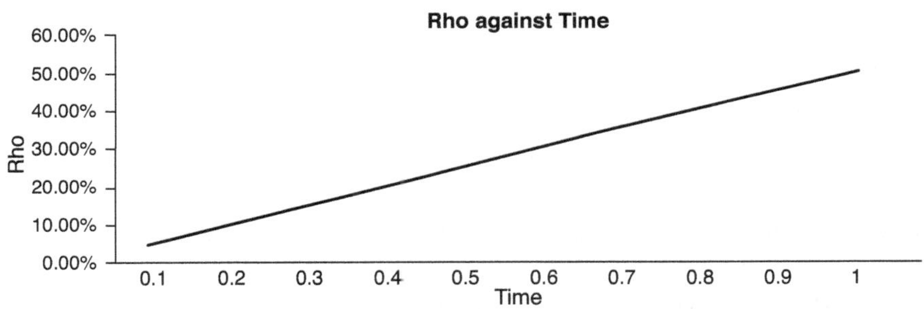

Figure 304 Rho plot against changing time for at the money call options

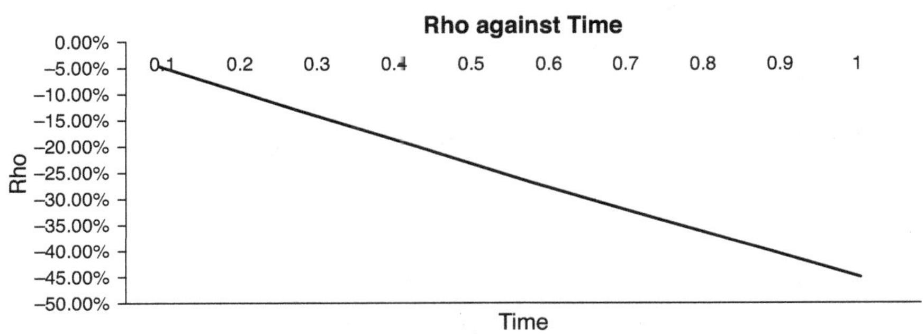

Figure 305 Rho plot against changing time for at the money put options

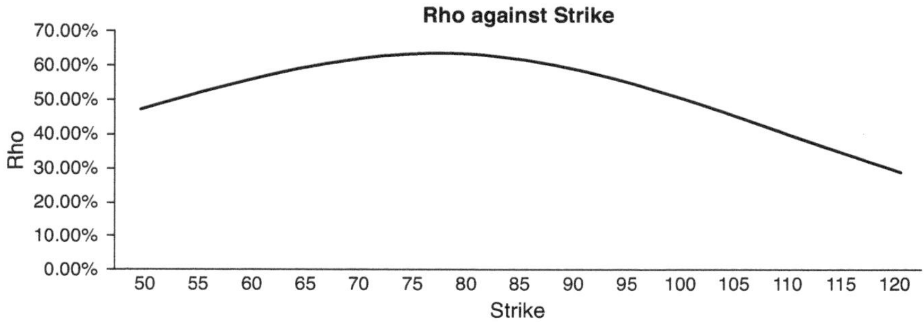

Figure 306 Rho plot against changing strike for at the money call options

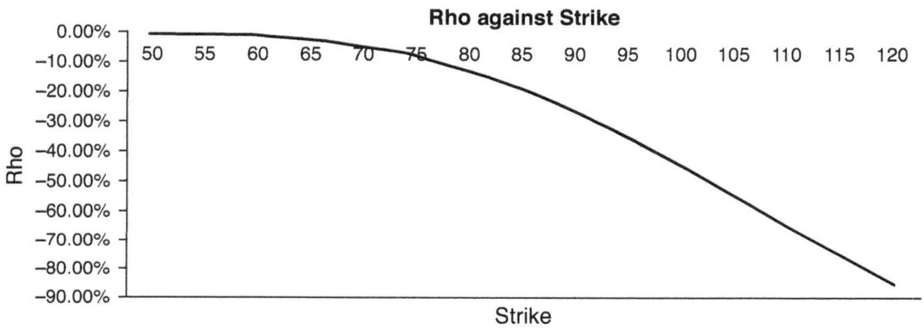

Figure 307 Rho plot against changing strike for at the money put options

Appendix 3 Drift, Diffusion and Volatility Drag Using MC Simulation

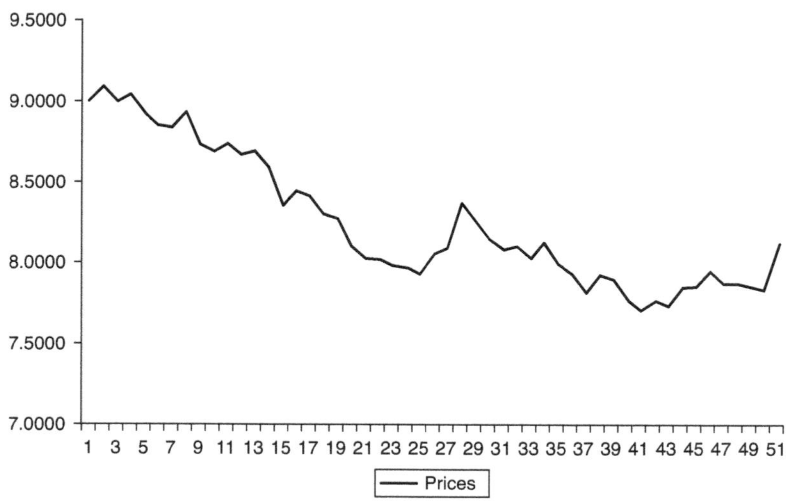

Figure 308 Price series generated using Monte Carlo simulation

Let's take a look at our standard rate of change equation for the change in price of a financial security from one step to another.

$$ds = \mu S dt + \sigma S dz$$

We introduce our friend mu (μ) as drift, and sigma as diffusion (or standard deviation or volatility, or vol for short). We use the process of Monte Carlo simulation to generate stock prices.[2] While the process assumes equity securities by default, the same underlying structure, with some tweaks, is used to generate rates and returns for currencies, commodities and (some) interest-bearing securities.

The solution for our equation is presented in discrete form below. In a risk-neutral world, the risk-free rate r replaces mu (μ).

$$S_t = S_0 e^{(\mu - \frac{1}{2}\sigma^2)t + \sigma\sqrt{t}z_t}$$

Let's run a simple experiment; we want to see how drift and diffusion interact using a simple base case. We have two variables that can each assume two values, hence four possible variations:

	EAN (MU, DRIFT, RISK FREE RATE R)	SD (SIGMA, DIFFUSION, VOL)
Zero drift, Zero volatility	0	0
Unit drift, Zero volatility	1%	0
Zero drift, Unit volatility	0	1%
Unit drift, Unit volatility	1%	1%

Figure 309 Parameters for thought experiments

Source: FinanceTrainingCourse.com

a MC simulation results – the drift and diffusion showcase

Here are the graphical results from a Monte Carlo simulator, built in Excel.

The simulated values have been plotted to give a more visual idea of the direction and trend of simulation results. The starting or initial spot price for the simulated security is 10. For each of the graphs, we plug in values from one of the rows provided in the table above.

To get the most out of the experiment, before you proceed, take out a flat sheet of paper and plot the four curves as you expect them. Then when you get the actual results compare your projections with them.

b The zero drift, zero diffusion case

The first case is zero drift and zero volatility. The simulation plot is a flat line going nowhere.

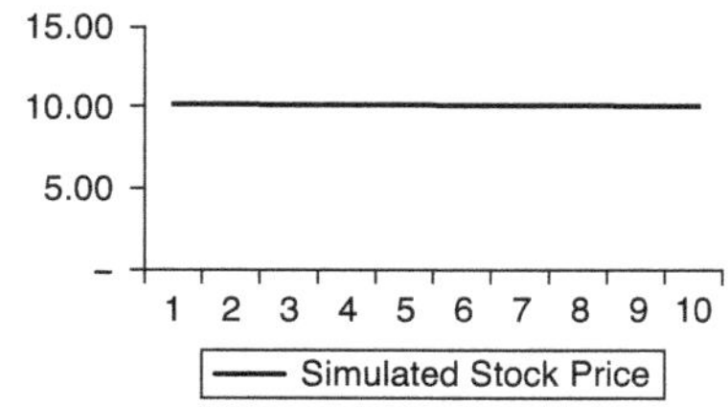

Figure 310 Zero drift, zero diffusion case
Source: FinanceTrainingCourse.com

c The unit drift, zero diffusion case

The second case is unit drift and zero volatility. The simulation plot is a flat line going upwards. The unit drift grows the trend at a 45% angle line per unit of time, and there is no uncertainty.

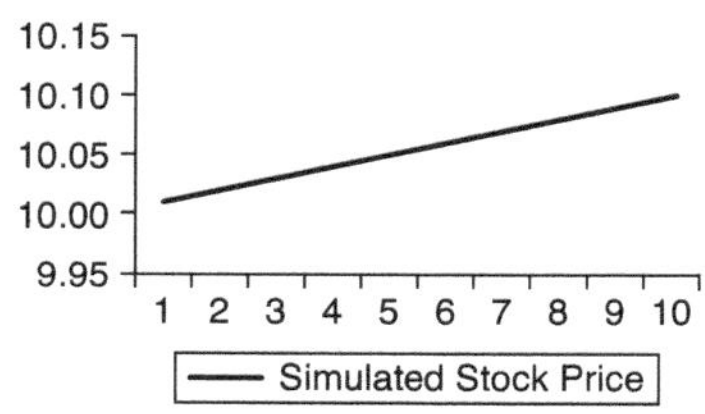

Figure 311 Unit drift, zero diffusion case
Source: FinanceTrainingCourse.com

This is similar to the exponential curve we see for bond pricing on a continuously compounded basis. There is a clear upward trend with no uncertainty or volatility. However, the shape is not exponential despite the fact that the underlying equation clearly belongs to that family.

The reason is the short time step combined with the low value of applicable interest rates in our simulation model. When you change both to higher values, the exponential curve become visible.

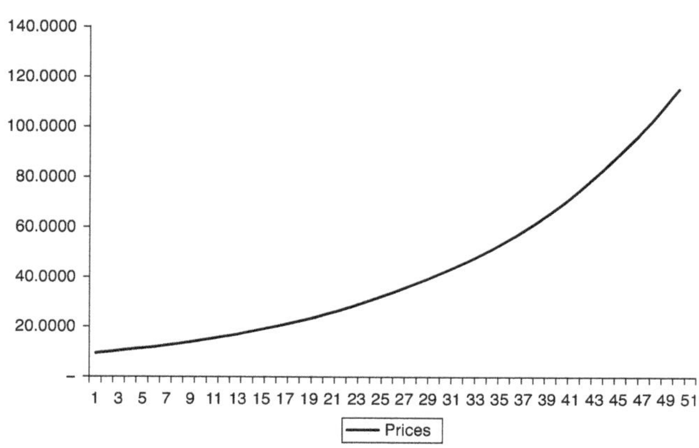

Figure 312 Unit drift, zero diffusion case
Source: FinanceTrainingCourse.com

d The zero drift, unit diffusion case

The third case is zero drift and unit volatility; we can now see that while the overall trend is flat there is now some uncertainty in results.

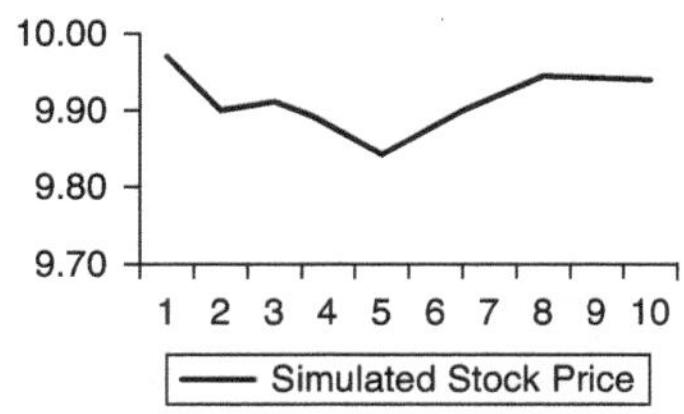

Figure 313 Zero drift, unit diffusion case – scenario 1
Source: FinanceTrainingCourse.com

Within our Excel Monte Carlo simulator, every time we press F9, the chart will change, and while with this level of volatility there will be instances of directional trends (both upwards and downwards), a large majority of cases will still have a flat trend.

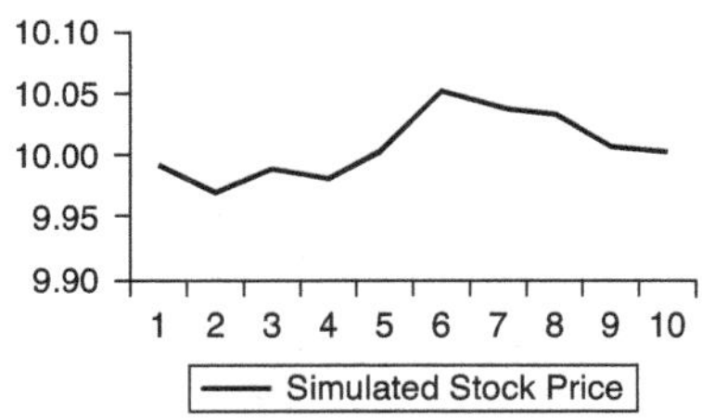

Figure 314 Zero drift, unit diffusion case – scenario 2
Source: FinanceTrainingCourse.com

e The unit drift, unit diffusion case

The final case is unit drift and unit volatility. A clear up trend is now visible. Once again, while there may be some instances of downward and flat trends for these values, in a majority of cases the price trend will be upwards and positive.

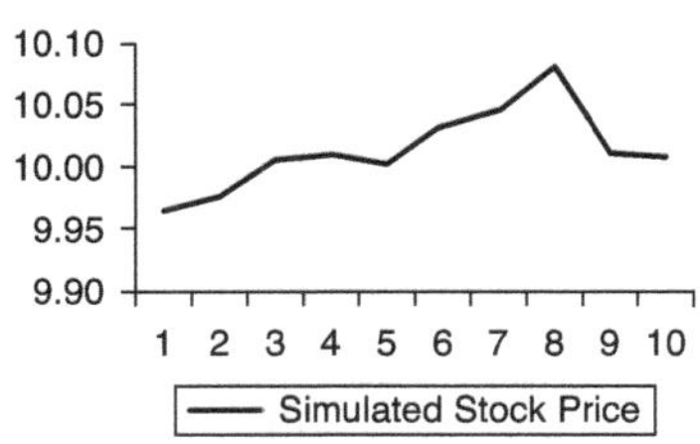

Figure 315 Unit drift, unit diffusion case
Source: FinanceTrainingCourse.com

f Understanding volatility drag or ½ sigma²

What happens if we increase the drift to five units from the original one? You will see that the up trend is now consistent across all iterations of the Monte Carlo simulation model. And the reason is that in the two-factor model, drift now dominates diffusion by 5 times.

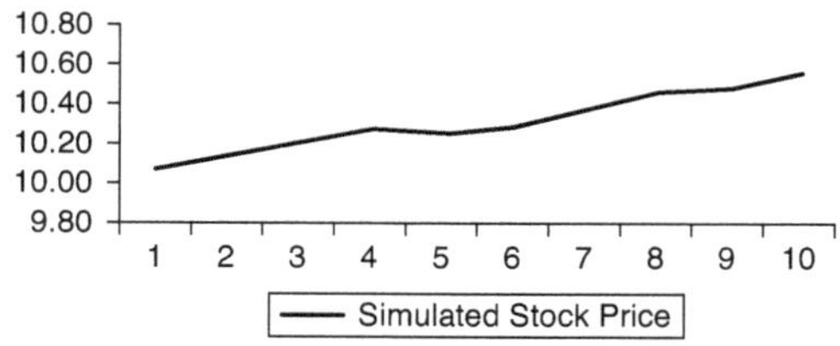

Figure 316 Drift dominates diffusion – positive returns
Source: FinanceTrainingCourse.com

If you increase volatility, in the same proportion, to five units and keep drift at the same level, you will still see a consistent up trend, but every once in a while a high enough dz (random) value will drag returns down, as in the simulation results below.

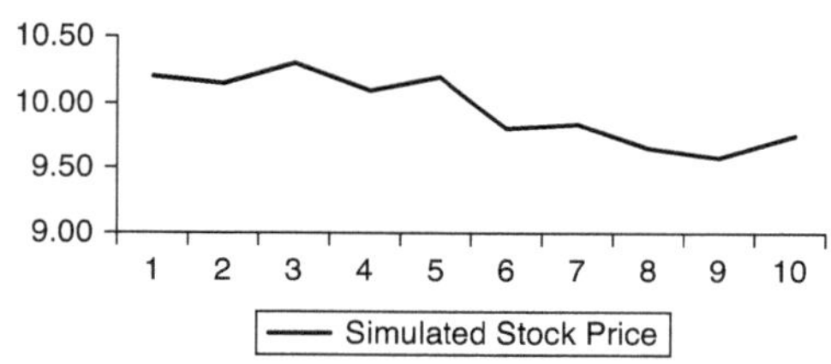

Figure 317 Equal higher values for drift and diffusion
Source: FinanceTrainingCourse.com

As you carry on increasing volatility (to 10 units and then 25) in proportion to drift, the frequency of flatter and downward returns will increase.

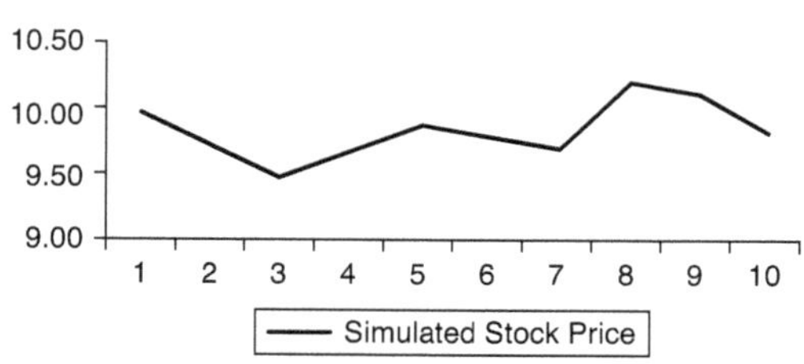

Figure 318 Higher volatility impact – scenario 1
Source: FinanceTrainingCourse.com

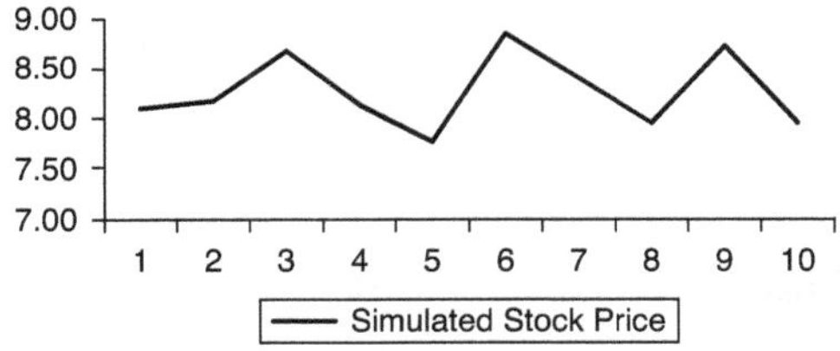

Figure 319 Higher volatility impact – scenario 2
Source: FinanceTrainingCourse.com

This is the impact of volatility drag or subtraction of the ½ sigma² term in our Excel Monte Carlo simulation model. For significantly higher values of sigma, the term ½ sigma² will dominate r, resulting in consistently negative returns.

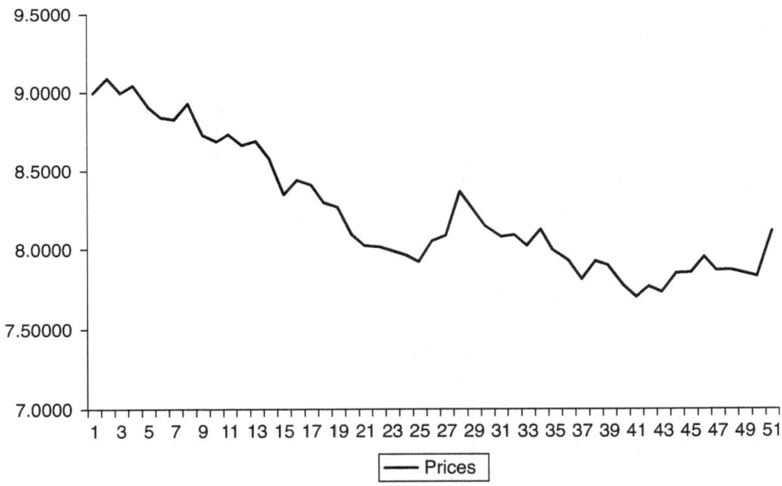

Figure 320 Diffusion dominates over drift – negative returns
Source: FinanceTrainingCourse.com

Notes

Introduction: Context

1. *Options, Futures and Other Derivatives* (Hull); *Paul Wilmott on Quantitative Finance* (Wilmott); *Models at Work* (Farid).
2. Convenience yield becomes a factor when options are written on commodities.
3. Informed Trading. See Joshua Turkington, David Walsh, 'Informed Traders and Their Market Preference' as well as Sugato Chakravarty, Huseyin Gulen & Stewart Mayhew, 'Informed Trading in Stock and Option Markets'.
4. *Models at Work*, Part II, Jawwad Ahmed Farid, Palgrave Macmillan, Dec 2013.
5. See 'The Holes in Black Scholes' by Fischer Black, *The New Corporate Finance*, ed Donald Chew.

1 Delta and Gamma

1. Taleb and others cover other Greeks.
2. *Dynamic Hedging, Section 2 – Measuring Options Risk*, Nicholas Nassim Taleb. John Wiley and Sons, 1997.
3. *Dynamic Hedging – Managing Vanilla and Exotic Options*, Nassim Taleb. Chapter 8: Gamma and Shadow Gamma, p.133.
4. *Derivatives Markets*, 3rd Edition, Pearson Series in Finance.
5. Common day-count conventions are Actual/360, Actual/365, Actual/Actual, 30/360 etc.

6 Understanding Volatility

1. Schmitz Abe Klaus, M. Giles and William Shaw, Pricing Exotic Options Using Improved Strong Convergence, Thesis, Oxford University, 2007.

8 Forward Implied Volatilities

1. *Dynamic Hedging, Managing Vanilla and Exotic Options*, Chapter 9, Nicholas Nassim Taleb, John Wiley & Sons.

9 Vega, Volga and Vanna

1. See *Dynamic Hedging, Vega and Volatility Surfaces*, Nicholas Nassim Taleb
2. Vanna, Eric Benhamou (ericbenhamou.net)
3. Volga, Eric Benhamou (ericbenhamou.net)
4. *Dynamic Hedging: Managing Vanilla and Exotic Options* – Nassim Taleb – Chapter 8: Gamma and Shadow Gamma, pp.138–142

10 Hedging Higher-Order Greeks

1. Based on and extended from Class Notes, Security Pricing, Professor Mark Broadie on multi period option portfolio optimization.

11 Reviewing the Solver Solution

1. See Numerical Analysis by Burden and Fairs or Numerical Methods for scientists and engineers by Hamming for a more detailed treatment of linear programming and the science of numerical optimization.

12 Rebalancing, Implied Vol and Rho

1. Riaz Ahmed, Paul Wilmott, 'Which free lunch would you like to have today, Sir...', Wilmott Magazine.

14 Option Prices and Time to Expiry

1. See 'A Closer look at Black–Scholes Option Thetas' – Douglas R. Emery, Weiyu Guo, Tie Su, October 2007.
2. For a detailed discussion of how to build Monte Carlo simulators in Excel, see *Models at Work*, Jawwad Ahmed Farid, Palgrave Macmillan, December 2013.

Further reading

Introduction

Bates, David S. "Empirical Option Pricing: A Retrospection." *Journal of Econometrics*, 116 (2003), 387–404.

Benhamou, Eric. "Option Position (risk) Management." Goldman Sachs International. Ericbenhamou.net.

Blamont, Daniel, and Pretty Sagoo. "Pricing and Hedging of Variable Annuities." Cutting Edge: 3944. Risk.net. Cutting Edge.

Christof Beuselinck, "Individual investors' Option Trading. Attention grabbing versus long term strategies." Tilbrug School of Economics & Management.

Holland, Allan. "Lecture 11: Black-Scholes and the 'Greeks'." Stochastic Optimisation and Derivatives for Energy Traders. University College Cork. <http://www.4c.ucc.ie/~aholland/bordgais/BG_Ch10.pdf>.

Hull, John C. *The Greek Letters, Options, Futures and Other Derivatives*. 6th ed. Pearson Prentice Hall, 2006, 363–396.

Joshua Turkington, David Walsh. "Informed Traders and Their Market Preference: Empirical Evidence from Prices and Volumes of Options and Stocks".

Liang Zhong, *Betting on Volatility: A Delta Hedging Approach*. Department of Mathematics, KTH, Stockholm, Sweden.

McDonald, Robert L. *Derivatives Markets*. 3rd ed. Pearson Prentice Hall, 2003.

Odegaard, Bernt Arne. "Financial Numerical Recipes." 9 September 1999. <http://cyber-bridgesfinancialderivatives.googlecode.com/files/recipes.pdf>.

Poulsen, Rolf. "Four Things You Might Not Know About The Black-Scholes Formula." *International Investor Journals*, 15 (2) (2007), 77–81.

Single, Saurab. "Option Greeks: A Detailed Graphical Treatment." Singapore Management University. QF 301. <http://www.saurabh.com/Site/Writings_files/qf301_greeks_small.pdf>.

Society of Actuaries. "Greeks." <rmtf.soa.org/greeks.pdf>.

Sugato Chakravarty, Huseyin Gulen & Stewart Mayhew. "Informed Trading in Stock and Option Markets." *The Journal of Finance*, LIX (3), June 2004.

Raju, Sudhakar. "Delta Gamma Hedging and the Black-Scholes Partial Differential Equation (PDE)." *Journal of Economics and Finance Education*, 11 (2), 2012, 51–62.

Yuhang Xing, Xiaoyan Zhang and Rui Zhao. "What Does Individual Option Volatility Smirk Tell Us About Future Equity Returns".

Zhong, Liang. *Betting on Volatility: A Delta Hedging Approach*. Department of Mathematics, KTH, Stockholm, Sweden. KTH, Stockholm, April 2011.

Hedging

Achdou, Yves, and Olivier Pironneau. *Computational Methods for Option Pricing*. Philadelphia: Society for Industrial and Applied Mathematics, 2005.

Alexander, Carol and Kaeck, Andreas. "Does Model Fit Matter For Hedging? Evidence from FTSE 100 Options." *Journal of Future Markets*, 2011.

Choudhry, Moorad. "Fixed-Income Securities and Derivatives." *Analysis and Valuation*. Bloomberg, 2010.

Chung, Pin and Evans, Kirk. "Equity-Based Insurance Guarantees Conference." Society of Actuaries, 18–19 November 2013.

Elder, John. "Greeks: Hedging with Options." Whoops – index.html <http://lamar.colostate.edu/~jelder/courses/derivatives/Lect_ppt/T15_Greek_Letters_HO.pdf>

Forde, Martin. "The Real P&L in Black-Scholes and Dupire Delta Hedging." *International Journal of Theoretical and Applied Finance*, 2003.

Horasanli, Mehmet. "Hedging Strategy for a Portfolio of Options and Stocks with Linear Programming." *Applied Mathematics and Computation*, 199, 2008, 804–10.

Jabbour, George, and Philip Budwick. *The Option Trader Handbook: Strategies and Trade Adjustments*. Hoboken, NJ: Wiley, 2010.

Kani, Iraj, Emanuel Derman, and Micheal Kamal. "Quantitative Strategies Research Notes." Goldman Sachs, August 1996.

Nielsen, Lars Tyge. *Pricing and Hedging of Derivatives Securities*. Oxford: Oxford UP, 1999.

Wilmott, Paul. *Paul Wilmott on Quantitative Finance*. Chichester: Wiley, 2006.

Woods, Brian. "On the Effectiveness of Edging Strategies for Variable Annuities." Society of Actuaries in Ireland, April 2014.

Higher-order Greeks

Alexander, Carol, and Leonardo M. Nogueira. "Hedging with Stochastic and Local Volatility." SMA Centre Discussion Papers in Finance, December 2004.

Alfred Lehar, Martin Scheicher, Christian Schittenkopf. "GARCH vs Stochastic Volatility: Option Pricing and Risk Management." Department of Business Studies, University of Vienna, Central Bank of Austria, Austrian Research Institute for Artificial Intelligence.

Benhamou, Eric. "Vanna." Goldman Sachs International. Ericbenhamou.net.

Benninga, Simon and Wiener, Zvi. "Dynamic Hedging Strategies." *Mathematics in Education and Research*, 7 (1), 1998.

Carr, Peter and Wu, Liuren, "Vega-Gamma-Vanna-Volga." Columbia University. 28 February 2011. <http://www.ccfr.org.cn/cicf2011/papers/20110108222110.pdf>

Castagna, Antonio. *FX Options and Smile Risk*. Hoboken, NJ: Wiley, 2010.

Castagna, Antonio and Mercurio, Fabio. "The Vanna-Volga Method for Implied Volatilities." Cutting Edge: 3944. Risk.net. Cutting Edge.

Catley Lakemen Securities. "A Jargon-Busting Guide to Volatility Surfaces and Changes in Implied Volatility." *Equity Derivatives Sales Market Commentary*, 23 April 2008.

Černý, Aleš. *Mathematical Techniques in Finance: Tools for Incomplete Markets*. Princeton, NJ: Princeton UP, 2004.

Crepey, Stephane. "Delta-hedging Vega Risk?" 10 January 2004.

Davis, Mark H. "The Dupire Formula." <http://www2.imperial.ac.uk/~mdavis/FDM11/DUPIRE_FORMULA.PDF>.

Duffy, Daniel J. *Financial Instrument Pricing Using C++*. Hoboken, NJ: John Wiley, 2004.

Emery, Douglas R., Weiyu Guo, and Tie Su. "A Closer Look at Black-Scholes option Thetas." 2007.

Feynman, Richard Philips. "Local Volatility Modelling." 13 July 2009.

Frederic Bossens, Gregory Rayee, Nikos S Skantzos, Griselda Deelstra. "Vanna-Volga Methods Applied to FX Derivatives: From Theory to Market Practice." May 2010.

Froyn, Sindre. "Computation of Greeks in Financial Markets Driven by Lévy Processes." Faculty of Mathematics and Natural Sciences, University of Oslo. May 2012.

Gatheral, Jim. *The Volatility Surface. A Practitioner's Guide*. John Wiley & Sons, Inc. 2006.

Gil, Miguel A. and Bennett, Colin. *Volatility Trading: Trading Volatility, Correlation, Term Structure and Skew*. Santander Investment Securities Inc., 16 April 2012.

Jackel, Peter. "Greeks with Monte Carlo." *Wilmott*, July 2001.

Jason. "Some Practical Issues in FX and Equity Derivatives." <http://www.iasonltd.com/FileUpload/files/pdf_res_1.pdf>

Kamal, Michael, and Jim Gatheral. "Implied Volatility Surface." <http://faculty.baruch.cuny.edu/jgatheral/ImpliedVolatilitySurface.pdf>.

Kapadia, Nikunj. "Negative Vega? Understanding Options on Spreads." *The Journal of Alternative Investments,* 75–79, 1999.

Louis H. Ederington, Wei Guan. "Higher Order Greeks." University of Oklahoma, University of South Florida, *Journal of Derivatives.*

Numerix. "Thinking Forward About Pricing and Hedging Variable Annuities." White Paper, Numerix.com. 2010

Pena, Ignacio, Gonzalo Rubio, and Gregorio Serna. "Why Do We Smile? On the Determinants of the Implied Volatility Function." *Journal of Banking and Finance,* 1151–1171, 1999.

Rakotondratsimba, Yves. "Modified Delta-Gamma Approximation." 28 April 2009.

Reisinger, Christoph. "Calibration of Volatility Surfaces." <http://people.maths.ox.ac.uk/reisinge/Students/volaNotes.pdf>.

Riaz Ahmed, Paul Wilmott, 'Which free lunch would you like to have today, Sir...', Wilmott Magazine.

San-Lin Chung, Weifeng Hung & Pai-Ta Shih. "On the Rate of convergence of Binomial Greeks."

Schmitz Abe Klaus E., M. Giles, and William Shaw. *Pricing Exotic Options Using Improved Strong Convergence.* Thesis. Oxford University, 2007.

Taleb, Nassim Nicholas. *Dynamic Hedging: Managing Vanilla and Exotic Options.* New York: Wiley, 1997.

Volatility Strategies. "Volatility Hedging – Turn Up the Static!" *The Volatility Exchange,* 10 (2), February 2013.

Weert, Frans de. *Exotic Options Trading.* John Wiley & Sons, Ltd. 2008.

Wystup, Uwe. "Vanna-Volga Pricing." Centre for Practical Quantitative Finance. Frankfurt School of Finance & Management, July 2008.

Xiong, Changwei. "Vanna-Volga Method for Foreign Exchange Implied Volatility Smile." January 2011. <http://www.cs.utah.edu/~cxiong/Files/Docs/Changwei_Xiong_VannaVolga.pdf>

Others

Kaminski, Thomas, Topper, Jürgen, and Giles, Mike B. "Efficient Computation of Hedge-Sensitivities via Automatic Differentiation." FastOpt. Oxford, November 2008.

Lee, Eileen. "Duality on Wall Street." Wilmott Magazine 50–59. April 2008.

Taleb, Nassim. Silent Risk, "Lectures on Fat Tails, (Anti)Fragility, and Asymmetric Exposures." Preliminary Incomplete Draft. January 2014.

Westerink, Joannes J. CE 341/441, Lecture 12. University of Notre Dame. "Derivation of Difference Approximations using Undetermined Coefficients." 2004. <http://ocw.nd.edu/civil-engineering-and-geological-sciences/computational-methods/eduCommons/civil-engineering-and-geological-sciences/computational-methods/readings/lecture-12>

Index

CPSIA information can be obtained
at www.ICGtesting.com
Printed in the USA
LVHW021221210523
747602LV00004B/236

9 781349 475728